CHICAGO STUDIES IN THE HISTORY OF AMERICAN RELIGION

Editors
JERALD C. BRAUER
AND MARTIN E. MARTY

A CARLSON PUBLISHING SERIES

For a complete listing of the titles in this series,
please see the back of this book.

An Unprov'd Experiment

RELIGIOUS PLURALISM IN COLONIAL NEW JERSEY

Douglas G. Jacobsen

PREFACE BY JERALD C. BRAUER

BR
555
.N5
J25
1991
West

CARLSON
Publishing Inc

BROOKLYN, NEW YORK, 1991

Please see the end of this volume for a listing of all the titles in the Carlson Publishing Series *Chicago Studies in the History of American Religion*, edited by Jerald C. Brauer and Martin E. Marty, of which this is Volume 9.

Copyright © 1991 by Douglas G. Jacobsen

Library of Congress Cataloging-in-Publication Data

Jacobsen, Douglas G. (Douglas Gordon), 1951-
  An unprov'd experiment : religious pluralism in colonial New Jersey / Douglas G. Jacobsen ; preface by Jerald C. Brauer.
    p. cm. — (Chicago studies in the history of American religion ; 9)
  Originally presented as the author's thesis (Ph.D.)—University of Chicago, 1983.
  Includes bibliographical references and index.
  ISBN 0-926019-46-5 (alk. paper)
  1. Religious pluralism—New Jersey—History. 2. New Jersey--Church history. 3. New Jersey—Religious life and customs.
I. Title. II. Title: Unproved experiment. III. Series.
BR555.N5J25 1991
277.49'07—dc20   91-25221

Typographic design: Julian Waters

Typeface: Bitstream ITC Galliard

Case design: Alison Lew

Index prepared by Scholars Editorial Services, Inc., Madison, Wisconsin, using NL Cindex, a scholarly indexing program from the Newberry Library.

Printed on acid-free, 250-year-life paper.

Manufactured in the United States of America.

Contents

An Introduction to the Series xi
Preface *by Jerald C. Brauer* xv
Acknowledgments xix

Introduction 1

I. The Legal Framework of Religious Diversity 19

II. Tribal Religion 53

III. Generic Religion 85

IV. Denominational Religion 113

V. New Jersey's Public Piety of Neighborliness 149

Conclusion 177

Notes 187
Bibliography 205
Index 215

for

James Thomas Jacobsen

and

Gloria Marie Jacobsen

An Introduction to the Series

The *Chicago Studies in the History of American Religion* is a series of books that deal with topics ranging from the time of Jonathan Edwards to the 1970s. Three or four deal with colonial topics and three or four treat the very recent past. About half of them focus on the decades just before and after 1900. One deals with blacks; two concentrate on women. Revivalists, fundamentalists, theologians, life in the suburbs and life in heaven and hell, the Beecher family of old and a monk of new times, Catholics adapting to America and Protestants fighting one another—all these subjects assure that the series has scope. People of every kind of taste and curiosity about American religion will find some books to suit them. Does anything serve to characterize the series as a whole? What does the stamp of "Chicago studies" mean?

Yale historian Sydney Ahlstrom in *A Religious History of the American People*, as influential as any twentieth-century work in its field, pays respect to the "Chicago School" of American religious historians. William Warren Sweet, the pioneer in such studies (beginning in 1927) at Chicago and, in many ways, in America at large represented the culmination of "the Protestant synthesis" in this field. Ahlstrom went on to name two later generations of Chicagoans, including the seminal Sidney E. Mead and major figures like Robert T. Handy and Winthrop Hudson and ending with the two editors of this series. He saw them as often "openly rebellious" in respect to Sweet and his synthesis.

If, as Ahlstrom says, "a disproportionate number" of historians have some connection with the Chicago School, it must be said that the new generation represented in these twenty-one books carries on both the lineage of Sweet and something of the "openly rebellious" character that scholars at Chicago are encouraged to pursue. This means, for one thing, that the "Protestant synthesis" does not characterize their work. These historians question the canon of historical writing produced in the Protestant era even as many of them continue to pursue themes shaped in a Protestant culture. Few of them concentrate on the old "frontier thesis" that marked the early years of the school. The shift for most has been toward the urban and pluralist scene. They call into question, not in devastating rage but in steady patterns of inquiry, the received wisdom about who matters, and why, in American religion.

So it is that this series of books focuses on blacks, women, dispensationalists, suburbanites, members of "marginal" denominations, "ethnics" and immigrants as readily as it does on white men of progressive urban bent in mainstream denominations and of long standing in America. The authors relish religious diversity and enjoy discovering the power of people once considered weak, the centrality to the American plot of those once regarded as peripheral, and the potency of losers who were once disdained by winners. Thus this series enhances an understanding of an America overlooked by the people of Sweet's era two-thirds of a century ago when it all, or most of it, began.

Rebellion for its own sake would not long hold interest; it might tell more about the psychology of rebels and revisers than about their subject matter. Revision, better than rebellion, characterizes the scholars. Re+vision: that's it. There was an original vision that characterized the Chicago School. This was the contention that in secular America and its universities religion mattered, as a theme in the national past and as a presence in the present. Second, it argued that the study of religious history belonged not only in the seminaries and archives of denominations, but also in the rough-and-tumble of the secular university, where no religious meanings were privileged and where each historian had to make a case for the value of his or her story.

Other assumptions from the earliest days pervade the books in this series. They are uncommonly alert to the environment in which expressions of faith occur. That is, they do not take for granted that religion comes protected in self-evidently important and hermetically sealed packages. Churches and denominations are porous, even when they would be sealed off; they cannot be understood apart from the ways the social environs effect them, but their power to effect change in the environment demands equal and truly unapologetic treatment. These writers do not shuffle and mumble and make excuses for their existence or for the choice of apparently arcane subject matter. They try to present their narrative in such ways that they compel attention.

A fourth characteristic that colors these works is a refusal in most cases to be typed in a fashionable slot labeled, variously, "intellectual" or "institutional" history, "cultural" or "social" history, or whatever. While those which concentrate on magisterial thinkers such as Jonathan Edwards are necessarily busy with and devoted to his intellectual achievement, most of the books deal with figures who cannot be understood only as exemplars in a sequence of studies of "the life of the mind." Instead, their biographies and circumstances come very much into play. On the other hand, none of these writers is a reductionist who sees religion as "nothing but" this or that—"nothing but" the working out of believers' Oedipal urges or expressing the economic and class interests of the subjects. Social history becomes in its way intellectual history, even if the intellects are focused on something other than the theologians in the traditions might like to see.

Some years ago *Look* magazine interviewed leaders in various denominations. One was asked if his fellow believers considered that theirs was the only true faith. Yes, he said, but they did not believe that they were the only ones who held it. The editors of this series of studies and the contributors to it do not believe that the "Chicago School," whenever and whatever it was, is the only true approach to American religious history. And, if they did, they would not hold that Chicagoans alone held it. To do so would imply a strange solipsistic or narcissistic impulse that would be the death of collegiality in the historical field. They have welcomed the chance to be in a climate where their inquiries are given such encouragement, where they find a company of fellow scholars in the Divinity School, the History Department, and the Committee on the History of Culture, whence these studies first emerged, and elsewhere in a university that provides a congenial home for massed and massive concentration of a special sort on American religious history.

While the undersigned have been consistently involved, most often together, in all twenty-one books, we want to single out a third person mentioned in so many acknowledgment sections, historian Arthur Mann. He has been a partner in two or three dozen religious history dissertation projects through the years and has been an influential and decisive contributor to the results. We stand in his debt.

Jerald C. Brauer
Martin E. Marty

Editor's Preface

For many years, historians have argued that both religion in America and the impact of religion on the shape of American culture have been determined largely by developments in Puritan New England. Their experience provided the myths and symbols that have come to identify the American nation and its people. From the Puritans arose the idea of a chosen nation with a special mission under God to the rest of the world. Supposedly, it was they who created a covenanted people banded together to create a new society under God. The Puritans instituted a system of checks and balances in their government, and though they did not create a democracy, they laid the groundwork whereby it was possible for democracy to develop. Many other virtues came from the Puritan experience. More attention has been given to this segment of American colonial life than to any other part. To be sure, the South, particularly Virginia, has had additional coverage because of the presence of such major figures as Washington, Jefferson, Madison, and Monroe.

Strangely overlooked in American historiography were the Middle Colonies. Some attention has been given to New York, and the presence of the Quakers and the importance of Philadelphia attracted minimal attention to Pennsylvania. New Jersey had been virtually overlooked. In recent years, the balance has begun to shift. Historians are showing more interest in colonial beginnings in the Middle Colonies and are exploring the relationship between their experience and the development of the American nation. Both New England and the South had more or less homogeneous cultures with a clear center and a well-integrated society. There was both unity and continuity within those two segments of American colonial life. Although they had little to do with each other until the coming of the Revolution, both New England and the South provided respectively neat pictures of social development. This was not so with the Middle Colonies. From the beginning, they were more complex, diverse, and seemed to lack coherence and aim. It was difficult to see how they could have exerted any kind of profound influence on what America was to become. In recent years, historians have exhibited second thoughts about the Middle Colonies.

Douglas Jacobsen has selected the least integrated and, supposedly, the least important of the Middle Colonies, New Jersey, in order to study the nature of religious life in that colony, and he has come up with surprising conclusions. It was common knowledge that there were many different religious groups in colonial New Jersey, but historians have assumed that each denomination had its own individual history and that there was little or no relationship among them. Consequently, many histories have been written about the particular groups, but most are from a parochial or limited point of view, centering only on the group under study.

Jacobsen argues that one can tell the story of *all* of the religious groups, not through individual stories but through a single story that binds all of them together within that particular colony. He seeks to provide a comprehensive framework in terms of which one can understand the overall religious developments in the entire colony. In spite of the particularity, denominations participated in a common history. It is this common history in which Jacobsen is interested, because, as he argues, not only is it unique in the colonies but it also provides the closest parallel to what actually happened when the United States was formed and pluralism was affirmed in principle through the reality of the separation of church and state and religious liberty.

Jacobsen adopts two basic concepts that have been widely employed in American history—religious diversity and pluralism—but he uses them in a quite new and exciting way. Though religious diversity exists in several forms, essentially it is a situation where a number of religious groups or denominations are present in or share a specific geographical area. Though they share the area, whether in a mixed or an isolated sense, they have little or nothing to do with one another and simply assume the right of each group to exist in its independence.

Religious pluralism is a quite different situation, because each of the different groups that share a common territory accepts the givenness, in a self-conscious way, of the other groups. They do not ignore them; they assume their presence as rightful. In addition, pluralism means that each of the groups not only understands itself in terms of its own beliefs and practices, self-consciously, but also attempts to see its particularity over against the other religious groups in their society. Both of these situations demand a constant reinterpretation on the part of each group, both with regard to its own tradition and how its own tradition relates to all other traditions. This is a considerable move beyond religious diversity.

Jacobsen analyzes various types or kinds of pluralism, differentiating between a pluralism that is limited in its applicability to a local situation, so that it is usually a pragmatic response that does not develop a self-conscious rationale, and a focused pluralism, which develops a set of assumptions and assertions concerning beliefs, values, or behaviors that "provides a focused point around which that pluralism can revolve." This focused pluralism becomes available to a much wider society than does the purely diffuse or pragmatic pluralism. Building on this distinction, Jacobsen constructs a sophisticated structure or typology with regard to religious diversity and religious pluralism in terms of which he can make sense out of the New Jersey religious experience.

He is well aware of the dangers of an abstract typology, and he makes clear that he uses the structure as a heuristic tool that enables him to make sense out of historical data. There is a danger that such a typology will force the historical materials into a preconceived mold, but it is equally possible that it will rather provide a framework of interpretation that enables one to make sense of the data. This is a classic case where the proof is in the pudding.

Jacobsen's analysis of religious experience in New Jersey makes eminent sense. He demonstrates that the wide variety of religious groups encountered from the earliest days initially accepted one another in terms of what he has called "religious diversity." He goes on to demonstrate how they moved from diversity to differing forms of religious pluralism. Because this is the way the New Jersey situation developed, it is possible to write a common or general history of all of the religious groups rather than individual histories of each group. That common story is to be found in the move from religious diversity to religious pluralism.

Jacobsen does not employ his categories as abstractions. He is concerned about the stuff and the raw events of New Jersey's religious history, and he devotes considerable attention to them. As a consequence, the various groups are seen to participate in a common history. This history reveals the New Jersey situation as something unusual in colonial American history. Though it is not unique in comparison with the situations in Pennsylvania or New York, it is, for a variety of reasons, somewhat different. Obviously, it is vastly different from the situations in either New England or the South. What is important about the New Jersey story is, first, the story itself because of its unusual and unique character. What is equally interesting and provocative is that this New Jersey experience is the closest in reality to what later happened in the other colonies and, especially, in the founding of the republic itself. New Jersey first embodied what other colonies later experienced and what the young republic itself came to exemplify in religious liberty and religious pluralism. It is a fascinating story. No longer can the Middle Colonies' experience be downplayed or overlooked, and this is now particularly true of New Jersey.

Jerald C. Brauer

Acknowledgments

Without the aid, encouragement and "harassment" of my wife Rhonda Hustedt Jacobsen, this book would never have been completed. She offered emotional support when needed and informed advice when requested. She is my best friend and most respected colleague. To her goes my first word of thanks.

I am also deeply indebted to my dissertation committee at the University of Chicago—Jerald C. Brauer, Edward M. Cook, Jr., and Martin E. Marty. Their corporate criticisms were always specific, constructive, and insightful. This study has been improved in more ways than I can easily enumerate by input from all three of these people as individuals. In particular, I should mention the skill with which Jerry Brauer always dismantled the arguments I proposed in the drafts I sent him and then reconstructed them in improved form. I am indebted to Ted Cook for keeping me historically honest by his meticulous attention to detail. And many times along the way, I was encouraged by Marty's ever present and infectious creativity and enthusiasm. Without their advice this study would be much more seasoned with faults than it undoubtedly still is.

The New Jersey Historical Commission deserves note for helping to defray some of my early research costs through a Grant-in-Aid for the year 1980. At an important point along the way I was encouraged by Peter O. Wacker's willingness to share an unpublished paper with me. Mary Suggs, in between her other secretarial assignments at Messiah College, managed gratis to transfer the text to computer disks several years ago. Had she not done that, the task of readying this manuscript for publication would have been almost impossible. Virginia Linden Hustedt Morse proofread the final draft of this manuscript for me before it was submitted to Carlson Publishing, and Cynthia Merman did the in-house editing. Without their help, numerous glitches, typos, awkward phrases, and simple errors would have remained in the text.

Finally, I am grateful to my three children, Kate, Anna, and Grant. Each in his or her own special way kept me anchored to present reality in the midst of the historical research and writing that went into this book. They above all others repeatedly remind me that living people are more important than dead people, no matter how interesting those people from the past may be.

An Unprov'd Experiment

Introduction

In 1765, when Samuel Smith wrote the first history of New Jersey, he spoke of the beginnings of the colony as "in a great measure an unprov'd experiment; and then much out of the common course of things."[1] Smith's description is correct and in no aspect of the colony is the unprovenness of the colonial experiment that was New Jersey more apparent than in its religious dimension. As much as or more than any other American colony, New Jersey was an experiment in religious freedom. Rhetoric about religious liberty was not as prominent in New Jersey as in some other colonies, but the reality of religious freedom is attested to by the amount of religious diversity the colony both attracted and produced.

This study represents one attempt to describe the freewheeling and "unprov'd" religious experiment that took place in the first seventy-five to eighty years of the colony's existence. My thesis is that the people of New Jersey very quickly adapted to the religious diversity that characterized their colony. By quickly, I mean that the residents of this small "backwater" province seem to have been the first colonists to internalize the diversity that later came to characterize the nation as a whole. And their adjustment to diversity was fairly sophisticated. Certain adjustments to diversity were made primarily on the local level and were essentially private-sector means of dealing with the situation. This kind of adaptation to the environment I label diffuse pluralism. Other adjustments were made on a more colonywide and public level. This kind of accommodation to reality I call focused pluralism. In this two-pronged approach to religious pluralism colonial New Jersey presages the dual solution that still characterizes American religion. Privately we compete in a peaceful and semicooperative manner; publicly we share and extol a common American civil faith. America is a land of "religions and religion."[2]

Significant in its own right as well as for its applications to the American experience, colonial New Jersey demands historical investigation. Unfortunately, colonial historians have overlooked New Jersey. Generally pictured as a backwater society that lacked a clear self-identity, the colony, if mentioned at all, has usually been relegated to the wasteland of scholarly footnotes or engulfed under that amorphous category "The Middle Colonies." A few recent works have begun to challenge this state of affairs, but the overall pattern remains.[3]

There are two major reasons why New Jersey has lacked attention from historians. One reason is simply that New Jersey's colonial history is not particularly dramatic. Whatever else they may be, historians are storytellers, instinctively attracted to times and places that seem to embody natural plots.[4] Viewed from this perspective, New Jersey would be less attractive to the historian than almost any other colony. Most of the American colonies developed and matured under the influence of a clearly defined center of society or goal of civil existence that had been enunciated by the colony's founder(s) or founding documents. Then, more often than not, the colony reacted against those guiding principles. By contrast, New Jersey stumbled through its colonial experience in constant search of a social center. Such a meandering historical path does not provide fertile material for an organized and aesthetically pleasing historical narrative.

A second reason for the lack of attention to New Jersey is that historians in a former generation of scholarship (most notably Perry Miller) looked for "laboratory" situations where they could observe the natural growth and development of American society and its foundational ideas. They wanted to discover the plot of American history, and to do so they sought coherent situations, pure and uncluttered, where America could be observed in embryo. An analysis of these controlled environments, it was hoped, would reveal a pattern by which to define, gauge, and narrate the later and more complex stages of American development. The complexity of colonial New Jersey obviously made the colony unattractive to this breed of historian.[5]

Attractive or not, colonial New Jersey now demands scholarly attention, and it does so precisely for the reasons it was previously ignored. Throughout its history, the crucial question for colonial New Jersey was how to cope with diversity. As post-melting pot historians are beginning to realize, diversity is and has been a major strand of the American experience. Yet diversity has not been a major theme of American historiography. A study of religious diversity in colonial New Jersey can help in this task.

Historiographic Review

A review of the historiography dealing with religious diversity in colonial New Jersey can serve as a helpful means of introducing the subject. Four particular works stand out as having signal importance. They are Nelson Burr's "The Religious History of New Jersey Before 1702" (1938), Thomas Jefferson Wertenbaker's *The Middle Colonies* (1938), Wallace N. Jamison's *Religion in New Jersey: A Brief History* (1964), and Peter O. Wacker's *Land and People* (1975).

Nelson Burr's short history of religion in early New Jersey is almost wholly descriptive. It is also a summary work as opposed to an exploratory one. Nonetheless, it has importance for the present discussion because it provided, when it was published, a needed reminder of the breadth and diversity of religious practice that had found representation in the colony. While important, the study is of limited helpfulness in coming to grips with the problem that pluralism posed for both the various religious groups in the colony and for the society as a whole.

Burr defined religious diversity solely as a multiplicity of institutional religious affiliations. As a result, he discussed religion in the colony in a highly compartmentalized fashion. His subsections, for example, are entitled "*The* Lutherans," "*The* Reformed Dutch Church," "*The* Presbyterians," etc. (emphasis mine). By segregating these various religious groups and treating them as if they had only private and distinct histories, Burr overlooked the radical internal significance that the pluralistic environment held for each group.

Even though he failed to see the importance of diversity for colonial New Jersey religion and society, Burr did recognize a certain historical precedent in the situation. He asserted at one point that the colony's "variety of religious belief and organization . . . was an epitome of the future American religious diversity."[6] While basically left undeveloped, this theme was first enunciated by Burr and he deserves recognition here. Burr's failure to develop the theme of diversity may have been due to his own agenda as a historian, which seems, in retrospect, more ideological than historical. Intent on defending "the religious character of New Jersey people" against the "sharp criticism" of all detractors, his own warmhearted and conservative religious sentiments finally led him to set up colonial New Jersey as a model of pietistic morality.[7] Burr at one point declared that colonial New Jersey, "although 'liberal' for that age, never slurred into the pragmatic humanism occasionally advocated at the

3

present day, which apparently sees no higher sanction for restraint than a purely worldly desire for social order."[8]

Thomas Jefferson Wertenbaker's *The Middle Colonies* represents a distinctly different type of history. Burr's interests were parochially confined to New Jersey; Wertenbaker's vision was, by contrast, broad-ranging. (The work considered here is actually only one volume of the author's three-volume *The Founding of American Civilization*.) Nonetheless, the two works are related by their shared, if differently emphasized, historical themes. Wertenbaker's study inverts Burr's concerns. Placing primary focus on what he terms the "Americanization" of transplanted European church traditions, Wertenbaker made diversity little more than a subsidiary theme that set the stage for these developments.

The primary importance of *The Middle Colonies* for the present discussion, as well as its major weakness, lies in Wertenbaker's understanding of the process by which the diverse religious groups in New Jersey were Americanized. On the positive side, Wertenbaker recognized the dynamism of the situation. Religion in New Jersey was not static but in the process of change. New emphases on piety and new institutional coalitions were emerging that differed distinctly from the European church traditions that had spawned the various groups in the colony. It is problematic, however, whether these developments can best be described as an "Americanization" of these groups.

Wertenbaker's presentation, like Burr's, ultimately seems more ideological than historical. At the close of the work he states his purpose:

> Just as it is necessary in studying a great cathedral or temple to examine its foundation to ascertain its strength, its proportions, the materials of which it is made, so we cannot understand the United States without a knowledge of the principles which governed the founding of American civilization.[9]

Wertenbaker is a classic conservative: past events explain and define the finished greatness of the present. For him, colonial history represented the development of a new form of human existence that culminated and was definitively announced in the founding of the nation. In this view of things events subsequent to the founding of the nation are of a different and inferior order than those which led to the creation of the nation.

The weakness inherent in this approach caused Wertenbaker to misunderstand religion in New Jersey in two different but related ways. First, he almost wholly ignored religious groups that did not fit his scheme of Americanization. For example, the Baptists, relatively "American" from their inception, and the Lutherans, who either remained decidedly Old World oriented or else associated themselves with the Anglican church, were not discussed. Second, his conceptualization of the situation led him emotionally to take sides in his historical inquiry. Wertenbaker wrote of the critical time when the Dutch Reformed church "had to determine whether it would perish with the old civilization or rise on the crest of the new," and when the Presbyterian church had finally to decide on "the old question of yielding to or resisting the forces of Americanization." For Wertenbaker the choice was clear: on the one side stood "vital and practical religion" and on the other "empty formalism."[10]

These criticisms do not negate the importance of his work. Wertenbaker mistook one aspect of New Jersey's adjustment to religious pluralism as the whole, and this seems obviously to have skewed his study. Still, his awareness of the dynamism of religion in the colony takes us far beyond the static picture of religion painted by Burr. Only after this fluid nature of the situation had been clearly enunciated could a more accurate analysis be attempted.

For twenty-two years no major work appeared that addressed religious diversity in colonial New Jersey. (The term "major" is used here both advisedly and relatively; in reality, there are no "major" works that deal with religion in the colony.) Several significant studies dealing with more restricted topics were published during this time. The two most significant were Leonard J. Trinterud's *The Forming of an American Tradition: A Re-examination of Colonial Presbyterianism* (1949) and Nelson Burr's *The Anglican Church in New Jersey* (1954). While each of these represents careful historical scholarship, neither is particularly helpful in enlightening the present concern.[11]

In 1964 this silence was broken with the publication of Wallace N. Jamison's *Religion in New Jersey: A Brief History*. Jamison's work was commissioned by the New Jersey Tercentenary Commission as part of a rather impressive attempt to provide a popular but academically respectable series of volumes that detailed various aspects of the state's history. Certain limitations were inevitable in this undertaking. The work, as the title warns, is too brief. It is also too broad, covering in just over 160 pages the entire history of the state from its inception in 1664. Primarily devoted to narrative, the analytical aspect of the work suffers and is considerably more suggestive than convincing in its appraisals. Despite these programmatic drawbacks, Jamison's study deserves attention for the creative proposals it makes about the structure of religion in the colony.

Jamison identifies one theme as central to the history of religion in New Jersey and provides two "keys" that he hopes will help make that story intelligible. The proffered theme is "the story of how the people of one state, New Jersey, have sought to discover their religious identity"; the two keys are diversity and polarity.[12]

Much more than Burr or Wertenbaker, Jamison saw the incompleteness and irony of New Jersey's religious story. The significance of this insight is made clearer when it is recognized that Jamison himself seemed somewhat surprised by its discovery. He labeled it "curious" that "New Jersey was one of the last colonies to develop a clear image of itself," but had enough sense of fidelity to his sources to declare that "the history of New Jersey might be described as the story of a state in search of its own identity." Jamison elaborated the central plot of this story as "a collection of widely diverse religious groups trying to learn to live in community."[13]

Having clearly articulated a major theme of New Jersey's religious history, Jamison unfortunately failed to develop its significance. Two reasons for this failure are: (1) the relative importance he assigned to the two keys (or subthemes) that he hoped would unravel the tangled skein of religion he saw in the colony, and (2) his adopted definition of religion.

Given the general storyline of Jamison's work, one would expect that diversity would be his primary subtheme, but it is not. Instead, he asserts that polarity is the "more serious" of the two keys.[14] Jamison seems to have fallen into what has become a typical way of talking about New Jersey. Ever since Benjamin Franklin metaphorically likened the colony to "a barrel tapped at both ends" (by the cities of New York and Philadelphia), it has been almost unavoidably tempting to repeat his imagery. Jamison's heavy weighting of polarity as a subtheme, however, seriously undercut his more important insight about the unity of the colony's religious history. By tearing the colony in two with his emphasis on polarity, Jamison foiled the plot of his proposed story of *one* colony seeking to discover its identity.

Perhaps an even more serious problem is Jamison's definition of religion. (In his defense and with gratitude, it should be acknowledged that Jamison, unlike his predecessors, at least tried to be clear about the subject with which he was dealing.) The definition he chose, like his emphasis on polarity, worked against a unified history of religion in the colony.

Two particular passages illustrate Jamison's conception of religion. In the preface he declares, "No history of a people is complete until careful attention has been given to its religious beliefs and practices."[15] And he begins his introduction by stating, "If we define religion as the attempt to relate human beings to the divine . . ."[16] Both of these suggestions, in addition to being restrictive definitions of the broad human phenomenon referred to as religion, seem antithetical to his main theme. Jamison's first proposal contains the inherent assumption that "religious beliefs and practices" represent only one type of an unspecified number of distinct types of human beliefs and practices. His second proposal defines the distinguishing aspect of this set of religious beliefs and practices as those which are directed solely to "the attempt to relate human beings to the divine."

If religion is understood in such psychologically segregated and otherworldly terms, Jamison's focus on community and the development of a corporate New Jersey religious self-identity seems out of place. What makes religious diversity a real problem, what made it a problem in New Jersey, is that, contrary to Jamison's assumption, religious beliefs and practices cannot be so easily compartmentalized. Furthermore, what first made religious diversity a pressing problem in New Jersey was the specifically human dimension (i.e., how was one to act in a pluralistic setting in a way appropriate both to one's religious self-understanding and to the dictates of human civility?). Jamison's explication of the story of religion in New Jersey suffered because of his inadequate definition. He initially describes the history of New Jersey as a poignant and publicly serious experiment in "trying to learn to live in community," but by the end of his treatment of the colonial period he can say nothing more about the results of that experiment than that there developed a " 'live and let live' attitude on the part of the laity which the sectarianism of the clergy was never able to eradicate."[17]

If Jamison's work ultimately fails to live up to its promise, it is not because the promise was lacking. I am profoundly indebted to Jamison's suggestion concerning the nature and importance of colonial Jerseyans' attempts to invest their common life in society with religious significance. It is, in fact, a high regard for Jamison's work that prompts consideration of the next study, Peter O. Wacker's *Land and People*. Wacker's work provides one corrective (and the adoption of a different definition of religion will provide another) that will allow us to salvage Jamison's most pregnant insight into religion in New Jersey.

Peter Wacker is not a historian of religion. Rather, he is a cultural geographer, and his work reflects that disciplinary commitment. The primary importance of his work for my discussion lies in his detailed elaboration of the nature and changing pattern of cultural diversity in the colony. There is a revisionistic as well as a constructive thrust to Wacker's work. First, he has shown that a New York-Philadelphia axial division of the colony, even though having some root in the political history and early land settlement pattern of the region, really misinterprets the cultural geography of the colony. Second, he has developed a much more complex cultural geographic matrix of the colony. This new map reveals at least six distinct "settlement regions," each with its own identifiable cultural distinctives. Around and between these regions there exists a grouting of culturally heterogeneous territory.[18]

By revealing a more complicated pattern of cultural and religious diversity in colonial New Jersey than was previously assumed, Wacker has shown that at least part of Jamison's quandary is avoidable. At the same time, Wacker has opened up the potential for a new sense of the unity of the colony to emerge. With regard to Jamison's work (or for that of any other historian dealing with religion in the colony in general) this implies two things: first, that a unified history of religion in New Jersey is possible; second, that that history can be unraveled only if one has as a primary subtheme a rather sophisticated understanding of the nature and scope of religious diversity in the colony. These two assertions represent critical assumptions for my work. Before outlining how they inform the overall structure of the study, however, it is necessary to address the issue of defining religion.

Defining Religion

Because of the looseness with which the term has often been used, it has become necessary to begin any discussion of religion with a clear definition. The primary purpose, as explained by Peter Berger, is not to establish whether a given definition is "true" or "false," but rather to employ a precise vocabulary and to choose a definition that will be maximally helpful in clarifying an otherwise muddled situation.[19] Such a choice cannot, of course, be arbitrary, and it would be foolish as well as self-defeating to ignore the major proposals that have emerged in the last century. Nonetheless, one important criterion in final selection of a definition must be how well that definition fits the data. Jamison's definition, regardless of the question of the accuracy with which it describes the breadth and variety of religious experience, proved inadequate—indeed even damaging—for his own study because of its inappropriateness for his projected theme.

I adopt, with some modifications, a definition of religion propounded by Clifford Geertz. Religion, he asserts, is metaphysics infused with ethics. It represents the link between a people's "ethos" and "world view."

> A people's ethos is the tone, character, and quality of their life, its moral and aesthetic style and mood; it is the underlying attitude toward themselves and their world that life reflects. Their world view is their picture of the way things in sheer actuality are, their concept of nature, of self, of society. It contains their most comprehensive ideas of order. Religious belief and ritual confront and mutually confirm one another; the ethos is made intellectually reasonable by being shown to represent a way of life implied by the actual state of affairs which the world view describes, and the world view is made emotionally acceptable by being presented as an image of an actual state of affairs of which such a way of life is an authentic expression. This demonstration of a meaningful relation between the values a people holds and the general order of existence within which it finds itself is an essential element in all religions.[20]

At the risk of gross oversimplification, Geertz's definition can be rephrased to read that "religion is a particular way of seeing the world and acting in it." A religion is not just one way among others of seeing and acting in the world, but a primordial one, and one, as Geertz says, that has a unique "aura of factuality" about it.[21] Taken in this sense, religion represents not a handful of propositions about the world and how one should act in it, but a conceptual and behavioral framework through which one looks at and acts in the world.

This definition of religion offers certain advantages over definitions that have guided earlier studies of religion in New Jersey. First, the definition adopted here portrays religion not as one type of human behavior and belief distinct and separable from other types of behavior and belief, but as an implicit dimension of *all* human behavior and belief. An individual's religious disposition informs all of her or his activity. Surely not all of a person's public actions are equally expressive of an individual's religious stance, but at the same time no public action is wholly devoid of the potential to reveal an underlying religious commitment. Second, this conception of religion seems to demand that any study of the subject ought to proceed in a phenomenological mode. One cannot assume that the observable religious disposition of any group or individual will conform to the normative model of any specific and/or institutionally organized "religion." A concentration on "religions" (or, in the case of New Jersey, on "denominations") has in fact often obscured the accurate observation of the actual religious dispositions of individuals and groups as manifest in their language and behavior.

By defining religion in this way, it seems possible to avoid a problem that has heretofore consistently befuddled historians' attempts to deal with religion in New Jersey as a single subject. Jamison's work serves as a case in point. Because of his definition of religion and his overattention to traditional and institutional categorizations of religion, his one story of religion in the colony quickly disintegrated into a telling of parallel and separate stories of different religious denominations. Relations among groups were treated as either oblique or inconsequential. If we phenomenologically bracket those traditional distinctions, however, and observe the behavior of colonial Jerseyans through a less rigidly institutional grid, it is possible to see a different pattern of religious behavior and commitment—one that allows more easily for the telling of a single story of religion in the colony.

The definition of religion proposed here has one other notable aspect to it. When religion is defined as that primordial dimension of existence through which one looks at and acts in the world, religious diversity becomes a foundational paradigm for all forms of social and cultural diversity. Seen in this light, a study of religious diversity in colonial New Jersey takes on a much more than antiquarian significance. What is important is not simply the clashing of a diversity of now largely discarded doctrines, but the fact that the colony presents a stage on which we can observe the early development of certain aspects of the contemporary American pluralistic environment.

A Definition of Religious Pluralism

One of the major claims of this study is that the people of colonial New Jersey very quickly adapted to the religious diversity of their environment—they internalized the diversity around them and became pluralistic in their view of things. Crucial to this thesis is a clear differentiation of religious diversity and religious pluralism. These phrases are often used in a basically synonymous manner; however, a few important distinctions can be made.

"Religious diversity" indicates a situation characterized by the copresence of a multiplicity of religious groups or traditions in a given geographical area. It is solely an objective and numerical designation. No interrelatedness among groups is implied. Rather, the term assumes a discrete, almost atomistic, separation of those groups. While all situations of religious diversity share certain characteristics, a helpful distinction can be made between two different forms in which the phenomenon can appear: at times, diversity can be segregated, and at other times, it can be integrated. Segregated religious diversity refers to a situation where a shared territory is geographically divided into discrete and identifiable regions, or neighborhoods, each of which is characterized by a relative homogeneity of religion. Integrated religious diversity, by contrast, indicates a situation where different religious groups do not find themselves in geographical isolation from other groups, yet each still maintains a distinct and separate social existence.[22]

"Religious pluralism" refers to a qualitatively different state of affairs than mere diversity. It defines a situation where the diversity of the external environment has been internalized by each constitutive religious group or tradition. This means, first of all, that each group has accepted the fact of diversity as an essentially permanent state of being. Second, it implies that each group has recognized a need to define itself not only in terms of its own peculiar vision or particular history, but also in terms of its distinctiveness vis-à-vis other religious groups in the society. The pluralistic environment becomes in effect an unavoidable and undeniable reality that all groups must confront in their ongoing and continual reinterpretations of their individual histories and rationales for existence. In a truly pluralistic environment, then, the developmental histories of all the participant religious groups become related.

With religious pluralism, as with religious diversity, it is helpful to distinguish two structural forms the phenomenon can assume. Religious pluralism can be either diffuse in nature, or focused. Diffuse religious pluralism indicates a situation where the need to take responsive cognizance of the proximate existence of alternative ways of being religious finds acceptable resolution wholly on the local level. The particular diversity of a local region gives rise to a particular pluralism that is inherently of only limited applicability beyond that specific situation. Diffuse religious pluralism tends to be more practical than analytical, and its expression is often more behavioral than theoretical.

In contrast to diffuse pluralism, focused pluralism refers to a situation where a more general and theoretical adjustment is sought. In instances of focused pluralism, an attempt is made to define a unifying core of beliefs, values, or behaviors that, while not wholly transcending the pluralism of the environment, provides a focused point around which that pluralism can revolve. Rather than being a local phenomenon, focused pluralism usually appears on the larger societal level. The most blatant examples can be found in pluralistic societies where "civil religions" have emerged. America is a prime example. Focused pluralism can, however, take a less theologically and institutionally developed form than that of a full-fledged "civil religion."[23] It can also exist in the form of a relatively uninstitutionalized public piety or religious sense of social community.

It is helpful briefly to outline the relations between these various types of diversity and pluralism. The four do not represent mutually exclusive categories of social organization; rather, they are basically compatible and hierarchical. Put simply, focused pluralism presupposes the earlier existence, or at least co-presence, of diffuse pluralism, and pluralism in general obviously presupposes diversity. The relation between integrated diversity and segregated diversity does not fit into this hierarchical scheme. Rather, these two concepts represent nodal points on a typological continuum along which different particular situations could be located as either more or less segregated in character.

Outline and Scope

The bulk of this study deals with the period before 1740. I began my work in New Jersey religious history with the intention of unraveling the background of the Great Awakening in that colony. My hope was to analyze the structures of religious behavior in New Jersey before that burst of revivalistic activity so that I would have a base from which to discover what really was new in the events of the 1740s and 1750s. It was in the process of researching that set of issues that my present interest was piqued. I discovered that the primary structure of religion in New Jersey both before and after the Great Awakening was diversity. The effect of the Great Awakening on this pluralism was, if anything, to simplify it—not to deepen, increase, or intensify it as the awakening seems to have done so many other places. Because of this fact, I decided to maintain my focus on the preawakening period. What is really surprising about New Jersey is how quickly this rural backwater colony adjusted to diversity. (Perhaps cities are not always at the cutting edge of history.)

The data referred to are almost entirely limited to readily available published materials. This seemed appropriate to the task at hand. My purpose in writing has not been to uncover a wealth of new information about religion in New

Jersey, but to provide a new way of looking at that religion. The study of religion in New Jersey cries out for more nose-to-the-ground local and archival historical investigation. Scholarship will not advance, however, unless such activity is combined with new ways of looking at what we find. This book is intended to prompt thinking about how to interpret the data we already have. Perhaps in doing that it will also suggest lines of inquiry for the future.

Let me sharpen the focus of this study by stating two things it is not. First, it is not an attempt to uncover the conscious sensibilities of people living in the past. Those are largely lost to us. Even if some individual's conscious awareness of religious pluralism in colonial New Jersey could accurately be recovered, that would not necessarily help us grasp the big picture of what was going on—most people are blind to the large-scale movements in their own societies. Rather, my task is to organize the explicit statements, implied attitudes, and observable behaviors of the colonists of New Jersey, which are preserved in the records that remain, into a coherent set of categories that defines the broad pattern of response to religious diversity. Second, this book is not intended to be a "scientifically" executed statistical analysis of pluralism in New Jersey. While I appreciate the insights that can be gleaned from such an approach when sufficient data are available (and I'm not sure an adequate data base could be constructed for an in-depth study of pluralism in New Jersey), my goal is more ethnographic in nature than rigorously sociological. The approach I take was chosen consciously. It fits the subject matter. Pluralism, after all, represents more an internal, qualitative sense of place than it does an external, quantitative description of a society.

I have done my best to balance simple observing with the need to organize what can be observed. While I did not come to my study with a blank slate, I did not approach the subject with a prepackaged theoretical model of understanding either. I began my research simply by reading everything I could get my hands on regarding religion in colonial New Jersey. The categories I employ were developed out of this reading as I looked for natural and repetitive patterns of religious behavior and belief. As much as possible, I use sociological and psychological theories only when they naturally fit the data, and then only as heuristic devices that help describe the behavior under examination. I do not use theory to try to predict what should have happened in the colony.

I have, to a large degree, ignored denominations. This is intentional. I have found it unhelpful to speak of denominations doing one thing or another. Denominational labels, in New Jersey, seem to obfuscate as much as they clarify. Especially in the early period (before 1702), they have almost no predictive power regarding how a given individual or local group will respond to pluralism. Baptists in one part of the colony do one thing and in another part of the colony they do something else. And so it is for all denominations. As the history of the colony progressed, and as the various denominations strengthened their institutional organizations, a certain homogenization of denominational behavior did take place. But this denominational uniformity was always limited and partial. Even without these misgivings about the helpfulness of denominational labeling, I would have felt free to ignore denominational institutions anyway because that aspect of New Jersey's religious history has been amply charted elsewhere.[24]

In organization, this book is put together like a sandwich. The "public" adjustments of the colony to religious diversity is the bread. Chapter One deals with the legal slice of this adjustment, while Chapter Five focuses on the shifts of "public piety" that took place in the colony. Layered in between is an analysis of three different ways the colonists of New Jersey made their "private" adjustments to diversity. In Chapter One, I deal with religion and the law. Seen from one perspective, New Jersey's relatively liberal laws concerning religion created the pluralism with which the residents had to struggle. Seen from another viewpoint, however, the legal code also represents one of the ways the colony adapted to diversity. The laws of a society never determine exactly what will happen in that society, just as they never perfectly reflect the actual state of affairs. However, laws do help push developments in certain directions and they do partially reflect historical realities. In colonial New Jersey, legislation regarding religion shows a back-and-forth movement. The earliest laws encouraged the growth of religious diversity; later laws tried to limit diversity through the creation of an informal establishment of religion; and, finally, legislation (or as the case is, the lack of legislation) during the royal period seemed designed to maintain the status quo regarding religious freedoms and diversity. The effect was twofold. First, it ensured the continuance of a limited but real religious diversity in New Jersey throughout the colonial period. Second, this pattern of legislation tended to relegate the most creative aspects of the colony's adjustment to diversity to the realm of "private" interpersonal relations outside the legal sphere of influence.

The second major section of this book (Chapters Two through Four) describes the development of several different types of diffuse religious pluralism in this "private" realm. I develop three categories, or ideal types, of private religious reaction to the diversity of the colony: some Jerseyans became religious tribalists, others religious genericists, and still others religious denominationalists.

Religious "tribalism" represents the attempt to stake out a piece of turf (sometimes literally, sometimes figuratively) where a person or group could establish a coherent sense of identity over and against the differing religious groups and individuals who surrounded them. Religious "tribalists" were not mere sectarians. They did not withdraw from society to form separatistic enclaves removed from the world. Rather, the presence of religious others (i.e., enemies) in the near environment was a necessary ingredient in any tribalistic vision of reality. Since other scholars have used the word "tribal" as an adjective for religious activity (especially in reference to the Society of Friends) in a much more quietistic and sectarian sense, I want to underscore the interactive element in my use of the term. In this study, "tribal" religion almost always involves self-definition over against other groups or individuals in the region—it is not a withdrawal from society into a separatistic and removed existence. More quietistic forms of tribalism did develop in the colony as it moved into the eighteenth century. But they were the exception rather than the rule.

A second "private" adjustment to the diversity of the colony I label "generic" religion. This attitude sought to dissolve the issue by ignoring it. A "generic" attitude toward religion reflects the belief that all religious institutions are flawed. If all are flawed, it is logical to conclude that while none is ultimately meaningful all can be used to meet the religious needs one might sense at different stages in one's life. The typical points at which one might feel these needs are crucial transitions—birth, puberty, marriage, sickness, and death. Since a great deal of "popular" religion (especially peasant religion) also hinges on these universal human experiences, one could easily question the label "generic." Why not just call the phenomenon by the more generally used term? While there may well be a significant dose of popular religion—peasant or otherwise—at work beneath the surface of generic religion in colonial New Jersey, generic religion cannot be reduced to that substrata. Generic religion was not just "popular" religion; it was popular religion bent to the purpose of coming to grips with pluralism, and as such it takes on its own distinctive hue and tone.

The third "private" adjustment that colonial Jerseyans made to the pluralism of their environment was to become "denominationally" religious. This too is a loaded term. By denominational religion, I mean an attitude of competitive interaction with other groups in one's local region. This denominational attitude did spawn the creation of actual institutional denominations—and New Jersey was one of the first regions of North America where this happened—but I focus on the underlying mindset that permitted, and in fact encouraged, institutionally defined denominations to develop, not on those institutions themselves. A great number of scholarly studies have analyzed the social reality of denominationalism in the modern world. My purpose is more humble. I only articulate the particular preunderstandings and attitudes that allowed denominationalism to emerge in one particular and small colonial society. In doing this, however, I want to stress that in New Jersey the growth of denominational religion was only one of three major reactions to the diversity of the environment. It was not the be-all and end-all of pluralism.

The third section of this book (Chapter Five) returns the discussion of religious pluralism to the public realm. I outline how New Jersey as a whole slowly came to grips with the pluralism of the colony by altering their perceptions of what their society ought to be and by modifying their expectations of how it ought to function—i.e., by changing their sense of public piety. In simple terms, the colonists of New Jersey slowly gave up the "vertical" notion that the health of their society was specially and conditionally determined by God and as a result they reconceived their societal self-definition largely in the "horizontal" terms of neighborly responsibility. New Jersey's changing public piety never became a civil religion of sufficient strength to override private adjustments to pluralism. But the public ethic of neighborliness that did develop became focused enough that it seems to have become a second faith of many people in the colony.

The importance of neighborliness as a unifying societal metaphor was that it accepted the diversity of the colony (in fact, it even sanctioned that diversity as good) while simultaneously providing a rationale for civility in public affairs. New Jersey's neighborly public piety thus forms a compliment to the legal realm. The colony's laws encouraged the "privatization" of New Jersey's adjustment to religious pluralism—that is, the colony tended to shy away from any legal-political solution to the problem of pluralism and allowed religious individuals and groups to come to grips with diversity in their own particular and various ways. At the same time, the colony's public piety provided a means by which public life could informally continue to have a religious aura about it that floated over and above those "private" pluralisms.

A word of caution is in order. This book is rather highly structured and systematic. At points, I have probably overreified the constructs of organization and explanation I have developed to help make sense of the cacophony of New Jersey religion. The actual flow of religion as experienced by the participants was undoubtedly more confused and muddy than it appears here. An awareness of that fact has constantly thrown the neatness of this systematic study back in my face. A hundred stories have been left untold and numerous byways have been ignored. All this is not without cost. The words of Bernard Berenson seem appropriate. "Every attempt at a system is made at the expense of facts, fancies, and ideas that clamor for notice like the denizens of Dante's *Inferno*. I can never get their cries out of my ears." Yet Berenson also notes that "systematizing is instinctive and useful."[25] The present task, I hope, falls into this useful category. It is not the total story of religion in New Jersey. But because it was their shared and common story, it is also part of our common story and by describing their "unprov'd experiment" we can maybe better understand our continuing American experiment in religion.

ONE

The Legal Framework of Religious Diversity

> Law in general is human reason, inasmuch as it governs all the inhabitants of the earth: the political and civil laws of each nation ought to be only the particular cases in which human reason is applied.
> They should be adapted in such a manner to the people for whom they are framed that it should be a great chance if those of one nation suit another.
> Montesquieu, The Spirit of the Laws

It may seem odd to begin a discussion of the relationship between religion and law in colonial New Jersey with Montesquieu's musings on the subject of law. However, Montesquieu provides a helpful glimpse into the general understanding of the nature and function of law as it was held by many western Europeans (including American colonists) in the seventeenth and eighteenth centuries. When Montesquieu wrote *The Spirit of the Laws* in 1748, he recognized the diversity of various national legal systems. Each nation, in Montesquieu's perception, had a unique individual character that was reflected in its laws. Yet Montesquieu wanted to retain a concept of universal natural law above and behind any particular national perception of law. He was, in short, a hybrid thinker, neither fish nor fowl, a man between two ages.

For well over one thousand years, natural law had been the dominant legal theory of Europe. The Greek Stoic philosophers provided one of the earliest statements of natural law theory. For this group of thinkers, law or the "logos" represented the ordering principle of the universe. Randomness in nature, such as that described by Lucretius and his fellow Greek materialist thinkers, was denied. The implications for human ethics were that man was to govern his life by reason and law, not by emotion or intuition. Human life was essentially public life, lived before men and for the good of one's fellow man. It was not a private endeavor.

Early in its history, the Christian church appropriated this model of law for its own purposes. As late as the 1600s, it was still the dominant model of the Christian world. The Reformation and the division of Christendom had begun to upset the sociological underpinnings of the theory, but this unrest often resulted only in more strict and comprehensive statements of the doctrine. In 1594, the Anglican divine Richard Hooker wrote:

> Here we may briefly end: of Law there can be no less acknowledged, than that her seat is the bosom of God, her voice the harmony of the world: all things in heaven and earth do her homage, the very least as feeling her care, and the greatest not exempted from her power: both angels and men and creatures of what condition soever, though each in different sort and manner, yet all with uniform consent, admiring her as the mother of their peace and joy.[1]

Montesquieu wrote as the "age of natural law" was crumbling. As the modern era began, the basis of legal reasoning shifted from the old myth of natural law to a new myth—that of a contractual understanding between the governed and the governing. This new understanding of law was often explicitly national, and it fed into and grew with the developing nationalism of the eighteenth and nineteenth centuries. Brought down from the heights in which Hooker had placed it, law came to be seen as a creation of this world, and rather than ruling all of creation, law was seen as the servant of the state. Law came to be viewed in terms of its practical usefulness rather than its moral truthfulness—as a restraining or policing force to keep the "war of all against all" within acceptable limits. John Stuart Mill expressed this view perhaps more baldly than anyone. He equated law with political power, and then sought to restrict severely the application of that power.

> The only purpose for which power can be rightfully exercised over any member of a civilized community against his will, is to prevent harm to others. His own good, either physical or moral, is not a sufficient warrant. He cannot rightfully be compelled to do or forbear because it will be better for him to do so, because it will make him happier, because, in the opinion of others, to do so would be wise, or even right.[2]

Montesquieu serves as an appropriate introduction to the subject of the legal framework of religion in colonial New Jersey because, like Montesquieu, the colonial period of New Jersey falls between these two ages. Most Jersey colonists did not come to America as proponents of a new age. Their reasons for settlement were more mundane and immediate than they were ideological.

They were basically a conservative group of people. In many ways, they were baffled by the new world that was being created, out of necessity, by them and around them. Like Montesquieu, they walked tentatively. This situation, not uncommon in the American colonies, has been described by Michael Kammen:

> The English settlements would at once salvage and selvage their culture of origin—conserve it as well as extend its boundaries. But more, in seeking to preserve the past under difficult circumstances, the colonists would move, crablike, sideways into the future.[3]

In New Jersey, the transition between ages was not felt as acutely as elsewhere, and for that very reason the colony's history reveals a much less neat dichotomy of spirit than is found in most other colonies. The laws of New Jersey do not show a clear progression toward liberty. Instead they seem to bend and adjust to more immediate problems. Behind these individual adjustments, however, a single concern informs the whole. Montesquieu distinguished between the letter and spirit of a nation's laws. This distinction, while obviously simplistic, helps explain the dynamics at work in the colonial New Jersey legal structure. The spirit of New Jersey's laws remained basically the same throughout the colonial period, even while specific laws were passed, revised, or rejected to meet the needs of a particular moment. New Jersey did not see itself as in an age of transition, and its leaders did not seek to program change. Nonetheless, the laws of the colony provide a means of cataloging that change.

The basic spirit or attitude that informed all of New Jersey's laws regarding religion was that religion should be denuded of its socially disruptive tendencies. To put the matter differently, the goal was to keep divisive issues of religion out of the public arena. New Jersey was not founded on any one religious vision of the world, and its colonists never viewed the colony as a whole as a religious Zion. Most Jerseyans did conceive of their society as "Christian," but such an attitude was construed in terms of civil peace rather than in terms of religious purity.

While this one spirit overshadows the entire legal history of New Jersey, the formation of the actual legal code of the colony can be divided into three periods. These separate periods are defined by their different central problems. The first phase of religious legal development began with the founding of the colony and lasted roughly until 1676. The major problem of this time was how to attract a base population to the colony. In order to achieve this end, the proprietors and their governors showed a liberal willingness to tolerate and even to encourage a diversity of religious practice. This set the foundation for all that was to follow.

A second phase of development began around 1675 and lasted until the turn of the century (although questions initially raised during this period continued to be asked throughout the entire colonial age). During this time the central problem of New Jersey society shifted from that of initial settlement to one of establishing a general public order. Issues of public religious comportment were addressed and minimal standards of religioethical conduct were enumerated in the law. In essence, this period can be defined as the erection of an informal religious establishment in the colony.

A final stage of development was inaugurated with the royalization of the colony in 1702. With this transition in government the central problem became that of coordinating and balancing the indigenous legal code of the colony with the laws and statutes of the mother country. Ironically the outcome of was a relative liberalizing of New Jersey law concerning religion; it did not result in a tightening of religious strictures, nor was the colony really brought into better line with English practice.

Foundations of Religious Liberty: 1660-1676

The initial phase of development in New Jersey's legal framework had as its central theme the flexibility of the proprietors and their governors in implementing a general policy of toleration toward all religious groups. The proprietors showed a willingness to accommodate themselves to a wide variety of religious expression and religious structure. In so doing, they laid the foundation for a religious diversity that very quickly came to characterize the colony.

A description of this period cannot be limited to a mere delineation of the laws enacted. Each law or proprietary policy must be examined to see if it was in fact implemented and, if implemented, to see with what leeway of interpretation. In colonial America there were two general views concerning the purpose of law. One view held that colonial law should be stricter than in the mother country and should be modeled on martial lines. Proponents of this view contended that the wilderness environment provided a temptation, indeed a compulsion, toward the barbarization of the populace. The presence of a potentially hostile Native American population also encouraged this view, since isolated European outposts were seen as necessarily both military-defensive and civil in nature. This view predominated in the American colonies founded before 1660. A second view asserted that colonial law should be less rigorous than in the mother country. It saw colonial social stability as a function of the size of population, and it was hoped that a liberal legal system would attract a large population to the colony. This view gained popularity later in the colonial period, generally after 1660, when the perceived threat of Native American hostilities had diminished, functional governments had been established in many independent colonies, and competition among colonies had increased. Though elements of the first view are evident in New Jersey, the second predominated. During its early years New Jersey was primarily interested in attracting settlers. Thus its legal code must be examined in the broad scope of its implementation.

Before looking directly at the colony's legal system, one caution is in order. The proprietary period, which lasted from 1664 to 1702, was a time of complex and complicated claims to governmental power both on the part of the various and changing proprietors of the colony and on the part of the crown.[4] Its complicated history resulted in a constant disputing of jurisdictions and authority in various areas and at numerous times in the colony's early history. It is therefore difficult to know exactly how much weight to put on different legal events. Added to this is the fact that all claims made by the proprietors about their right to govern the colony were finally disallowed by the monarchy. This disjuncture in the legal history of the colony created a problem of precedent for the rest of the colonial period. Despite this caution, it is possible to sketch the developing legal definition of the place of religion in colonial New Jersey society. While governors and governments changed, the overall framework of the legal system as it related to religion had a tendency to become more solidified with time.

A. Governorship of Colonel Richard Nicolls

New Jersey was founded on a practical economic and political vision. Determined to unite their landholdings in North America, England launched, in 1664, a military expedition against the Dutch colony in New Amsterdam. Under the leadership of Colonel Richard Nicolls, the venture was a success: the Dutch surrendered on September 7. Even before Nicolls and his fleet had left England, Charles II had granted to his brother James, duke of York, a vast territory in the New World, including that land still ruled by New Netherlands. Having conquered the territory, Richard Nicolls, by prior arrangement, assumed the governorship of all the duke's land.

Nicolls's primary responsibilities centered on the military security of the newly conquered region and the stability of its civil government. He had also received certain "secret instructions as to religion" from the duke. Essentially these were a recognition of the de facto religious diversity of the area, coupled with a policy of nonoffense against Dutch Reformed sensibilities. The ultimate ideal expressed in these instructions was for "one faith and one way of worship" in the new colony, but Nicolls was cautioned against starting in this work until he had "made some progress in less difficult business." Over and over again Nicolls was cautioned to be circumspect in all his actions bearing on religion and in no way to do anything to arouse Dutch suspicions of religious discrimination. The general tenor of these "secret instructions" makes clear that the English had little concrete hope of ever realizing the ideal of "one faith."[5]

Nicolls's instructions dealt specifically with already settled areas and did not outline policies to be followed in unsettled lands such as New Jersey. When the English took over the New Netherlands, only one permanent settlement was intact west of the Hudson. The town, Bergen, had been established, complete with church, in 1660, but four years later it remained a relatively small frontier settlement. As far as records indicate, Bergen received no instructions from Nicolls concerning either military, civil, or religious matters.

Nicolls was not, however, indifferent to the region west of the Hudson. He regarded New Jersey as the most prized of the duke's vast landholdings. When informed at a later date that the duke had given away that part of his territory, Nicolls wrote begging James to reconsider his decision, since, he argued, that was the "most improveable" of all his lands.[6]

While Nicolls took steps to encourage new settlement in the duke's land, a special attraction to Jersey spawned early efforts regarding the area. Nicolls had a ready base on which to build, since Puritan settlers from New England had sought entrance to the fertile region even before its English conquest. As early as 1661, a group of Milford, Connecticut, residents had been invited by Peter Stuyvesant, the Dutch governor of New Netherlands, to explore the territory for possible resettlement.[7] Religion was never a point of contention between these Dutch and English, as evidenced by Stuyvesant's comment "that there is noe at the least differency in the fundamentall points of religion, the differency in churches orders and government so small that wee doe not stick at it, therefore have left and leave still to the freedom off your owne consciences."[8] While an agreement between the governor and these potential Puritan settlers was never reached, religion was certainly not the cause.

The New England Puritans' vision of westward expansion was invigorated with news of England's success. One particularly eager group from the Jamaica vicinity of Long Island pressed Nicolls into issuing, in late 1664, a list of "conditions for New Planters." Seven of the conditions dealt strictly with land acquisition and development, two defined judicial rights and duties, and two related to religious matters. The two articles that address religious concerns read as follows:

> In all Territories of his Royal Highness, liberty of conscience is allowed; Provided such liberty is not Converted to licentiousness or the Disturbance of Others in the exercise of the Protestant Religion. . . .
> Every Town-ship is Obliged to pay their Minister, according to such Agreement as they shall make with them and No man to refuse his Proportion, the minister being Elected by the Major Part of the householders, Inhabitants of the Town.[9]

The orderly governance of the duke's realm seemed always predominant in Governor Nicolls's mind. For the purpose of defensive solidarity, Nicolls required, as had his Dutch predecessor, that new planters organize themselves into compact town settlements.[10] Within these close quarters, the divisive potential of religious differences needed to be held in check. At the same time, Nicolls realized that religious uniformity could hardly be coerced in the Jersey frontier; the governmental machinery to do so was nonexistent. Nicolls, therefore, chose to walk a middle path. A certain liberty of conscience was assured, but liberty of practice was not. Considerable freedom was granted each town to regulate itself, but each town had certain clearly defined religious obligations. The "conditions" stipulated that each town was to have one corporately supported minister, chosen by majority vote of the freeholders. Additional ministers, or ministers for minority religious groups, were not mentioned.

Nicolls's provisions handily met the situation he faced. His regulations were designed to ensure civil orderliness, but were also couched in language attractive to the variety of New England settlers he sought to draw to the area. Puritan zealots could, if they held a local majority, erect new "Zions" in the New Jersey wilderness. Likewise, New England dissenters were promised freedom from persecution, and could even organize their own towns with their own establishments.

As wise as Nicolls's conditions seem, only one town was ever founded under them. And that town was never fully organized according to his provisions. Elizabethtown was settled in 1665. The inhabitants then spent several years waiting for the Rev. Thomas James of East Hampton to join them and to lead them in their local theocracy. He never arrived, and in 1668 the Elizabethtown Puritan congregation finally accepted the former Newark schoolmaster Jeremiah Peck as their minister.[11] By then, however, conditions in the town had changed drastically, and the type of religious oligarchy they sought to erect was no longer legally sanctioned.

One other tract of land, the Navesink (later Monmouth County), was patented during Nicolls's tenure, but the religious provisions of the "conditions" were not applied to this region. Unlike the settlers at Elizabethtown, the original twelve patentees of the Navesink did not share a common religious commitment (although most were either Baptist or Quaker). In light of these religious divisions, Nicolls allowed in the patent for the land that all "shall have free Liberty of Conscience without any Molestation or Disturbance whatsoever in their way of worship."[12] Thus, the patent specifically freed all groups and individuals to practice their religion in worship as well as in conscience, a provision considerably more liberal than any previous conditions.

Nicolls's flexibility in the Navesink situation underscores the primacy he assigned to public order. Nicolls, the Englishman that he was, would probably have preferred to have some sort of publicly maintained religious establishment. He may have intended to imply broad freedom in his earlier "conditions," but the documents seem to indicate his desire to maintain certain restrictions in the practice of religion. In the Navesink, however, such restrictions seemed impractical and unenforceable. Therefore, Nicolls, pragmatic soldier, set aside his ideal of an established church in the interest of orderly government.

Colonel Nicolls's rule over New Jersey did not last long, but the practical adaptability to real situations that guided his tenure in office set a tone that echoed throughout the subsequent history of the colony. Nicolls's official role ended in August of 1665, when Philip Carteret arrived in Elizabethtown and announced himself governor of New Jersey, appointed by the lords proprietor of the colony, Lord John Berkeley and Sir George Carteret. This came as a shock to Nicolls and many resident Jerseyans, but the two had in fact held title to the land for over a year. James had given them ownership through a deed of lease and release dated 23/24 June 1664—almost three months before the area had been seized by British troops.

B. Governorship of Philip Carteret

The arrival of Carteret threw into question the legality of all actions taken by Nicolls since the Dutch surrender. In addition to generally rocking the boat of governmental authority, Carteret's presence had an impact on the Jersey religious scene. Carteret was no Puritan. He came from a Royalist family and had been appointed by two Royalist proprietors. Carteret, however, had no desire to be purposely contrary. He made no attempts to disallow Nicolls's grants of land to either Elizabethtown or Monmouth, nor did he move to curtail any privileges. Nevertheless, Carteret managed to have a dramatic and immediate impact on the development of Elizabethtown. By purchasing the rights of John Bailey, one of the original patentees, Carteret joined the town association. His presence broke the religious homogeneity of the town, and, by fiat, he opened the town to settlement by members of diverse religious commitments.[13] Furthermore, he made Elizabethtown his seat of government. T. J. Wertenbaker has aptly noted the change: "The Elizabethtown Associates thus found that they had prepared, not an isolated religious community, but a capitol for a province."[14]

Carteret's new government was to be based on the document he brought with him, *The Concession and Agreement of the Lords Proprietors of the Province of New Caesarea, or New Jersey*. The seventh and eighth articles relate to the exercise of religion in the colony.

> Item. That no person qualified as aforesaid within the said Province, at any time shall be any ways molested, punished, disquieted or called in question for any difference in opinion or practice in matter of religious concernments, who do not actually disturb the civil peace of the said Province; but that all and every such person and persons may from time to time, and at all times, freely and fully have and enjoy his and their judgments and consciences in matters of religion throughout the said Province, they behaving themselves peaceably and quietly, and not using this liberty to licentiousness, nor to the civil injury or outward disturbance of others; any law, statute or clause contained, or to be contained, usage or custom of this realm of England, to the contrary thereof in any wise notwithstanding.

> Item. That no pretence may be taken by our heirs or assigns for or by reason of our right of patronage and power of advouson, granted by his Majesty's Letter's Patents, unto his Royal Highness Duke of York, and by his said Royal Highness unto us, thereby to infringe the general clause of liberty of conscience, aforementioned: we do hereby grant unto the General Assembly of the said Province, power by act to constitute and appoint such and so many ministers or preachers as they shall think fit, and to establish their maintenance, giving liberty beside to any person or persons to keep and maintain what preachers or ministers they please.[15]

These articles outline a religious policy that parallels but is much more liberal than that which then existed in England. They indicate that a colonywide religious establishment ought to be constituted by the General Assembly, but a broad toleration of religious opinion and practice should be maintained. An article relating to division of land spells out some of the details of this religious establishment, by stipulating that the proprietors should "grant convenient proportions of land . . . for churches . . . and to each parish for the use of their ministers two hundred acres, in such places as the General Assembly shall appoint."[16] The proprietors would thus provide the established church with a means of material support.

The promise of religious toleration contained in *The Concession and Agreement* is clear and has been duly noted by historians since colonial times. The document implies that a broad spectrum of religious belief and practice would be countenanced provided that such behavior did not threaten the civil peace. Equally clear is an intention to form a religious establishment. Philip Carteret assumed such when he issued his proclamation summoning the first assembly:

> I have thought fit with the advice of my Councell to appoint a Generall Assembly . . . for the making and Constituting such wholsome Lawes as shall be most needfull and Necessary for the good government of the said Prouince, and the maintayning of a religious Community and ciuil society one with the other as becometh Christians without which it impossible for any boddy Poloticq to prosper or subsist.[17]

Provisions for religious establishment, however clearly outlined and intended, seem to have been overlooked in colonial times as well as by later chronicles of New Jersey history. Whatever the design of the proprietors, it remains true that laws intended are not always laws enacted and enforced. The colonial assembly never created the machinery of a religious establishment.

This type of independent behavior is paradigmatic of what later became a general pattern. The proprietors, and later the Crown, discovered that the practice of religion in New Jersey followed its own path with only glancing acknowledgment of higher authorities. The local legal framework of religion accordingly grew in an ad hoc manner, reflecting historical realities in the colony as much as or more than any policy decision imposed on the colony from above.

The settling of the town of Newark provides an early example of Jersey's independence of spirit and of the various motives, perceptions, and realities that influenced religious developments in the colony. Theological and political ideals were melded together in the formation of the town, begun in 1666 after five years of negotiations with the Dutch and later with Philip Carteret. The original Newark associates came from an assortment of towns in old New Haven Colony. New Haven had been founded in 1638 by the Puritan minister John Davenport and with the financial backing of Theophilus Eaton. Designed to be a successful commercial enterprise, New Haven was also intended to serve as a bastion of truth and conservatism against what Davenport saw as a lax and weakening New England witness to Puritan ideals. At one point Davenport "nominated God the Supreme Governor" of the colony, and in 1656 he championed the acceptance of John Cotton's *Moses, His Judaicalls*, a strict systematization of Old Testament law, as the basis for New Haven's legal system.[18] As was often the case, these otherworldly and ascetic Puritans were also good businessmen. As early as 1641, the colony had established a trading post on the Delaware River (later abolished by the Swedes) and soon after began founding towns all along the north shore of Long Island. While energetic and growing, New Haven always owned a precarious existence because it had never had a royal charter. This shaky standing was further weakened during the early Restoration when the colony protected two Puritan regicides from royal prosecution. In 1662 New Haven was formally disbanded and the territory was placed within Connecticut's jurisdiction.

The early New Haven vision still burned in the hearts of some of the colony's residents, however, and the thought of being absorbed into Connecticut with its relatively lax governance was anathema to them. While most of the residents accepted the dissolution of their government as uncontestable, a remnant felt settlement in a new area was in order. With this in mind, Robert Treat and two associates from the town of Milford began negotiating with Peter Stuyvesant as early as 1661. Their hope was to reorganize the whole town somewhere west of the Hudson.[19] A general agreement was reached but no action was taken while Stuyvesant was in power. This was possibly because the Milford representatives had heard rumors of an impending English takeover and thought they could obtain more favorable terms from their own government.

A year after the Dutch surrender in late 1665, Treat reopened negotiations with the New Jersey governor.[20] Carteret had hopes of quickly populating his new jurisdiction, and he was willing to lend himself to a broad range of schemes in order to accomplish that goal. Both sides seem to have bargained in good faith; a site on the Passaic River was selected and fifteen articles of agreement were drawn up.[21] While the strict ideals of the Milford people may have waned and this allowed for compromise, it also seems likely that Carteret employed a loose interpretation of *The Concession and Agreement* in order to entice settlement. The fifteen articles have been lost, but if the structure described in them was similar to that later allowed to the Milford settlers when reorganized as the Newark Associates, it hardly fit the framework provided in *The Concession and Agreement*.

The structure of government that finally emerged in Newark was influenced by a compact jointly confirmed by Milford, Guilford, and Branford. The inclusion of Branford seems especially significant, because it was the only New Haven town that had not yet submitted to Connecticut jurisdiction.[22] This resistance-minded town provided a new leadership core in the Newark Association. Branford also sent the greatest number of settlers, though not the earliest and not a majority. Newark's first fully installed minister, Abraham Pierson, hailed from Branford. Most important, it seems to have been the Branford émigrés who coaxed the Newark Associates into declaring a strict civil rule in the town to be overseen by visible saints alone. Two resolutions were declared on 30 October 1666:

> 1st. That none shall be admitted freemen or free Burgesses within our town upon Passaick River in the Province of New Jersey, but such Planters are members of some or other of the congregational Churches nor shall any part of civil Judicature, or as deputies or assistants, to have power to Vote In establishing Laws, and making or Repealing them or to any chief Military Trust or Office. Nor shall any But such Church Members have any Vote in any such elections; Tho'all others admitted to Be planters have Right to their proper Inheritance, and do and shall enjoy all other Civil Liberties and Privileges, According to all Laws, Orders, Grants which are, or hereafter shall be made for this Town.

> 2nd. We shall with Care and Diligence provide to the maintenance of the purity of Religion professed in the Congregational Churches.[23]

The franchise in Newark was restricted to church members, and anyone who was not a member of some Congregational church was heartily discouraged from settling in the town. This theocratic structure seems inconsistent with the range of allowable practices described in *The Concession and Agreement*, but Carteret's goal of rapidly populating the colony apparently allowed him casually to connive with the letter of the law in order to make settlement appear more attractive. Carteret may have justified Newark's restrictions by couching them in terms of the guaranteed condition not to be disturbed in one's manner of worship. The Newark settlers themselves framed their parochialism in such terms, labeling any and all dissenters from within or without as those who would "disturb us in our Peace and Settlement."[24] Carteret seemed content to let the town choose its own way, and the proprietors also seemed to have no problem with this situation. The proprietors' main desire was for the colony to provide revenue. They had no great ideological commitment to religious liberty. Newark's deviation from proscribed practices was easily countenanced, as long as the town showed promise of prospering.

Comparison of Newark with other Jersey settlements emphasizes the fact that the legal structure of religion was never uniformly applied or enforced. Carteret apparently felt free to handle each town's situation differently. Newark was allowed a relatively undisturbed and parochial existence, but Elizabethtown had had its Puritan hegemony broken by Carteret. Meanwhile, Carteret confirmed the rights of the Monmouth patentees as they had been granted by Nicolls and, in 1672, further ordered that in Monmouth, "no Ministerial Power or Clergyman shall be imposed on any the Inhabitants of the said land, so as to influence any that are contrary minded to contribute to their maintenance."[25] In Bergen, however, Carteret allowed the following clause to be included in the town's charter of 1668:

> ... that all the freeholders aforesaid, or the major part of them, have power to choose their own minister for the preaching of the word of God, and the administering of his holy sacraments; and being so chosen, all persons, as well the freeholders as the inhabitants, are to contribute according to their estates and proportions of land for his maintenance, or to lay out such a proportion of land for the minister ... as they shall think fit. ... Notwithstanding, it shall and

may be lawful for any particular person or persons, to keep and maintain any other minister at their own proper cost and charges.[26]

Though variously interpreted, the original *Concession and Agreement* of the proprietors still served as the final legal guide regarding the breadth of allowable religious behavior, and in 1672 the proprietors reasserted their commitment to the basic provisions of that document. The occasion, sparked by a revolt of sorts during the years 1670 to 1672, was the issuance of "A Declaration of the True Intent and Meaning" of the original concessions. The fundamental point of contention had little if anything to do with religion. Rather, the "rebellion" stemmed from a host of conflicting claims over land titlement rights and local governmental privileges.[27] While religion was not directly involved, the proprietors did take the occasion to enunciate one minor change in their stated religious policy.

> As to the 8th article, it shall be in the power of the Governor and council, to constitute and appoint such ministers and preachers as shall be nominated and chosen by the several corporations, without the General Assembly, and to establish their maintenance, giving liberty besides to any person or persons to keep and maintain what preachers or ministers they please.[28]

The change proposed was that the governor and council, as opposed to the General Assembly, were to be given the task of erecting whatever religious establishment they deemed fit. The point, of course, is ultimately moot, for no establishment was ever organized. The change in legal form is nonetheless instructive. In a disorderly situation, the proprietors iterated their endorsement for some sort of colonial religious establishment. Possibly they hoped that a religious establishment overseen by the governor and his council would aid social control. Yet they also seem to have approved of Carteret's varied and freehanded interpretations since they gave him even more power in religious matters. The proprietors also continued to insist that a broad toleration of religion be maintained. Perhaps their reasoning was that such a policy would serve to lessen the homogeneity in those towns that tended to be more resistant to proprietary claims. Whatever their motives, the proprietors maintained a call for both religious establishment and religious toleration in their document of 1672.

C. Dutch Rule, Reconquest, and Division of the Colony

The Dutch repossessed the territory from August 1673 to November 1674. In October 1673, the "Provisional Instructions for the Schouts and Magistrates" contained a statement that,

> The Sheriff and Magistrates shall, each in his quality, take care that the Reformed Christian Religion be maintained in conformity to the Synod of Dordrecht without permitting any other sects attempting any thing contrary thereto.[29]

However, the Dutch reconquest had little effect on religious matters, and only in the predominantly Dutch town of Bergen were these instructions carried out at all. Like the English, the Dutch had no desire to antagonize a foreign population living in their midst. They felt a compulsion to state their ideals, but winked at almost all non-Dutch transgressions against them.

With the restoration of English rule, earlier statutes and privileges were reintroduced, and there was a general return to the situation immediately prior to the Dutch invasion. That configuration was significantly altered in 1676. New Jersey had originally been deeded as a unit to the two proprietors Berkeley and Carteret, but Berkeley had tired of his colonizing ventures. In March of 1674, he agreed to sell his half-share of the colony to two Quaker friends, Edward Byllynge and John Fenwick. Carteret agreed to a partition of the province in 1676. By the Quintipartite Deed (so named because of its five signers: Carteret, Fenwick, and, acting as trustees for Byllynge, William Penn, Gawen Lawrie, and Nicholas Lucas), the formerly unified colony was divided into East New Jersey and West New Jersey.

This division had little immediate effect in East New Jersey, for it represented basically a truncated continuation of the early New Jersey colonial venture. In the western half of the old colony, however, the division created a new colony. As such, the West Jersey proprietors, upon assuming title to the land, issued their own set of "concessions and agreements." It is likely that William Penn composed this statement, but the question of authorship is relatively unimportant since all the proprietors were staunch and devout Quakers. This West Jersey constitution represents one of the most liberal legal documents ever issued in the American colonies, and its description of religious and civil life differs dramatically from the plan in East New Jersey.

That no men, nor number of men upon earth, hath power or authority to rule over men's consciences in religious matters, therefore it is consented, agreed and ordained, that no person or persons whatsoever within the said Province, at any time or times hereafter, shall be any ways upon any pretence whatsoever, called in question, or in the least punished or hurt, either in person, estate, or privilege, for the sake of his opinion, judgment, faith or worship towards God in matters of religion. But that all and every such person, and persons, may from time to time, and at all times, freely and fully have, and enjoy his and their judgments, and the exercises of their consciences in matters of religious worship throughout all the said Province.[30]

The framers of this document saw religion as distinct from any civil governing of society. Religious practice was not even restricted in terms of public order. There are no references to any kind of religious establishment; indeed, religion is not placed in any institutional framework. The theology of the new Quaker proprietors resounds throughout the document, but there were also several practical considerations working to make such a structure feasible. By 1676, the threat of Native American hostilities was considered relatively small, and the Quaker rulers of the colony took pains to maintain good relations with the Native Americans of the region. Because of this lessened threat, close town settlements were not as necessary for defense. The proprietors had also inherited a basically unoccupied land, had formulated a set of fairly well-controlled immigration plans, and had encouraged a religiously and culturally fairly uniform group of people to settle the region. All of these factors freed the West Jersey proprietors to draw up concessions consistent with their own religious convictions.

While divergent in theory, the frameworks of religion that developed in East and West Jersey exhibit certain parallels. In both provinces, religion became a local concern, although that had been the plan in only the West. Each locale worked out its own religious organization with minimal or no direction from the central government. Religion in East and West Jersey became relegated primarily to the private, as opposed to the civil or public, realm.

An Informal Protestant Establishment: 1675-1702

The second period of legal religious development centered on the need, felt by both the proprietors and the colonists alike, to announce certain moral and/or religious boundaries for society. Earlier legal developments had tended to relegate religion to the private sector. This period can be understood as a reaction against that tendency. Jerseyans now felt the need to address issues of religious diversity on a public level.

The attempt was made to unify the legal code regarding religion and to systematize it in practice. The general pattern of legislation that emerged can appropriately be described as an informal establishment of religion. This statement must, however, be qualified. No institutional ecclesiastical establishment was ever erected. Nor were any significant attempts made to limit the range of religious opinion present in either of what were after 1676 the two colonies of New Jersey. Rather, what were primarily called for in the legislation were restrictions on irreligious behavior. In the world of the late seventeenth century, the ties between religion, morality, and civil order were rarely questioned. The law was still conceived in terms similar to those described by Samuel Purchas, who wrote in 1619 that law is a "Hedge about our Persons, and States, to keepe out the Robber and Cheater, the violent Intruder, and Fraudulent Insinuator."[31] As a hedge around the state, law kept the public peace, and as a hedge around each person, it controlled individual conduct and helped each person ready himself for the life to come.

While scrambling for practical ways to attract settlers and seeking different and localistic solutions to deal with the developing religious pluralism, the colony had never lost sight of Carteret's goal of maintaining "a religious Community and civil society one with the other as becometh Christians."[32] This injunction by the colony's first governor was never explicitly addressed by the colonial legislation, but in 1675—the year before the division of the colony into the two colonies of East New Jersey and West New Jersey—four laws were passed that seem to have had the governor's concern in mind. Taken as a group these laws sought to impose a more pointedly religious and morally ordered facade on society. The first law forbade "prophaning of the Sabbath." All "servile work, unlawful recreations, or unnecessary travels on that day, not falling within compass of works of mercy or necessity, either wilfully or through careless neglect" were to be severely punished "according to the nature of the offense." A second law stipulated that no one "shall disturb any public minister in time of divine service." The third and fourth laws reenacted laws previously passed in 1668. These proscribed witchcraft as a capital offense, and made all forms of blasphemy and profanity in general punishable by a fine of one shilling per offense.[33]

The passage of these four laws by the then still singular New Jersey Assembly indicates a willingness on the part of the legislators to move the colony in the direction of an informal establishment of religion. Subsequent developments in both East New Jersey and West New Jersey reveal the depth and breadth of such sentiments.

A. *East New Jersey*

In 1676 Sir George Carteret reached an agreement with the purchasers of Lord John Berkeley's share of the proprietorship to divide the colony in two. Carteret retained control over the eastern area of the colony while two Quakers, Edward Byllynge and John Fenwick, took charge of the western region. This division gave the Puritan-oriented population of East New Jersey a relatively greater say in provincial affairs and this was accordingly soon reflected in the statutes of the colony. In 1677, the year after the division of the colony, the East New Jersey Assembly tightened restrictions on irreligious behavior even further than those enunciated in 1675. Having received several complaints regarding "some persons who suffer disorders in their houses on the Sabbath Day," the assembly enacted a Sabbatarian Law that stated that any Jerseyan who "shall entertain or suffer to be entertained, in his house on the Sabbath, or first day of the weeks, any person or persons that shall behave themselves disorderly . . . namely staggering, reeling, drinking, cursing, swearing, quarreling, or singing any vain songs or tunes of the same" were to be fined ten shillings for the first offense and twenty shillings for all further offenses. The revelers themselves were to endure "two whole hours, without relief," in the pillory.[34]

As East New Jersey progressed through its first independent decade of existence, it became increasingly clear that while a certain freedom of religion was allowed, irreligious behavior was not. The proprietors were willing to countenance a wide range (for the time) of religious belief and practice, and most inhabitants were pleased with such leeway. Yet neither the proprietors nor the locally elected officials wanted to condone publicly irreligious behavior. Under the provisions of *The Concession and Agreement*, liberty of conscience had been given to all who did not "actually disturb the civil peace," but no debauchery—not even private debauchery—was allowed a free hand under such a clause.

This last point was forcefully iterated by the Assembly of East New Jersey in 1682. As a concluding statement to a law denouncing a somewhat strange assortment of twenty-eight different forms of misconduct—ranging from "drinking of healths" to rape and from "Murthers" to cockfighting—the legislators asserted that all such "offenses against God . . . shall be respective discouraged and punished by the judges and courts of justice in this province."[35] According to the assembly, public immorality was one religious issue within their purview.

The residents and leaders of East New Jersey shared a concern to improve the religious/moral atmosphere, but there were also limits beyond which they would not pass. Two anecdotes illustrate the dynamics of this period. Both took place in the year 1683. The first example is that of a law *not* passed, the second that of a new constitution refused ratification.

On 24 March 1683, the governor and Council of East Jersey considered "a Bill for the Better observation and keeping holy the first day of the week or Lord's Day," which had been sent to them by the deputies of the assembly. No copy of the bill exists, but the journal of the governor and council indicates that it sought to enforce Sunday worship throughout the colony by requiring "all persons to worship in publick or private or pay five pence."[36]

The council rejected this bill, voicing four specific objections. First, the bill was redundant, since several laws already on the books ensured public respect for the Sabbath. Second, it was potentially harmful, because the bill made no provision to distinguish true from false worship. The council was wary of forcing worship in the abstract, since they considered the absence of worship preferable to false worship. In their words, "Better to be silent than offer the sacrifice of fooles. The worship of the wicked is Abomination to the Wholy God." Third, the bill was unenforceable. Authorities could not demand to witness private worship. Such a provision was problematic and unreasonable. Finally, the council thought the bill simply too fanatical. The observance of the Sabbath was not, in the eyes of the council, a fundamental law of God. Arguing theologically they asserted that, "Everyday is holy to the Lord—hee has no profane Dayes." Quoting the apostle Paul, the council reminded the assembly that it is a personal matter to "esteeme one day above another."[37]

In addition, the council noted that the proposed bill violated a basic principle of New Jersey life and law. The council felt that the purpose of religious law was to maintain a delicate equilibrium between the extremes of coercing uniformity of practice or belief and encouraging "irreligiousness." Reflecting on the particular bill before them, the council did not find this proper balance. Their final judgment was that "Liberty of conscience ought to be preferred and Licensciousness punished which this Bill seemes not equally to secure."[38]

One month after the New Jersey Council rejected this piece of legislation the New Jersey Assembly opened consideration of a new constitution—the "Fundamental Constitutions" proposed by the new East New Jersey proprietors in 1683. In the previous year, the proprietary rights over East New Jersey had been bought by a group of twelve well-to-do, and mostly Quaker, English merchants.[39] George Carteret, former sole proprietor of the East, had died in January 1680, and the colony fell to his heirs, who had scant interest in his grandiose colonization ventures. The colony was put up for sale at an asking price of £10,000. The actual purchase price amounted to only £3,400, which reflects the generally wretched state of the colony.[40] Civil unrest associated with unstable land titles had given New Jersey an unattractive reputation that tended to squelch rapid immigration and accordingly drive down the market price of the enterprise.

East New Jersey's new proprietors were businessmen. They bought the colony at a bargain price and hoped to reorganize the colony along more stable lines in order to begin once again attracting large numbers of settlers. The time had come in their understanding of things to shift colonial gears from an expansionist mentality to one of orderly consolidation. Slowly, New Jersey was changing from a fluid frontier settlement to a more stable way of life.

As one of their first acts of business, the English businessmen proposed a new constitution to replace the *Concession and Agreement* of 1664. They had great hope that this document would find joyful reception, and even stipulated that the approval of the General Assembly would be necessary for its adoption. It was the stated intention of the proprietors that this new constitution would only refine the spirit and clarify certain points in the older document. They eschewed any intention of drastically changing any of the people's rights or privileges. Nonetheless, on 19 April 1686 the General Assembly voted not to ratify the proposed constitution, giving the opinion that the document did not "agree with the Constitution of this province," that is, *The Concession and Agreement* of 1664.[41] Religious issues may well have played a part in the rejection of this new constitution. The new "Fundamental Constitutions" in many ways reflected the prevailing religious status quo in the colony, but on a number of points its provisions distinctly altered the conditions of the original *Concession and Agreement*. For example, religious liberty in the new document was limited to theists alone, whereas formerly it had been a right of all residents. Granted, there were few atheists living in the colony at this time, and few of those atheists would have been public in their opinions, and hence the change in the letter of the law would have had a negligible effect on the population; still, the shift in language is significant.

The "Fundamental Constitutions" also called for a religious test for public office, the first proposed in the history of the colony. The test was latitudinarian: one had only to "profess faith in Christ Jesus" and declare that one would neither seek to alter the government nor religiously or morally slander any public officer.[42] This is a mild test indeed. But its implementation would have allowed a two-tiered division of the citizenry to arise based on religion. The provisions of the new constitution were liberal for the times, but not sufficiently broad to meet the situation that had developed by that time. Although the General Assembly seemed hesitant to adopt a more traditional model of church-state relations, it must be pointed out that the colony's original breadth of religious freedom was, in fact, not being maintained. In 1698, the assembly did adopt a two-tiered religious model for the colony when it voted to bar Roman Catholics from the franchise and from public office.[43]

B. West New Jersey

Developments in West New Jersey did not parallel those in East New Jersey, but they led to a similar state of affairs. In the west as in the east an initially wide range of religious freedom was slowly narrowed and much more stringent guidelines of morally and religiously acceptable behavior were announced.

When the colony was divided in 1676 it was not at first clear whether the right to govern went with the ownership of the land. In fact, the duke of York, the original proprietor of the colony did not recognize Edward Byllynge's right to govern the colony until 1680.[44] Even after Byllynge had established this right, the residents of West New Jersey continued to look at him with distrust—and this despite the fact that Byllynge appointed Samuel Jennings (a man whom the colonists later came to respect and trust) as his first deputy governor.[45] To protect themselves and their legal rights, the West Jersey Assembly adopted in 1681 ten "fundamental" laws designed to limit Byllynge's ability to interfere in the life of the colony. The law that had to do with religion states:

> That liberty of conscience in matters of faith and worship towards GOD, shall be granted to all people within the Province aforesaid; who shall live peaceably and quietly therein; and that none of the free people of the said Province, shall be rendered uncapable of office in respect of their faith and worship.[46]

By this act the assembly sought to place religious liberty on a more secure and definable base. By binding religious liberty to peaceable and quiet civil comportment, the assembly hoped to protect that liberty from direct encroachments by Byllynge. The fact that the legislation also barred any religious test for public office is an indication that the law's intent was not primarily restrictive.

Two years later, continued fears of Byllynge's plans sparked another spate of legislation. This time the immediate concern was a rumor that Edward Byllynge himself might arrive in West New Jersey to assume direct governorship of the colony.[47] At this point, West New Jersey was still primarily settled by members of the Society of Friends—though a small minority of other religious groups were also present. Perhaps fearing that Byllynge's commercial goals might inundate the colony with disreputable types of people, thus diminishing the influence of Quakers, the assembly passed in 1683 a series of laws relating to morality and religion.

The first law outlawed "drunkenness, whoredom, and other prophaneness," and forbade the above practices "in the presence or hearing . . . or sight or knowledge of a magistrate within the colony." Coupled with another law passed four months later, the first bill's religious implications become clearer. This second act was designed "for the better preventing of such as are prophane, loose, and idle, and scandalous from settling amongst us, who are, and will be not only unserviceable, but greatly burdensome to the Province." It demanded that "all person and persons who shall transport him or themselves, into this Province, shall within eighteen months . . . procure and produce a certificate under the hand of such of that religious society to whom he or they did belong, or otherwise from two magistrates (if procurable) or two constables or overseers of the poor, with three or more creditable persons of the neighborhood, who inhabit or belong to the place where he or they did last reside . . . [showing] that he or she, are such as live soberly and honestly to the best of their knowledge" A third law completes the picture, punishing by a fine not to exceed two shillings per offense all "cursing or using any other brutish, abusive, or reviling speech or speeches, either in the hearing of a magistrate or by the testimony of one or more creditable witnesses."[48] More important than any specific action proscribed by these laws is the general context in which they were set. The stated reason for the last act speaks for them all. They were enacted for "the preventing of those heathenish practices and words, which are unbecoming people professing to know God, and which are dishonourable to his name."[49]

West New Jersey had begun its history with a more liberal statement of religious freedom than the East. However, these laws reflect a move toward a type of two-tiered socioreligious class structure similar to that which had been proposed in the "Fundamental Constitutions" of 1683 and rejected by the East Jersey Assembly. West Jersey had what East Jersey lacked: one religious group that could claim absolute majority status. The Society of Friends ideologically might have opposed any civil establishment of religion, but in practice and in law an informal establishment was being erected. This did not financially aid the Society of Friends or enforce any mandatory religious worship, but it did seek to discourage and even bar from the colony any and all who would not adjust their public behavior to accord with Quaker sensibilities.

For a decade after 1683, the West Jersey Assembly passed no laws that directly related to religion. Then in 1693 an act was passed "for preventing Profanation of the Lord's Day." The preface of this bill indicates that the developmental trajectory of the colony had not changed.

> Whereas it hath been the practice of all societies of Christian professors to set a part one day in the week for the worship and service of God, and that it hath been and is the antient law of England, (according to the practice of primitive Christians) to set a part the first day of the week to that end, and finding by experience that the same good practice and law, hath been greatly neglected in this Province, to the grief of such as profess the Christian religion, and to the scandal thereof. Be it therefore enacted . . . [50]

West Jersey was rapidly moving away from its original commitment to religious liberty toward the erection of an informal establishment. In one sense, the actual conditions in the colony had changed little, the law had only become more reflective of those realities. Religious liberty in West New Jersey had never really been tested beyond the Christian fold. In another sense, however, everything had changed. Few West Jerseyans of the 1690s, it seems, would have agreed with the statement in the original West Jersey concessions that "no men, nor number of men upon earth, hath power or authority to rule over men's consciences in religious matters." Less than twenty years from the founding of the colony "the grief of such as profess the Christian religion" was a sufficient warrant to restructure the code of public behavior for the entire colony.[51]

Despite Quaker ideals to the contrary, the sociological fact of Quaker domination in West Jersey continually pushed the colony's informal religious establishment into a more and more narrow mold. By 1696 an act can be found on the books indicating that a test of religious orthodoxy had been imposed on officeholders for some time.[52] (No record of its passage remains.) The required oath, or affirmation for Quakers, was more lenient than that later passed in East New Jersey that specifically banned Roman Catholics from the franchise and public office.[53] The West's oath required only a profession of trinitarian belief in God and the acceptance of the divine inspiration of the Holy Scriptures. Nonetheless, it is significant that it was in "liberal" West Jersey that such legislation was first passed.

By the mid-1680s, the Jerseys, East and West, had definitely effected a marriage of sorts between religion and the state. It was as much a common-law marriage as a more formal one, but it was of lasting consequence. Although new problems came to the fore after the Crown assumed direct governance in 1702, a close accord between civil and religious concerns remained. Beginning with Lord Cornbury, the first royal governor, a linkage of religion and virtue is prominent in almost every governor's instructions to the General Assembly. For example, John Lord Lovelace, upon his arrival in 1708, assured the gathered assembly that he would "always be ready to give my Assent to whatsoever laws you shall find necessary for promoting Religion and Virtue."[54] Robert Hunter, successor to Lovelace, encouraged the assembly to be as concerned for public virtue and religion as he was himself, and then exhorted them, "Never want will and power to punish wickedness and vice and Encourage true Religion and Virtue."[55] The surrender of proprietary government to the Crown in 1702 had a marked effect on developments in New Jersey, but the tie between religion and civil order built in the years 1675-1700 was a theme that would frequently be echoed throughout the rest of New Jersey's colonial history.

Royalization and Religious Diversity: 1702-1730

A third phase in the development of New Jersey's legal code regarding religion was inaugurated by the cessation of proprietary claims to govern the colony and by the subsequent surrender of the colony to direct rule by the English monarch. The resultant royalization and unification of the colony set the stage for all developments during this period and ironically the main theme that emerged was a renewed emphasis on religious diversity.

Royalization had long been seen as inevitable. Conflicts among the proprietors combined with a growing distrust of the proprietors by residents of the Jerseys were contributing factors, but the immediate reason for royalization was England's desire to impose a stronger and more workable empire structure on its truculent and often less than cooperative American colonies. *Quo warranto* proceedings had been inaugurated against both East and West Jersey as early as May of 1687, but for one reason or another these proceedings languished until the mid-1690s. At that time, a disagreement between East New Jersey and New York over rights to custom revenue reopened the case. By 1699, the proprietors of both East and West Jersey sensed defeat, and they began to negotiate the surrender of governmental claims over both Jersey colonies. Ultimately the proprietors waived all claims and submitted unconditionally to the Crown. In response, they were allowed to retain title to the land and were granted the privilege of making recommendations they thought might be profitable.

The East Jersey proprietors were more vocal, and in 1699 they made several recommendations to the Lords of Trade regarding their colony. One of these relates to religion. They requested that in any settlement:

> No person or persons whatsoever to be molested or deprived of any civil right or privilege, or rendered uncapable of holding any office or employment in the Government because of their religious principles, the Province being planted by Protestant people of divers perswasions, to whom that liberty was an original encouragement.[56]

The phrasing shows that the proprietors were eminently aware of the actual state of religion in the colony, as well as of its more formal legal tradition. They reaffirmed the historical liberty of the colony, but also noted, apparently to reassure the Crown, that such liberty had been extended in fact only to Protestants.

The formal document of surrender was more restrictive and more specific in its recommendation concerning religious rights. Both East and West Jersey proprietors signed this document, and the concerns of each are reflected in it.

That all Protestants may be exempt from all penal laws relating to religion, and may be capable of being of the Governor's Council, and of holding any other publick office, though they do not conform to the discipline of the Church of England, or scruple to take an oath; and that an instruction be given to the governor for procuring a law to pass in the General Assembly for substituting some proper declaration in the place of an oath.[57]

A. The General Impact of Royalization

Royal policy regarding religion was announced by the queen in instructions to her cousin, Edward Lord Cornbury, when he assumed the governorship of the reunited colony in 1702. In keeping with the English Toleration Act of 1689, the queen expressed a terse and rather Erastian commitment to liberty of conscience. She wrote, "You are to permit a Liberty of conscience to all persons (except Papists) so they may be contented with a quiet and peaceable enjoyment of the same, not giving offense or scandal to the government." At considerably greater length, she instructed Cornbury on her desired purpose and place for religion in the society.

> You shall take especial care, that God Almighty be devoutly and duly served throughout your government, the book of common prayer as by law established, read each Sunday, and holy-day, and the blessed sacrament administered according to the rights of the church of England.
>
> You shall be careful that the churches already built there, be well and orderly kept, and that more be built, as the colony by God's blessing be improved; and that besides a competent maintainance, to be assigned to the minister of each orthodox church, a convenient house be built at the common charge for each minister, and a competent portion of land, assigned to him, for a glebe and exercise of his industry.
>
> And you are to take care, that the parishes be so limitted and settled, as you shall find most convenient, for the accomplishing this good work.
>
> You are not to prefer any minister to any clesiastical benefice in that our Province, without a certificate from the right Reverend Father in God the Lord Bishop of London, of his being conformable to the doctrine and discipline of the church of England, and of a good life and conversation: And if any person already prefer'd to a benefice shall appear to you, to give scandal either by his doctrine or manners, you are to use the best means for the removal of him, and to supply the vacancy in such manner as we have directed.
>
> You are to give order, that every orthodox minister within your government, be one of the vestry in his respective parish, and no vestry be held without him,

except in case of sickness, or that after the notice of a vestry summon'd he omit to come.

You are to enquire whether there be any minister within your government, who preaches and administers the sacrament in any orthodox church or chapple, without being in due orders, and to give account thereof to the said Lord Bishop of London. And to the end the ecclesiastical jurisdiction of the said Lord Bishop of London, may take place in our said Province, so far as conveniently may be, we do think fit that you give all countenance and encouragement to the exercise of the same, excepting only the collating to benefices, granting licenses for marriage, and probate of wills, which we have reserved to you our Governor, and the commander in chief of said Province for the time being.

And you are to take especial care that a table of marriages established by the cannons of the church of England, be hung up in every orthodox church, and duly observed, and you are to endeavour to get a law passed in the Assembly of our said Province, (if not already done) for the strict observation of the said table.

You are to take care that drunkeness and debauchery, swearing and blasphemy, be discountenanced and punished: And for the further discountenance of vice, and encouragement of virtue and good living, (that by such example the infidels may be invited and desire to partake of the Christian religion) you are not to admit any person to publick trusts and employments in our said Province, under your government, whose ill fame and conversation may occasion scandal.[58]

What these instructions very clearly call for is the erection of an Anglican establishment of religion in the colony. Still, there seems to be considerable reluctance on the part of some scholars to admit that the queen's instructions amount to an approval of, and order for, a religious establishment. Richard Hofstadter, for one, has labeled these lines "nebulous instructions" that were purposely misinterpreted by "the extravagant and corrupt governor Lord Cornbury, who was also an Anglican zealot . . . as a mandate for creating an establishment." Cornbury might have been extravagant, corrupt, and psychologically unstable to boot, but the instructions he received were not nebulous; they call for the creation of a religious establishment. Hofstadter goes on to note that "neither the Crown nor the legislature ever erected one [an establishment]."[59] This is true, but what he fails to note is that such independence of actual practice from stated policy had come to characterize New Jersey society, especially in its religious aspects, long before 1702. Despite these facts, royalization did have a marked effect on thinking about religion in that it brought the issue of religious establishment to the level of conscious public awareness. During the early years of royal government, New

Jersey was forced to determine its mind about the issue in a more exacting way than it had ever previously done.

The real threat of an Anglican establishment being erected in the colony was, at least in the Cornbury years, minimal. The Church of England did not have a strong presence in New Jersey before royal rule (only one Anglican chapel existed in the colony before 1702), and it grew only slowly after royalization. Anglican missionaries from the Society for the Propagation of the Gospel entered the colony in 1702 (the same year as Cornbury) and they could have been used to help erect an establishment, but friction between Cornbury and the missionaries hampered the efforts of both to strengthen the church.

Later royal governors received instructions identical to Cornbury's, and they all, more or less, worked to make the church's presence increasingly more noticeable, but numbers were always against an Anglican establishment. If the threat of an Anglican establishment had any affect at all it was that it crystallized forces in New Jersey opposed to such developments and helped spawn a conscious religious reaction to the informal establishmentarian pattern of legislation that had been concocted in the colony in the late seventeenth century.

The royalization and the simultaneous unification of the colony religiously affected New Jersey in two other ways. On the sociological side, no one religious group could now dominate public life. This was felt especially by the Quakers of the western half of New Jersey. As late as 1700, the major part of the West New Jersey population was still Quaker. This demographic fact had provided a basis for the earlier push in that region for the creation of an informal establishment of religion. After 1702, however, Quakers were set on a par with all other religious groups. In the unified assembly of the colony no one group held a majority. A second effect of royalization was primarily political. The legal code of New Jersey now had to be examined in the light of the entire weight and history of English law. New Jersey could no longer go its merry way, existing in its own narrow and isolated understanding of the law. Ostensibly, this should not have been a problem, since the rights of government, even as they had originally been granted to James, duke of York, had stated that all colonial legislation must "be as near as may be agreeable to the laws, statutes, and government of this our realm of England."[60] Nevertheless, zeal had often outrun mandate, and proprietors from Berkeley and Carteret on down had tended to overlook this injunction. Perhaps the most blatant example is the earliest one. In the original *Concession and*

Agreement of 1664, the proprietors assured settlers that religious liberty would be maintained, "any law, statute . . . usage or custom of this realm of England notwithstanding."[61]

B. *Legal Rights of Quakers*

Even with a royal governor seated in the colony, the liberty enjoyed by Jerseyans with regard to religion did not cease. The people continued quietly to ignore English religious legislation where it seemed antithetical to conditions in the colony. During the royal period of New Jersey colonial history few new laws relating to religion were passed. Whatever new statements were made tended to be examples of the colonists using pressure to adjust colonial law to English precedent as a force for furthering religious liberty—and this despite attempts by numerous royal governors to do just the opposite. Nowhere is this more evident than in the question, posed frequently after 1702, of the proper place and rightful privileges of Quakers in the government of the colony. This "problem" was first addressed by Cornbury. Besides having a strong personal antagonism toward the Quakers, he also thought their presence and strength posed some very real legal problems. One question was whether Quakers should be allowed to sit on juries. In November of 1704, Cornbury wrote to the Lords of Trade:

> [Quaker] consciences are soe tender that they can't suffer an oath to be taken in their presence soe that either Quakers must not be admitted to sit in Courts of Judicature, or else all causes must be tried by Jurys who have taken noe oaths, and upon the Evidence of witnesses not sworn.[62]

Cornbury and his associates feared that having a large number of Quakers in the assembly might doom any militia bill. The governor also felt that the informal Quaker establishment in West New Jersey, still a potent force, would use their bloc voting in the assembly to prevent the formation of an Anglican establishment. Cornbury and his successors therefore sought to restrict Quaker participation in the government.

One hindrance, however, had been placed in the governor's way. His official instructions had included an article devoted exclusively to the Quaker issue:

> And whereas we have been informed that divers of our good subjects inhabiting those parts, do make a religious scruple of swearing, and by reason

of their refusing to take an oath in courts of justice and other places, are or may be liable to many inconveniences, our will and pleasure is, that in order to their ease in what they conceive to be a matter of conscience, so far as may be consistent with good order and government, you take care that an act be passed in the General Assembly of our said Province, to the like effect as that past here in the 7th and 8th year of his Majesty's reign, entitled, An act, that the solemn affirmation and declaration of the people called Quakers, shall be accepted, instead of an oath in the usual form, and that the same be transmitted to us, and to our commissioners for trade and plantations as before directed.[63]

The instructions further noted that Quaker scruples might make them unwilling to serve in office, and in such cases they were to be pressured to serve.

These explicit instructions could not blatantly be ignored. Still, Cornbury and his immediate successors were adamant in their desire to rid the Jersey legislature of Quakers. The records that remain are full of their spleen. Over and over again it was asserted that Quaker thought and behavior were intrinsically antithetical to the interests and goals of the Crown. Such sentiments were voiced both within the colony and in overseas correspondence. Cornbury's successor, John Lord Lovelace, was repeatedly advised by his counselors to take action against Quakers in the Assembly. It was charged that "their Insolencies in Government are Intollerable . . . they become mischievous and daring even to the affronting Magistrates and contemning the laws, and Particularly Pride themselves on being able to Cramp and Confound Government."[64] (The Quakers responded that they were free to act because of the instructions to the governor, and also because "the old Established Magna Charta of New Jersey" [the "Fundamental Laws" passed in 1681] securely protected their rights.)[65] And Governor Ingoldsby wrote to the queen in 1709 that unless the "Quakers be restrained from the management of Publick affairs . . . your Majesty can never expect to see an end of Confusions and Divisions which have so long reigned among us."[66]

Ingoldsby's request apparently went unheeded, and the Quakers scored a major victory five years later. At that time, *An Act that the Solemn affirmation and declaration of the people called Quakers Shall be accepted* . . . was passed by the New Jersey legislature, which fully qualified Quakers for public office. Some delicate political trading may have contributed to the passage of the act, since *An Act to Settle the Militia* sailed through the legislature at the same time, apparently with only minimal Quaker resistance.[67]

The Quakers had succeeded in obtaining the right to hold office, but anti-Quaker sentiments continued. As late as 1729, Governor John Montgomerie was still voicing opposition to Quaker power. In that year he wrote to the Lords of Trade asking them "to delay obtaining His Majesties Assent to the Quakers and Triennial Acts," with the hope that he had "convinced your lordships that the Quakers do not deserve His Majesties assent to the Act past in their favours."[68] But the Lords of Trade were not convinced and wrote back to Montgomerie in July 1729:

> As to first of these [i.e., the Quaker bill] We see no Reason for repealing it either from the Impropriety of the Diction or from the small variance between the Quakers Affirmation prescribe'd by this Law And that prescrib'd by the Law of England, and therefore purpose to let this Act lye by Probational, and hope the Behaviour of the People, will never induce the Crown to Repeal it.[69]

This decision of the Lords of Trade basically guaranteed full legal rights for New Jersey Quakers. The Crown could have repealed the act, but it never did, even though Quakers constantly hindered the passage of militia bills, refused to accept offices in the militia, and even laughed at the complying citizenry when they assembled for military exercises.[70] These actions could justly have been interpreted as disruptive of the civil peace. In spite of such injudicious behavior, the right of Quakers to hold positions of public trust in the colony was never again seriously questioned.

Conclusions

The legal framework of religion in New Jersey was basically complete by 1730, and from 1730 to 1760 the assembly only rarely dealt with religious matters. This underscores the colony's renewed attentiveness to the breadth of religious diversity that existed within its bounds. It also reveals the colonists' basic commitment to religious liberty. The primary means of maintaining religious liberty during the royal period was, except in the most pressing cases, simply to ignore religious questions in governmental debate.

During the time of royal government, the colony in many ways turned back to its original position. The first proprietors had attempted to free society from the disruptive influences of religion in order to get on, as Nicolls's instructions had stated, with "easier business." After experimenting with several methods of trying to tie together religion and society, the residents of New Jersey returned to the wisdom of the founders of the colony. This spirit is illustrated by an example of a bill that in 1721 did *not* become law in New Jersey.

In that year, a "remarkable bill"—to use Samuel Smith's words—was introduced in the assembly by the pious Puritan Governor William Burnet.[71] All we have is the title, but that speaks eloquently by itself: "An Act against denying the divinity of our saviour Jesus Christ, the doctrine of the blessed trinity, the truth of the holy scriptures, and spreading atheistical books."[72] Possibly the governor envisioned this bill as the first of a series by which he would redirect the colony into a more specifically religious and godly state. If so, he was in for an education about the place of religion in New Jersey life. The few comments that have survived speak clearly and loudly. Assembly member Nathaniel Jenkins, an ordained Baptist minister, immediately labeled the bill "ill-designed." Jenkins asserted that he heartily agreed with all the doctrinal statements in the proposed legislation, but felt it should be defeated since religion should make its case in society with no "weapon save that of argument."[73] Samuel Smith, a Quaker, expressed a historically informed awareness: "Assemblies in the colonies have rarely troubled themselves with these subjects, perhaps never before or since."[74] In Smith's estimation, silence should have been, and in fact was, the appropriate response of the assembly.

In the preface to their collection of New Jersey law published in the early 1750s, Aaron Leaming and Jacob Spicer wrote that the colony's first proprietors "were wise and happy enough to hit upon that system which of all others is the most worth pursuit of a rational being, namely, the security of the religion, liberty, and properties of the adventurers and their latest posterity."[75] Leaming and Spicer overstate the case; the founders were not quite that wise. But in time the colonists and the leadership of the colony together came to what in retrospect seems a very wise working solution to the problem of religious diversity. The model inherent in the policies they developed would find explicit expression only later. It was not until 1748 that Montesquieu would write:

> When the legislator has believed it a duty to permit the exercise of many religions it is necessary that he should enforce also a toleration among these religions themselves. . . .
> It is necessary, then, that the laws require from the several religions, not only that they shall not embroil the state, but that they shall not raise disturbances among themselves. A citizen does not fulfill the laws by not disturbing the government; it is requisite that he should not trouble any citizen whomsoever.[76]

This theoretical announcement was, in fact, practice in the colony well before 1748.

TWO

Tribal Religion

General Characteristics

The earliest and perhaps the most natural reaction to the multifaceted religious environment of New Jersey was religious tribalism. The first impulse of tribalism was to deny diversity by attempting to establish a homogeneous order—or at least a sense of homogeneous order—in the local environment. The goal was to provide a "shelter of sameness" for the colonists who saw themselves living in the midst of what they perceived as dangerous diversity. A second aspect of tribal religion was authoritarianism in the tribal group. Tribalism was, in many senses, more a subjective way of envisioning the world than it was a reflection of objective sociological realities. As such it was necessary to police attitudes among members of the tribe to ensure that divergent visions of the world not be allowed casually to circulate, weakening resolve and threatening tribal uniformity. Finally, religious tribalism functioned as a mediating structure. It provided a buffer protecting individual identity and meaning from erosion by the acids of diversity.

Tribal religion was rooted in the natural human desire to live among the like-minded—to live within a seemingly "natural" social uniformity. There is a certain shelter in sameness. We are all more comfortable (if sometimes bored) with the familiar than we are with the new. This is especially true of the radically new, those situations for which experience has not prepared us. Most immigrant religious groups entering New Jersey found the religious diversity of the colony new; for some it was radically new. Tribalistic developments should not, therefore, be looked down on. Religious tribalists were not so much bigots as they were uncertain about how to act in a new sociological environment.

While tribalism should not be scorned, it is important to note the irony that is inherent in it. By seeking to deny the diversity around them, tribalists ultimately ended up being the most intractable supporters of diversity. Active tribalism prompts reactive tribalism; separationism on the part of one group encourages a counterseparatism on the part of other groups as these groups come to sense the outsider status conferred upon them by the original tribe in an area. The depth of irony found in religious tribalism goes beyond the incidental perpetation of diversity. Tribalism ultimately needs diversity in order to survive. Tribes define themselves over against other tribes. They cannot exist in a social vacuum; indeed, the end of diversity would be the death knell of tribalism. The felt presence of otherness in the near environment is necessary.

Much of the strength and appeal of religious tribalism in colonial New Jersey derived from its function as a mediating structure in society. Situated between the individual and the total social system, the tribe provides an immediate, personal, and comprehensible unit of meaning and belonging. Peter Berger has convincingly argued that reality is a social construction built upon a foundation of conversation with "significant others."[1] Through fellowship with like-minded people we assure each other that our own "reality" is indeed "the reality." The comfort of such assurance is never cheap. Numerous moral and material demands are inherent in all tribal associations. But many people—perhaps most—prefer security to freedom. In New Jersey, many settlers preferred the restrictive comforts of the tribe to the anomie of freedom contained in diversity.

Religious tribes in New Jersey usually did not exist as legally and/or institutionally defined organizations. This points to the fact that religious tribalism was really more an attitude than an objective evaluation of the environment. A tribe existed primarily in the shared worldview and shared self-definition of a flexibly bounded group—in other words, tribes existed as corporate perceptive fictions. In order to maintain this type of existence, it was necessary that an authoritative pulpit of some sort exist where the definitive shared characteristics could be enunciated. The continued existence of tribes hinged on this task and usually it was delegated to the clergy. It was the minister's job to announce the limits of opinion and action that would be tolerated within the tribal orb and it was the minister's responsibility to do this with sufficient verve that the plausibility of the tribal vision of the world would appear self-authenticating. As in more primitive forms of religion, so also in tribal religion, it was the priest/shaman/minister's job to portray the tribe, convincingly, as residing at the middle of the world—the *axis mundi*—and thereby to infuse the concerns of the tribe with a proper aura of sacredness. Similarly, it was the minister's task metaphorically to relegate all outsiders to the fringe—to the end of the earth.[2]

Tribal religion in New Jersey—or at least a rough approximation of it—has not suffered for want of scholarly notice. If anything, modern scholarship has tended to overemphasize its prevalence and importance. Larry Gerlach has stated this position as forcefully as anyone.

> Religious heterogeneity, a conspicuous characteristic of the Mid-Atlantic provinces, tinctured every phase of life in New Jersey. Sectarian rivalries contributed to and compounded the numerous tensions and divisions that beset the Jerseys....
> The facade of apparent religious harmony, more expediential than ideological, must not obscure the fundamental fact that spiritual passions always ran high in this ecclesiastical Babel.[3]

Descriptions such as these misrepresent conditions as they prevailed. Tribalism was not the be-all and end-all of religion in New Jersey. In fact, religious tribalism in the colony was, in terms of its geography, distinctly restricted, and, in terms of its general existence, always tenuous. Religious tribalism was a prominent feature of life, but it was not ubiquitous. The conditions necessary for the development of tribalism were not present everywhere, and some regions reveal almost an absence of religious tribalization. Where religious tribalism is found, it varies by locale in intensity, duration, and degree of strength.

A. Demography

In many ways religious tribalism can be discussed as a special kind of subculturalism. Recent studies on the development of subcultural groups indicate that a certain critical mass of people must be assembled to touch off the formation of a distinct group.[4] Many locations in New Jersey (for example, the sparsely settled Atlantic coast) simply could not provide such numbers. The experience of the French Huguenots of Hackensack illustrates the need for this critical mass. Under the leadership of a local resident layman, David DesMarest, the Huguenot settlers of Bergen County broke away in 1682 from the local Dutch Reformed Church (with which they shared an essentially identical theology) to form their own French Reformed church. They called Rev. Pierre Danielle to be their pastor and under his leadership the congregation remained intact. In 1696, however, Danielle relocated to Boston. Shortly thereafter, the church folded. Despite the fact that the original impetus for the French church's formation had been local and lay, this Huguenot group, when deprived of clerical leadership and inspiration, was quickly reabsorbed by the local Dutch Reformed congregation. Theological affinities between the two groups surely paved the way to a merger, but a basic lack of numbers seems to have been the real reason for the collapse of the separate Huguenot church.[5]

Regions containing a highly diverse population also seemed relatively immune to tribalistic religion. In Monmouth County, where Anglican, Presbyterian, Baptist, Quaker, and Dutch Reformed groups had all established regular services by the first decade of the eighteenth century, tribal religion was practically nonexistent. The diversity of Monmouth with its actual and undeniable pluralistic religious panorama defused the development of all narrow tribal visions. It seemed that tribal religion flourished best in situations of face-to-face competition between two or, at the most, three groups.

Religious tribalism seems to have developed most readily in areas where a distinct religious and cultural group early had staked out a claim and later found itself surrounded by a different group or groups. The cultural clustering that set the necessary stage for these developments was prevalent in New Jersey. Historical geographer Peter Wacker has noted a strong "tendency on the part of whites [in New Jersey] to settle in a locale where those of similar cultural origins had already located."[6] Cultural factors in land settlement decisions were not, of course, unique to the colony, nor were they by themselves always decisive. But New Jersey's cultural diversity did tend to increase the relative importance of such considerations.[7] Newly arrived immigrants did not face a neutral choice: either one settled among those of his or her own cultural group or one ended up living amid strangers.

A brief look at the Swedish Lutherans of South Jersey provides a good example of how religious and culturally motivated geographical clustering could develop into religious tribalism. Swedish Lutherans had originally settled in southern New Jersey when that region was under the control of the Swedish crown. The New Sweden colony failed, but many settlers stayed on. Soon, however, these recalcitrant Swedes found their territory being inundated by English Quakers. In reaction, they increasingly wore their religion, culture, and nationality as a badge to distinguish themselves from these intruders. They refused assimilation and in 1693 they wrote home to assure their friends and families that they had not deserted either Swedish culture or religion:

> . . . as regards our general condition in this country, we are almost universally farmers who plow and sow and practice agriculture, and live according to the lawdable old Swedish customs. . . . For we do not believe that God will forsake us, although we are in a strange and heathen land, far away from our own dear fatherland.[8]

Personal as well as cultural factors were also important. Immigrants tended to spread out over the land. They did not settle in neat little towns. Robert Redfield has observed that where "there is no community centering upon town or village; there is only a double network of kinship connection and neighborly connection to hold together, loosely, people who dwell separate from each other."[9] The lineaments of tribal religion often followed this "double network" of connections. Neighborly connections and kinship connections, however, would often reinforce each other through intermarriage. The result sometimes bordered on the creation of an independent "primitive society"—defined by the "circulations of goods, wives, or messages"—such as that described by Claude Levi-Strauss.[10] This type of social arrangement does seem to have existed in eighteenth-century Essex County. The depth of familial social interrelatedness was revealed when prosecutors of participants in the land riots of the 1740s found they could not bring the offenders to trial in the local court because "there is scarcely a man in the county of Essex but what is related by blood or marriage to some one or other of the rioters."[11]

B. Actions of Defense and Offense

"Primitive societies," such as those described by Levi-Strauss, and cultural concentrations of population are, of course, necessary but not sufficient explanations for the tribalism that dotted New Jersey's colonial map. A tendency on the part of Jerseyans to "cluster into separateness"[12] only provided a foundation. The real trigger for religious tribal developments was the diversity of the colony. It was the feeling of being surrounded by potentially, and sometimes actually, hostile strangers that prompted tribalization when and where this occurred. Tribalism is, after all, a reactionary strategy. It seeks to restore to a group a strengthened sense of unity in the face of outside threats. Because of this, early tribalistic developments in New Jersey were usually defensive in nature.

A poignant illustration of one such defensive response is again provided by the Swedish Lutherans. In the same letter from 1693 already quoted, they asked for assistance from their countrymen:

> We, therefore, beg that there may be sent to us two Swedish ministers, who are well learned and well exercised in the Holy Scriptures, and who may well defend both themselves and us against all the false teachers and strange sects by whom we are surrounded, or who may surround us on account of our true pure, and uncorrupted service to God and the Lutheran religion, which we shall now confess before God and all the world, so that if it should so happen, which, however, may God avert, we are ready to seal this with our blood.[13]

It is a piece of practical wisdom that the best defense is a good offense and such reasoning was not lost in New Jersey. Defensive postures often metamorphosed into offensive ones and social conflict between groups quickly developed. Lewis Coser defines social conflict as "a struggle over values and claims to scarce status, power, and resources in which the aims of the opponents are to neutralize, injure, or eliminate their rivals."[14] New Jersey law prohibited the physical elimination or injury of rival religious groups, but in their struggles against one another the different tribes quickly devised a variety of techniques designed proficiently, yet nonviolently, to neutralize the claims of their opponents.

C. Communication and Conversion

One of the most effective means of neutralizing the religious claims of an antagonistic tribe was to label one's opponents irrational or, better yet, crazy. The Presbyterian Francis Makamie was a master of this technique. In the preface to his work against the then Quaker George Keith, he states:

> Such is, not only the impiety, irreligion, and contradiction to clear Scriptural Light, which the Doctrine of the Quakers is stuffed withal; but the Unreasonableness, Nonsense, and Self-contradiction which it carries with it, that it may well seem a wonder to men of understanding that it hath not long since been exploded.[15]

John Talbot, missionary of the Society for the Propagation of the Gospel (SPG) stationed at Burlington, favored a somewhat less confrontational, more pastoral, approach. He warned his parishioners, for their own sakes, to avoid all Quaker meetings lest they "be bewitched and forced out of their Faith and senses, too."[16]

Quakers were often the objects of more traditional and churchly tribal invectives. Seizing the opportunities offered to them by their opponents, however, Quaker tribal apologists could sometimes turn a supposed weakness into an asset. John Delavall, in a response to criticism by the then "Christian Quaker" George Keith, calmly asserted that the "profound logick" of his antagonists "cause[d] him not to stagger."[17] Like all Quakers, he claimed the assurance of an "Inner Light" that transcended human rationality. Quaker adversaries often found themselves frustrated by subjective responses such as Delavall's. Keith's attempted repartee to Delavall's quick-witted assertion undoubtedly fell on deaf Quaker ears. He did not understand his opponent when he protested:

> I used no profound logick in the case, but one or two of the easiest and plainest Rules in that called Logick, belonging to the rudiments of it, and as I told him true Reason teacheth it, without all Art of Logick.[18]

Events at Elizabethtown illustrate the same point. Seth Fletcher, the Congregational minister of the town, was a rabid anti-Quaker. In 1681, he agreed to meet some of his foes for what he assumed would be a scholarly debate over the ultimate destiny of convinced Quakers. He was mistaken. On 25 March 1681, he penned the following description of the meeting to Increase Mather at Boston:

> I proceeded to six severall Arguments by which to make good my Assertion, viz. that a Quaker living and dyeing as a Quaker (without repentance) according to what God hath revealed in his work, he could not be saved. I in every argument demanded what part of the Arguments they would deny but instead of answer there was railing and threatening mee that my destruction was nigh at hand. To prove the Minor I continually produced their own authors and several things out of their Rabbie's books, which so exceedingly gauled them that then they set themselves to Humming, singing, reeling their heads and bodies (Antique like) whereby both to disturb me and to take off the people from attending to what I had to say for the maintaining the Assertion.[19]

That event illustrates more than merely a clash between rational and irrational forms of argumentation. It also reveals that in order to maintain strong tribal ties, true communication with other tribes or outside elements could not be allowed. At Elizabethtown, Quakers resorted "to Humming, singing, [and] reeling their heads and bodies" to distract themselves and others from Rev. Fletcher's diatribe. An easier means of blocking communication was simply to avoid all unnecessary contact with nontribe members. In *A Brief Exhortation to all who profess the Truth* (1691), John Willsford of Burlington voiced a distressed prayer to his fellow Friends:

> Oh! the Lord help all his People well and truly to consider this weighty thing, in all our commerce with all sorts of People, that God's pure witness may be reached and every appearance of Evil born testimony against. . . .
> . . . it concerns our Monthly Meetings to inspect well into this matter that we may not become a mixt People, lest the Lord be angry and spue us out.[20]

Cessation of communication with outside elements served as a hedge around the purity of the tribe. For many tribalists, purity seemed necessary lest, as Willsford warned, "the Lord be angry and spue us out." Such demands for purity were often tinged with apocalyptic fears and fervor. Willsford, in the same exhortation, informed his fellows that "the Lord is about to make a clear separation, he will not bear much longer, as he hath done in the time of ignorance."[21] In other instances, purity was seen as an end in itself. The Newark patentees, for example, conceived of it as a part of "God's blessing."[22] These tribalists did not need apocalyptic threats to keep them in line. Given the option of strict tribal purity or learning consciously to live with diversity, purity was an easy yoke to bear.

The same kind of attitude prevailed in early Newark. The second item of the "fundamental agreements" of the Newark patentees avows:

> That in case any shall come into us or arise up amongst us that shall willingly or wilfully disturb us in our Peace and Settlements, and especially that would subvert us from the true Religion and worship of God, and cannot or will not keep their opinions to themselves or be reclaimed after due Time and means of Conviction and reclaiming hath been used; it is unanimously agreed upon and Consented unto as a fundamental Agreement and Order, that all and Persons so ill disposed and affected shall after Notice given them from the Town quietly depart the Place Seasonably.[23]

Contemporary scholars have noted another effect of stressing tribal purity. Mary Douglas writes, "Rituals of purity and impurity create unity in experience."[24] An emphasis on purity provides the last link in the circular reasoning of tribal identity. An initially shared history and vision of the world drew people together. Having congealed into a distinct group, these people found that the mere fact of separateness accentuated their peculiar distinctives. Those distinctives in turn were elevated to the level of moral imperatives. Such an imperative was, of course, essentially a demand for purity. And this came to define ever more sharply the shared history and religious vision of the group.

Despite all attempts to build strong walls, no defense was unassailable. Chinks in a tribe's armor allowed messages from outside to penetrate the mental cosmos of the tribe. Intrusions of this nature might create new tensions, or increase existing tensions, but they could still usually be ignored; the conversion or apostasy of a member, however, could not.

The initial problem faced by tribes from which individuals had converted was one of explaining how God (in this case functioning as the tribal deity) could allow such a thing to happen. The real threat of conversion or apostasy was that it revealed the volitional basis of tribal association and thereby threatened the sense of organic cohesion—the grounding myth—that held the tribe together. To defuse this threat, it had to be shown that the convert had in some way been coerced. Religious tribalists reasoned inventively, but ultimately all deemed the convert either deluded by enemies or duped by the devil. John Talbot thought converts "bewitched."[25] Francis Makamie perceived tribal defectors as lying under God's "awful and righteous Judgment" because they had "Believe[d] a Lie . . . [and] received not the truth in the love of it."[26]

A General Epistle issued by the Philadelphia-Burlington Yearly Meeting of the Society of Friends in 1686 contains an extended discussion of the matter. Deserters of the faith are first disowned and then called devils. Finally the faithful of the tribe are reassured that such evil individuals are relatively few in number.

> That all may know, we own none to be of our Fellowship, or to be reckoned or numbered with us, but such as fear the Lord and keep faithfully to his heavenly Power, that with a holy Conversation they may adorn that Truth they profess, otherwise what experience soever they have had of the Truth, and are fallen from it, we account them as so many Judasses or Demasses, and own such no more than the primitive Christians owned them. . . . [I]f amongst the twelve Disciples there was one become a Devil, and fell by Transgression, so now if amongst every twelve who Profess the same Truth with us called Quakers, one should become a Devil, and fall by Transgression, we cannot help it.[27]

Religious tribes that gained members through conversion were in a rather different position from those that lost members. Edward Vaughn, Anglican rector at Perth Amboy, wrote to England in December of 1709 describing the situation he had found on his arrival in the colony as the successor to the SPG missionary John Brooke.

> Here are a vast number of Deists, Sabbatharians and Eutychians as also of Independents, Anabaptists, and Quakers from which absurdities Mr. Brooke brought a considerable number to embrace our most pure and holy religion. I hope that my labors also will be attended with no less success, and observe that those late converts are much more zealous for promoting the interest of our church and more constant in the public worship of God, than those who "sucked her milk in their infancy."[28]

Vaughn perceived the zeal of new converts as an advantage. In a sense it was, but such fervor could cut two ways. Lewis Coser describes the positive results:

> The renegade contributes to the strength of the out-group to which he transfers his allegiance not only, as Simmel points out, because, unable to go back, he will be more firm in his loyalty to the new group than those who have belonged to it all along, but also because he gives it the increased conviction of the righteousness of its cause.[29]

Tribal convictions were undoubtedly strengthened by the addition of these "true believers"[30]—individuals who had burned their religious sociological bridges behind them. All converts, however, come with a price. The inevitable result of an individual's conversion from one group to another was that intergroup conflict took on a new and more bitter note. Coser quotes Georg Simmel concerning this effect:

> . . . the renegade hates and is hated. The recall of earlier agreement has such a strong effect that the new contrast is infinitely sharper and bitterer than if no relation at all had existed in the past. . . . "Respect for the enemy" is usually absent where the hostility has arisen on the basis of previous solidarity.[31]

Incidents of conversion were mixed blessings for all concerned. Conversion provided opportunities for strengthening tribal solidarity, but it simultaneously increased the degree of hostility between tribes.

D. A Variety of Conflicts

Violence between opposing religious groups was legally prohibited in New Jersey. Despite this, many tribal groups still harbored apocalyptic visions of their enemies' destruction. Given the right circumstances, these desires could burst forth in action. Most frequently this occurred on a local level, but given conducive political conditions, it could also appear colonywide. Occasionally, these disputes erupted into actual violence; more frequently they did not. The goal of all, however, remained, in Coser's terms, the injury of all competing tribes and the effective elimination of all nontribal or antitribal elements within one's territorial bounds.

A mild example of this kind of intertribal strife comes from Cohansey in Salem County. In 1715, a number of inhabitants submitted an affidavit to Governor Robert Hunter, informing him that they were refusing to pay their assessed taxes.

> Wee have been Illegally Assesed by an Asseser who being a Known and open profest Roman Catholick which is Utterly Repugnant to the Laws of Great Brittain and Contrary to the Rights and Liberties of his Royall Majesties faithfull Subjects and if wee Submitt To Suffer or Acknowledge any such Roman Catholick to Usurp or bare any place in office or proffitt or trust Among us wee Should Count our Selves Traytors to his Majestie our King and all True Protestants.[32]

The appointment of a Roman Catholic to a position of public authority infuriated the Congregationalists of Cohansey. Tribal disgust at the perceived strength of an opponent (there were hardly enough Roman Catholics in the colony to spark any justifiable fear) motivated them to action. Since they could not claim any chartered legal right to homogeneity, such as that possessed by the Puritans of early Newark, they had to manufacture another kind of legal case against their opponent. As the case turned out, however, Governor Hunter would have none of it. The impartial governor stated in correspondence with the Lords of Trade that he saw "no real ground for their [i.e., the Congregationalists'] uneasiness." (This reveals considerable toleration on the part of the governor, since Roman Catholics were legally prohibited from holding public office in the colony.) He further noted that the real cause of the squabble appeared to lie elsewhere than in a strict concern for legal propriety. Hunter's personal conclusion was that the reason for the conflict was "in their nature, for they are all from New England who have signed it."[33]

Events in Burlington illustrate a more heated kind of intertribal conflict and underscore the ever present potential for violence. John Talbot, the SPG missionary stationed at Burlington, reports two separate and revealing incidents.

> At the time of Election of representatives at Burlington there was a Man Came to him [Talbot] And said they would pull down the Quakers meeting house and Dwelling Houses or burn them . . . an old Fool (as he called him) advised with him at another time and asked him if they should not break all the Quakers Glass windows for not putting out of Lights.[34]

The issue here is not defensive in nature, but offensive. These anti-Quaker Anglican tribalists, existing as a very small minority amid an overwhelmingly Quaker population, appear to have viewed violence as one of the few means available to combat their enemies. Talbot, though himself a vehement opponent of the Quakers, dissuaded the individuals involved from putting their plans into action. Talbot was sensitive enough to the letter and spirit of the colony's law to know that no good could result from such actions.

At least one more example deserves note, not because it was violent, but because it was colonywide in scope. This occurred during the gubernatorial tenure of Jonathan Belcher. Belcher was a Puritan, a Harvard-educated Bostonian who before coming to New Jersey had been governor of Massachusetts. Once in New Jersey, he experienced little difficulty recognizing the Presbyterians as his natural religious cotribalists. Belcher quickly developed the habit of naming only Presbyterian ministers to be justices of the peace. He markedly increased the preeminence of his coreligionists in general, and also strengthened the financial resources and social prestige of the individual ministers appointed to office. Presbyterians were so encouraged by Belcher's presence that the Anglican minister Edward Vaughn reported they "stick not to say they are the established church in this province and all others are only tolerated."[35] Belcher was also an indefatigable proponent of the College of New Jersey (later Princeton University), and often complained about the anti-intellectual truculence of Quaker members of the assembly who repeatedly blocked the use of public funds to aid this almost wholly Presbyterian endeavor.[36]

In this situation, where violence was not an option and where Presbyterians were able to wield significant political clout, opponents of Presbyterians became adept at using nonconfrontational means to taunt their adversaries and to vent their anger. Freud noted that "wit permits us to make our enemy ridiculous through that which we could not utter loudly or consciously on account of existing hindrances" and "is used with special preference as a weapon of attack or criticism of superiors who claim to be in authority."[37] Edward Vaughn, the Anglican rector of Perth Amboy, provides an amusing anecdote of witticism so used against his Presbyterian foes.

> On one occasion, when Mr. Vaughan was riding on a fine horse, handsomely caparisoned (being fond of such equipments), he was met by two of them i.e., Presbyterian Justices of the Peace who, relying upon his presumed ignorance of their names, accosted him rudely with, "Why Parson, you are not like your Lord and Master, for he was content to ride upon an Ass"!—"So would I be, brethren" was the quick reply, "but our Governor has made them all Justices of the Peace."[38]

E. Authority Within Tribal Religion

The responsibility of intellectually defending the tribal mental cosmos against outside elements was almost wholly delegated to the clergy, and almost all intertribal sparring was conducted by ministers. There are, of course, exceptions, but a dichotomy of clergy and laity is basic to tribal religion.

The preeminence of minsters in tribal religion derives from several sources, but all relate to the connection between authority and group identity. Tribal existence has as its ultimate goal the total socialization of all members into tribal reality. Peter Berger notes, however, that such a goal is in fact unattainable. "Socialization is never completed. Not only children, but adults as well 'forget' the legitimating answers. They must ever again be 'reminded.' In other words, the legitimating formulas must be repeated."[39]

Legitimating formulas of reality must indeed be repeated if tribal solidarity is to be maintained, but such repetition is not automatically efficacious. Depending on the perceived authority of the one who intones such canons, formulas can either strengthen unity or fall on deaf ears. The setting apart of a specially designated priestly class is a primary means of granting authority to the orators of legitimating formulas, i.e., to those who provide the rationalization for beliefs and ritual. Max Weber has commented on the apparent historical necessity of such a development:

> The full development of both a metaphysical rationalization and a religious ethic requires an independent and professionally trained priesthood, permanently

occupied with the cult and with the practical problems involved in the cure of souls. . . .

Moreover, . . . the rationalization of religious life was fragmentary or entirely missing wherever the priesthood failed to achieve independent class status.[40]

Authority is not a simple concept, and Weber's basically circular reasoning is not a sufficient explanation for clerical importance in New Jersey tribal religion. Richard Sennett lays out some of the complex dynamics of how authority is actually exercised.[41] He notes that authority is two-sided for all involved, having both a passive and an active aspect. Authority is not unidirectional, and true authority cannot be achieved through coercion. Individuals *choose* to *submit* to authority, and those who become authorities attain their status, at least partially, by learning to follow their followers, so that they in turn can lead them.

This was definitely the case regarding the relation between ministers and congregations in New Jersey's tribal religion. Ministers who did not deign to follow the lead of their parishioners were, in fact, occasionally ousted by their congregations. Two cases in particular stand out. In 1736 the Newark Congregational Church dismissed Joseph Webb after eighteen years of service, and in 1752 the Congregational Church at Woodbridge discharged John Pierson after thirty-eight years. While age may have been a contributing factor in both cases, the stated reason for the dismissals was a lack of fervor in attacking local religious competitors (especially Anglicans). If religious leaders chose to ignore the particularistic and separatistic desires of their tribal group, they quickly became expendable.[42]

Authorities—leaders—are born as well as made. Richard Sennett employs the example of conductor Pierre Monteux. Monteux, he relates, "had a relaxed, complete control of himself, and that assurance was the cornerstone of his authoritativeness." Monteux could inspire fear and enforce discipline because his self-assurance and superior judgment gave him "the strength to see through you, to refuse what your peers had accepted."[43] Monteux-like charisma was clearly a factor in authority in colonial New Jersey tribal religion. John Talbot seems to have almost singlehandedly kept Anglican tribalism alive at Burlington by the dint of his own abilities. His self-assurance, good judgment, expertise at discipline, and aptitude for inspiring fear combined to hold together a coalition that all but disappeared shortly after his departure.

In a significantly different case, Johann August Wolf experienced years of strife with his Lutheran congregants in the Raritan Valley because his pulpit presence lacked any sense of strength and assurance. Wolf's general problem was an inability to preach "extempore." Upon his arrival in New Jersey, he preached three sermons to the satisfaction of his parishioners, but "the fourth time . . . he stopped short in the middle of the sermon, and from that time on he has always read from his manuscript." Wolf claimed his preaching disabilities resulted from a "sickness of mind caused by the evil circumstances which I am subjected to and the acts of unrighteousness of my hearers. I cannot preach because of sadness and melancholy." Wolf was a wholly unsatisfactory pastor in the eyes of the Raritan Lutherans. Not only did his pulpit readings lack the authority of self-assured knowledge, his justification for that weakness destroyed his credibility as a defender of their faith and tribe. Despondent leaders breed little sense of security.[44]

Historical Patterns

Despite the depth and strength of tribal religion in New Jersey, the phenomenon ultimately represented an unstable form of association. The diversity that prompted tribal developments often later became an acid eating away at loyalties. Groups did continue throughout the colonial period, but after an initial phase lasting into the first decade or two of the eighteenth century, the general characteristics of tribal religion changed significantly. Intertribal conflict declined after this time and internal tribal wranglings assumed a new importance.

In order to understand these later developments, it is helpful to treat churchly and sectarian tribalism separately. The distinction should not be exaggerated, for no religious group exists wholly in the form of either ideal type, but the distinction is still a helpful heuristic device. My use of these terms basically follows the definition enunciated by Ernst Troeltsch:

> The Church is that type of organization which is overwhelmingly conservative, which to a certain extent accepts the secular order, and dominates the masses; in principle, therefore, it is universal, i.e. it desires to cover the whole life of humanity. The sects, on the other hand, are comparatively small groups; they aspire after personal inward perfection, and they aim at a direct personal fellowship between the members of each group. From the very beginning, therefore, they are forced to organize themselves in small groups, and to renounce the idea of dominating the world. Their attitude towards the world, the State, and Society may be indifferent, tolerant, or hostile, since they have no

desire to control and incorporate these forms of social life; on the contrary, they tend to avoid them.[45]

In New Jersey, different patterns of development characterized the different tribal religious groups. Over time, sectarian groups—especially the Quakers—became increasingly uncomfortable with the active, aggressive nature of religious tribalism as it typically existed. The primary reaction in such groups was to seek to return the communal life of the group to a more traditionally sectarian separatistic and quietistic mode. For churchly groups, the ineradicable diversity of the environment tended to force a tempering of any and all expectations of actually dominating the whole society—even if the desire to do so sometimes remained strong.

A. Sectarian Tribalism

Quakers came to New Jersey as a persecuted sect. West Jersey, in fact, had been established by William Penn and his associates as a haven for Friends fleeing the Old World. Once established in the colony, however, Quakers found themselves in an unprecedented situation. No longer could they exist and define themselves as a pure minority—a sect—living in opposition to corrupt governmental and ecclesiastical authorities. They were, by dint of numbers and by ownership of land, the rulers of the region.

Originally the Quakers sought to maintain their sectarian ideals while simultaneously governing the colony. The West Jersey Concessions of 1676, for example, argued for religious freedom on the basis "that no men, nor number of men upon earth, hath power or authority to rule over men's consciences." Furthermore, Quakers always remained ambivalent toward some aspects of the exercise of governmental authority. As late as 1693, the Philadelphia-Burlington yearly meeting issued *A Testimony and Caution*.

> The which [corporal punishment] although proper and necessary to be executed by Worldly Rulers and Judges, yet seeming Christ hath forbid it unto his followers . . . it is our Judgment and Persuasion that those of our Profession . . . should not meddle or be concerned with any other part or office of worldly Rule or Government, as to be Justice, Sheriff, or Constable or Jury-man in any Criminal Causes, or to chuse or be chosen to sit in an Assembly or Provincial council to make laws against Criminal Offenders, extending either to the taking away of life, or any other corporal punishment.[46]

Despite warnings of this nature, Quakers—like any group that has tasted the intoxicating potion of political power—were rarely hesitant to grasp for dominance, governmental or otherwise. Indicative is the passage in 1683 by the Quaker legislators of West New Jersey of a law preventing all "such as are prophane, loose, and idle, and scandalous from settling amongst us." In place of this descriptive enumeration of the unwanted, one could, in effect, substitute the phrase "all non-Quaker elements."

Intoxication with political power easily spilled over into the more strictly religious realm, and numerous Quakers readily entered intertribal lists for ascendancy. Despite the vigor with which individual Friends attacked their enemies, Quakers as a group always remained ambivalent about these aggressive religious forays into foreign territory. Most Quakers considered internal issues of the society more important than outward relations. The single most important concern voiced by the Society of Friends was that a "witness for truth" be maintained within the fellowship. To that end, anyone who repeatedly swerved from the moral expectations of the Quaker community was unhesitatingly disowned.

For almost twenty years, Quakers in New Jersey maintained a fragile balance between their sectarian heritage and the realities of power, but disturbances associated with the career of George Keith during the early 1690s dramatically unveiled the instability of this equilibrium. The essence of Keith's threat to the Society of Friends was that he revealed to the society how far it had drifted from its original moorings. This happened in two ways: first, Keith's own behavior seemed inimical to traditional Quaker emphases on peaceableness; perhaps more important, the reactions Keith elicited from his Quaker foes displayed to the leaders of the society how much they themselves had imbued a spirit of violence.[47]

As a Quaker apologist before the schism, Keith showed a violent temper anathema to many Quakers. In debate, Keith went for the jugular. In doing so, he repelled many Quakers who had previously assumed that a passive and submissive witness in the face of opposition was a more appropriate testimony to truth.

If offended by Keith's attacks on outsiders, Quakers were all the more taken aback when he turned his guns on adversaries within the society's own ranks. Jon Butler says that "Keith's behavior tore at the heart of Quaker decorum."[48] Public Friends in particular were incensed by what they perceived as the unnecessary harshness of Keith's condemnation of fellow Quaker and Public Friend William Stockdale. Thus, even while sustaining Keith's complaint of unorthodoxy against Stockdale, the Philadelphia meeting of ministers censured Keith for his language and withdrew his ministerial status.

Keith's debate with Stockdale had revolved around the necessity of belief in the historical existence of Jesus. Stockdale denied that any such belief was necessary for salvation, holding that "the Inner Light alone brought salvation."[49] Keith held the contrary. Theological points of contention, however, do not define all the issues involved. As a tribal warrior, Keith was not content to answer an enemy attack solely with a nonrational appeal to "Inner Light." Such a response may have protected Quaker tribal identity, but it did little to injure or eliminate Quaker opponents. Rather than following traditional Quaker practices, Keith had increasingly built his personal apologetic system on an appeal to the same scriptural foundations that his opponents used. Keith hoped not only to preserve his Quaker tribe intact, but also to overwhelm his enemies with the power of his rational arguments based on a shared ground of accepted facts. More than any other Quaker of his time, Keith had adopted as his own the churchly goal of dominating society. (The fact that he finally became an Anglican indicates the direction in which he was headed.) Rational argument was the tool he thought could be used to achieve those goals. When opposed by other Public Friends, not on the basis of logic but by appeal to the uncontestable authority of the ministerial meeting, George Keith revolted.

As a result of his insolence toward Public Friends who were also Pennsylvania magistrates, Keith was eventually arraigned on political charges and convicted "of Transgressing the 29th Chapter of Laws of this Province, viz. against speaking slightingly of a Magistrate."[50] Keith and many Quakers recognized the hypocrisy of these charges. His real crime had been religious. In *New England's Spirit of Persecution Transmitted to Pennsylvania* (1693), Keith accordingly castigated his prosecutors for being, in reality, persecutors.

While most of these events took place in Pennsylvania, Jersey Quakers were also deeply involved in the dispute. In the schism that resulted from Keith's trial and condemnation, several Quaker meetings in New Jersey separated themselves from the Philadelphia-Burlington yearly meeting. In fact, Keith's strength was probably proportionally greater in New Jersey, his original residence in the New World, than it was in Pennsylvania.

The Keithian schism did not, by itself, immediately shock the Quakers into a more sectarian mold. For years after the split, Keith's Quaker antagonists hurled published invectives in his direction. These tirades were met, in turn, with slander for slander. But such conflict was increasingly seen by Quakers as opposed to their true mission in the world, i.e., having a quiet reputation for truth.

The case here should not be overstated. Keith is not single-handedly responsible for the resectarianization of the Society of Friends. The Keithian schism and its aftermath, however, do illustrate very clearly the tensions of the situation. Ultimately the strain produced by acting one way while simultaneously claiming to follow a different ideal—i.e., the strain of cognitive dissonance—became too great to ignore. A choice was called for, and the Society of Friends withdrew from combat and re-evoked the separatistic ideals on which the group had been founded.

In the pluralistically charged atmosphere of New Jersey, of course, no return to pristine sectarianism was possible. But as numerous scholars have observed in different ways and on different levels, Quakers in the Pennsylvania—New Jersey region did become increasingly more provincial and withdrawn as the eighteenth century progressed.

> The Society became ingrown. The early sectarian ideal of being a chosen people whose bond of unity was an experience of God was replaced by a policy of birthright membership. While the goal of evangelism toward outsiders never faded, the meeting became tribalistic. For social and business activities, Friends associated mainly with members of their own denomination. The education of children proceeded from the premise that exposure to the world resulted in contamination. Home, school, and meeting combined to mold the child into a virtuous person. A man became religious not only by the grace of God but from the force of habit. At the end of the seventeenth century, the dwindling number of outsiders joining the meeting prompted Friends to emphasize the family. Pious parents would guarantee the survival of the faith by implanting religious norms in the next generation.[51]

Rather than deny the founding ideals of the society, the Quakers early in the eighteenth century decided to forfeit the offensive. Falling back to defensible boundaries, they sought the protection of a cloistered existence where a tribal identity could be maintained more easily. The cost was high. It entailed the renunciation of all desires for cultural domination and amounted to an admission of public irrelevance, but it did preserve a continuity, if not a consistency, of the Quaker tribal world.

B. Churchly Tribalism

Churchly tribalists faced a more complex situation than their sectarian counterparts. By nature, churchly religious groups seek a dominant position in society. In New Jersey, however, no such domination was possible. Tribal adherents of the various churchly traditions thus found themselves, like their sectarian counterparts, in a situation of cognitive dissonance. Their ideals simply were not compatible with the realities they faced. For churchly tribalists, however, no falling back to safer turf was possible. Churchly goals *are* to dominate. Struggling to come to grips with their situation, New Jersey's churchly religious tribalists explored a varied range of adaptive strategies.

Leon Festinger has observed that faced with a situation of cognitive dissonance, individuals and groups invariably strive to develop some kind of strategy that will allow them to reduce the dissonance without facing the necessity of giving up any cherished beliefs. A frequent initial step in this process is to repeat with increased fervor the shibboleths of the group, disregarding any need to adapt to the environment. If the repetition of slogans does not assuage the dissonance, the tribe must either modify its ideals in recognition of environmental realities or else attempt to restructure the local environment so that it will be in closer accord with preconceptions. Both of these methods were used in colonial New Jersey.[52]

Elizabethtown, the oldest of the "Puritan towns" of East Jersey, provides one example of how religious tribalists could adjust their own self-understanding to fit the environment. In this case, what was really called for, however, was the cessation of tribal pretensions. This was not necessarily an uncommon event. Adjustment to the environment often came to mean a conscious recognition of being only one equal among other equals. This recognition in and of itself was the death knell of tribalism.

Elizabethtown was one of the few settlements that had originally seen themselves as potential religious Zions. It was established in 1665 by a group of staunch Puritans from East Hampton. But the town had hardly gotten off the ground when the dreams of its founders were dashed. Philip Carteret arrived and declared Elizabethtown the official seat of government. With Carteret came a small but significant host of non-Puritans—"strangers" in New England parlance. The appearance of these religious enemies (Anglicans) acted as a catalyst releasing Puritan tribal inclinations. Puritan tribal spirits still appeared fairly healthy in 1705 when the Anglican missionary John Brooke reported to England that the Congregational minister John Harriman was often heard "railing against the Church." (Brooke's perception of Harriman seems to have had a bit of tribalism in it itself, for Harriman probably thought himself a moderate. He claimed that he encouraged his parishioners "to live at peace with people of Episcopal persuasion." Still, he always carefully "urged his congregation to hold fast to their Independent Church doctrine." Coexistence should never come to cooperation.[53])

A significant change in Anglican-Congregational relations occurred in 1706. In that year the Anglican congregation outgrew its meeting place in Colonel Townley's house. In their need, the Anglicans requested of the Congregationalists the use of their building for religious services. John Harriman had died the year before, and his replacement, Samuel Melyen, was in Boston. In the absence of ministerial leadership, the ruling body of the church approved the request with only a minor list of conditions. The result was hardly less than revolutionary. John Brooke recounts what happened:

> The dissenters . . . would not suffer me upon my request to officiate in the meeting-house unless I would promise not to read any of the prayers of the Church, which I complied with upon condition I might read the Psalms, Lessons, Epistle, and Gospel, appointed for the day, which I did and said all the rest of the service by heart, the doing of which brought a great many to hear me who otherwise, probably, would never have heard the service of the Church, and (through God's blessing) hath taken away their prejudice to such a degree as that they have invited me to preach in their meeting-house till our church be built.[54]

Even after Samuel Melyen returned from Boston, cordial relations continued.

> Their Teacher begins at eight in the morning, and ends at ten, and then our service begins, and in the afternoon we begin at two. The greatest part of the Dissenters generally stay to hear all our service.[55]

As soon as these two formerly antagonistic congregations began to cooperate—even on this minor level—Elizabethtown was permanently changed. Both Anglicans and Congregationalists lost and then secured new pastors within three years after these events, but in spite of that, warm relations endured and were even strengthened. In 1709, Edward Vaughan assumed the Anglican pulpit and John Dickinson the Congregationalist. Their friendship was renowned. While Vaughan in other locations appears as an Anglican tribalist, he never wore that visage in Elizabethtown. The same can be said of Dickinson's Presbyterian convictions. The two men served their respective congregations until 1747, and then died within hours of each other. The following story may be more hagiographical than historical, but it indicates the degree to which many people believed the tribal hostilities of the past had been buried.

> The news of the death of Mr. Dickinson (the clergyman of the first Presbyterian Church with whom Mr. Vaughan's "personal relations were always of the pleasant character" was carried to Mr. Vaughan just as he was dying, and, amongst the last audible words that he was heard to utter were these, "O that I had hold of the skirts of brother Jonathan."[56]

Not all churchly tribalists followed the path of accommodation taken by Elizabethtown's Anglicans and Presbyterians. Many groups refused to recognize any bias against tribalism in the pluralistic environment of the colony. These groups, in defense of their peculiar ideals, tended to become more narrowly tribalistic as the realities of the environment impinged on their clusters of separateness. Like sectarian groups, these churchly tribalists sought to make a stand against the world. Falling back to defensible geographic and mental barriers, they tried to construct a private reality where undesirable "facts" could be ignored. Such measures were seen as dictated by immediate necessity. Churchly hopes of dominating the culture did not necessarily wane, but at least temporarily such goals became secondary to the more immediate task of maintaining a tribal existence.

Some of the groups that followed this second route of development were longtime residents of New Jersey, but more seem to have been relative newcomers. Entering the game late, they never enjoyed the security afforded by geographical isolation. Some groups came to the colony prepared for a fight; others developed their attitudes only after planting their feet on the Jersey soil. In either case, it was the colony's pluralism that encouraged the full blossoming of such tendencies.

William Skinner, Anglican rector of Perth Amboy, penned the following description of one group of immigrants who arrived in the colony (in 1728) already festooned with the characteristic ornaments of this style of tribal religion:

> Swarms from New England and Ireland settle yearly among us but an unhappy education has rendered them so adverse to better information that they seem resolved to persist in their own way. They pretend to be so nicely acquainted

with the Almighty's counsels and Decrees a that at first sight they can distinguish between Saint and Sinner and tell the Person of a truth, whether the white stone in the Revelation shall be his portion or not. These wild notions have so prevailed in some parts of the province that several families have been ruined. Husbands have been separated from their wives and wives from their husbands. Children have thrown off their duty to their parents and parents have cancelled the bonds of nature toward their children and that by the particular advice and injunction of their teachers, prohibiting as they word it "Babes of Grace to cohabit or have fellowship with Sons of Belial."[57]

By the time these groups arrived in New Jersey, the very real diversity of the situation seems to have blocked the development of more typical forms of churchly tribalism. Instead of clustering together in their separateness, vis-à-vis the heterogeneous population around them, they turned their vision and judgmental propensities inward and divided among themselves. They seem to have entered upon what Coser calls "the search for enemies." They found their enemy among their own group.

The central problem faced by these new tribalists was essentially the opposite of their earlier counterparts. Instead of building a vision on an already existing sociological and cultural foundation, they faced the task of constructing a sociological foundation for a previously arrived at psychological tribalism. This task was to prove more difficult by far than the earlier one. New Jersey's acids of diversity were ultimately to tarnish and then to corrode almost all tribal enclaves.

C. The Case of Theodorus Jacobus Frelinghuisen

Dutch Reformed minister Theodorus Jacobus Frelinghuisen arrived in New Jersey in 1720. Very soon after his arrival, a number of his parishioners became disenamored with him. For three years this disaffected group bore their animosity in relative silence, but in 1723 they took their case to the Dutch ministers in New York. Going first to Bernard Freeman on Long Island and later to Henricus Boel and Gualtherus DuBois in New York City, these individuals sought advice concerning how they should act toward their minister, whom they claimed was a "teacher of false doctrine." When Frelinghuisen became aware of this, he and his supporters issued three citations that condemned the actions of those whom they termed "Heads and Leaders of the seceded congregation" and threatened excommunication if they persisted in their ways. This threat was in fact executed late in 1723. In response to what they perceived as an unjust judgment, the excommunicated members published in 1725 a *Complaint* against Frelinghuisen.[58]

Most scholars have assumed that opposition to Frelinghuisen developed in response to his pietistic preaching and to the revival it supposedly spawned.[59] In reality, it is difficult if not impossible to prove that a revival ever occurred in the Raritan Valley during this time.[60] Furthermore, while Frelinghuisen did preach the need for personal regeneration—a characteristic element of later revivalistic preaching—this particular doctrine was not a central issue in the resistance he met, nor was it solely definitive of his own theology. One of the individuals whom Frelinghuisen most hotly opposed was the Rev. Joseph Morgan of Freehold, who also preached the need for personal regeneration.[61] The primary issue in the dispute between Frelinghuisen and certain of his parishioners seems more to have revolved around Frelinghuisen's claim to be able to discern the spiritual state of each member of his congregation—a claim similar to that advanced by the group of immigrants William Skinner had observed at Perth Amboy. Frelinghuisen's assistant Jacobus Schuurman spoke for both Frelinghuisen and himself when he informed Gualtherus DuBois that the "regeneration of a person was obvious, except to an unconverted teacher."[62]

James Tanis locates the roots of Frelinghuisen's judgmental tendencies in his Dutch associations. For almost two years, from late 1717 to mid-1719, Frelinghuisen had served as pastor of the Reformed Church at Harkenroht near Emden in East Friesland. At Emden, where he was ordained, Frelinghuisen became acquainted with "a group of intense strivers after 'rebirth' and 'experimental divinity,' " a group labeled by its opponents "the sanctimonious" or, in Dutch, *fijnen*. Tanis reports that "in this theology of 'experimental divinity' one finds a categorizing of Christians, a methodology which placed the pastor in the role of judge." He further postulates that it was this role that later "brought sorrow and conflict to Frelinghuisen" in New Jersey.[63]

Tanis's argument is highly circumstantial, but his presentation nonetheless represents a distinct advance over previous revival-oriented explanations of the dissensions that were so prominent in Frelinghuisen's early career in New Jersey. In reality, however, Tanis has just opened the door to a new interpretation of Frelinghuisen. Not only do Frelinghuisen's specific Dutch pietistic roots have to be uncovered, his specific program of action in the New World has to be explained. The methodology of *fijnen* piety that Frelinghuisen may have acquired in Emden represents no more than a technique. What needs to be analyzed is the sociological use to which Frelinghuisen put that technique.

Seen from a tribalistic viewpoint, Frelinghuisen's project in the Raritan Valley seems threefold. First, he sought to isolate the Dutch Reformed churches, to cut them off from all outside influence. This was a necessary prerequisite for any internal molding of the community/tribe. Second, Frelinghuisen attempted positively to announce what he understood to be the real identity of the group he led. That identity was, as described by Frelinghuisen himself, to be the embodiment of "the true Reformed Church."[64] When Frelinghuisen thought his efforts to establish this "true Reformed church" were meeting resistance within his congregations, he launched a third phase of his project—the search for internal enemies. This search accomplished two things at once. It symbolically established purity in the tribe by finding and expelling three traitors, and it created a sense of solidarity by providing a common enemy for all to oppose.

Frelinghuisen's attitude toward "outsiders" was announced in one of the first sermons he preached in New Jersey. Frelinghuisen described "the people of God" as "lowly in heart," and then expanded this definition.

> They exhibit this in their amiable and quiet intercourse with other people, without yielding to wrath and revenge. They show this also in docility, and in readiness to do the Lord's commands; in patient enduring of all kinds of reviling, wrongs, adversities and oppressions, etc.[65]

While at first glance this seems almost diametrically opposed to the type of rigid tribalism that Frelinghuisen otherwise seemed to encourage, in reality it is not. Throughout his ministry Frelinghuisen assumed a disinterested stance toward those whom he deemed outside the pale of this tribal purview. He encouraged his parishioners to follow his lead in simply avoiding all situations that demanded real communication with outsiders. Frelinghuisen's attitude of disinterest toward outsiders is illumined by his behavior toward Ary Molenaar. Molenaar was the husband of one of his parishioners and, more important, he headed the family with whom Frelinghuisen had lived for six months during the early period of his ministry in the Raritan region. Molenaar testified that:

> Rev. Frelinghuisen, in the course of his six months' stay at his house, had no conversation with him in regard to the Word of God, nor did he particularly

admonish him, even though shortly after his arrival there, Molenaar had announced himself to be a worldly person.[66]

Molenaar was perplexed by Frelinghuisen's behavior because he seems to have expected the dominie's harsh criticism. Molenaar did not understand Frelinghuisen's motivation. It may well be, however, that the minister had not left him alone *"even though . . .* [he] had announced himself to be a worldly person," but precisely *because* Molenaar had so labeled himself. Once Molenaar had voluntarily placed himself outside the bounds of Frelinghuisen's religious tribal world, the minister's religious responsibilities to him, and religious authority over him, had ceased.

In another incident Hendrik Vroom upbraided Frelinghuisen over his selection of Hendrik Fisser to be deacon at the Three-Mile Run Church. (Fisser was at the time under suspicion of adultery.)[67] Vroom stated, "Dominie, I am of opinion that if you continue in this wickedness, I shall leave you; I shall stop paying you: I shall have nothing more to do with you!" Frelinghuisen responded to Vroom's threat with a simple, "Do as you like."[68] In Frelinghuisen's eyes, Vroom too had ceased to be part of the tribe.

Frelinghuisen's lack of interest in nontribal members had a territorial, as well as a personal, dimension. Excluded from the orb were *all* distant groups and individuals regardless of the degree of their cultural and theological affinity with the Raritan group. Tribal identity thus became thoroughly localistic, and the authority structure of the tribe became absolute. It was this circle of reasoning that prompted Frelinghuisen and his followers to lash out at their opponents for consulting various individuals in New York—especially Rev. Henricus Boel and his brother—about how to react to their new dominie. The first citation declares that: "Mr. Boel and his brother, the lawyer, have not been set over us as popes or bishops, yet you correspond with these gentlemen and consult with them." These outsiders had no right to meddle in local affairs. This same attitude is reflected in the demand of Frelinghuisen and his consistories that their opponents appear before them and them alone to explain their actions. A local tribunal was, in their minds, the only court of appeal.[69]

While Frelinghuisen took pains to restrict the contacts of his parishioners with the outside world, isolation itself was not his final goal. Within the protected bounds of the Raritan Dutch Reformed domain, Frelinghuisen sought to forge a new sense of tribal identity. He hoped to establish "the true Reformed Church" in the Raritan Valley, and beneath that banner, he worked to restructure the institutional organization of the Reformed congregations within his jurisdiction. This overall project reflects Peter Berger's dictum that individuals who wish to "stay converted" (in this case, those who wanted to maintain their tribal identities) must "engineer their social life in accordance with this purpose."[70]

Frelinghuisen's engineering of the social life of the tribe began with the appointment of new consistories for each of his congregations. Rather than following the standard method for electing members of these bodies, Frelinghuisen placed a heavy hand on the operation. The *Complaint* reports:

> Instead of allowing the male communicants, or the ruling consistory, to elect (according to Articles 22, 24 of Church ordinances) such persons as each one might nominate as suitable candidates, their minister, being joined in this by the summoners, wished the election to be made only from a number whom he, according to his own mind, should propose in writing.[71]

Frelinghuisen essentially drew up his own slate of officers and pushed their election through the congregation without allowing any public voicing of dissent.

The weekly pattern of religious life was also reconstructed. It had been common practice to have a lay reader lead services in the absence of a minister. After Frelinghuisen settled in the area, this practice continued on a lesser scale. The Raritan charge consisted of four congregations spread out over a good fifteen-mile circle. It would have been extremely difficult for the members of all these congregations to trudge across the terrain each Sunday to attend services at whichever church the dominie was present. This seems to have been especially the case for the North Branch parishioners who lived at the farthest extremity of the area. In response to this situation, Lucas Schermerhoorn, a ruling church master at North Branch, took it upon himself to lead "worship at one place and another, on occasions when Rev. Frelinghuisen had preached in a distantly located church."[72]

Later Schermerhoorn appears in the record as an opponent of Frelinghuisen, but at the time of these events there is no evidence to indicate that Schermerhoorn either considered himself an opponent of Frelinghuisen or was so considered by the dominie. Despite Schermerhoorn's apparently good intentions, Frelinghuisen soon forbade this practice. He reasoned "that people should come to him; or in case the church was too far off, should remain at home reading good books." Schermerhoorn protested Frelinghuisen's ruling, but was unable to convince the dominie "that a service in church was more edifying, was more convenient for the old and weak, and had the effect of keeping the children off the street." In this light, Frelinghuisen's determined decision to stop the practice appears as an integral attempt sociologically to structure tribal unanimity. In Frelinghuisen's scheme, two leaders spelled disunity regardless of whether they agreed or not. What was important was to have a single focus of authority.[73]

Frelinghuisen's emphasis on his singular authority as dominie is as evident in his dealings with individuals as it is in institutional matters. In several instances, he demanded that members make new confessions of faith to him before he would confirm their status as members in good standing. Frelinghuisen's stated rationale was biblically based, but it was out of line with typical Reformed practice. He said, "one should always be ready to render an account [of one's faith] to everyone, especially to a new minister, in a place where a pastor never before was settled."[74] When several people refused his unusual request, Frelinghuisen insisted that they had to be catechized anew by him before he would serve them the Lord's Supper. He seemed to see himself as the sole determiner of tribal membership.

This same attitude is reflected in Frelinghuisen's general style of handling the celebration of the Lord's Supper. He began a practice of inviting only certain individuals to partake in the service while he specifically discouraged some others from coming forward. Usually he did this without giving any public reasons for his behavior. Some parishioners apparently disregarded their minister's advice and took upon themselves the prerogative of determining their readiness for participation. Frelinghuisen was appalled by the presence of such individuals. He once greeted those who had come forward to receive the cup and bread with the words, "The unconverted also dare draw near the table?"[75] Frelinghuisen's behavior at the Lord's Supper irritated his opponents more than any other facet of his ministry, and their irritation reflects the fact that such behavior was central to Frelinghuisen's plan of ministry. It is also a significant indicator of the tribalization process that was underway.

Frelinghuisen's concern for sole authority is also evident in his attitude toward families in his churches. While Frelinghuisen did not specifically attack family loyalties, family religious responsibilities were consciously lessened in the ongoing process of tribal organization. With the exception of his assistant, Jacobus Schuurman, Frelinghuisen considered himself the only proper religious instructor of the children. But his formulation of the content of that religious education differed from that of many parents and tensions developed. The main issue was that neither Frelinghuisen nor Schuurman would instruct the children in the Lord's Prayer. The dominie also, however, forbade parents from teaching the prayer to their own children.

Most likely Frelinghuisen's justification for this practice would have been that only the truly regenerate should be taught how to pray, and in his judgment most, if not all, of the children of the church were unregenerate. Regardless of motivation, Frelinghuisen's orders greatly reduced the degree and scope of in-family religious education for those who obeyed. Some individuals rejected Frelinghuisen's injunction and encouraged their children to learn and recite the prayer. One of these parents, Nicholas Hayman, stated that "the Devil laid such a prohibition upon the children to keep them altogether from praying." Frelinghuisen reportedly "never called him [Hayman] to an account." He was simply ignored. As in previous incidents, here too, those who refused to listen were relegated to a position outside the tribe.[76]

Tribal developments in the Raritan Valley not only weakened family ties, but in some instances resulted in the painful severance of them. One example is a letter written by Pieter Woertman to his parents in July of 1723. Pieter was a follower of Frelinghuisen while his father, Jan Woertman, was later to sign the *Complaint* published against Frelinghuisen. The dominie reviewed Pieter's letter before it was sent to his parents and he approved its message. He also encouraged Pieter in his resolve. The general tone of the correspondence is captured in the following excerpts.

> Oh father and mother, pause and consider your everlasting condition. Whither shall you go when you leave this life?
> Oh, how sad it is that such old persons refuse to reflect. I cannot express the sorrow wherewith I lament over your poor souls. Why do you, in your old age, allow yourselves to be so grievously led astray by people who have no knowledge of the truth, but are slanderers, mockers, drunkards and murderers of their own souls?
> Oh father and mother, I entreat you again, attend to your poor souls, for such people are as crafty as the Devil. But what shall I say? You are resolved to deceive yourselves for you hold with them, and think that your way is the right way? But what says Proverbs 14? "There is a way which seemeth right unto a man, but the end thereof is the way to death." . . .
> . . . I fear that this letter, instead of promoting friendship, will create enmity. But, as for myself, I am not concerned about this. I hope that my father and mother will come to reflection.[77]

It is only a short step from Pieter Woertman's attitude toward his parents to the identification of internal enemies—traitors.

Frelinghuisen discerned very soon after his arrival that not all the Dutch Reformed settlers in the area were amenable to his tribalistic vision of religion. He attracted some loyal followers, repulsed others, and probably found most members of his four congregations, like most members of churches today, basically noncommittal in their stance. The Raritan was not, in other words, a seedbed of tribalistic fervor. Properly tribalistic attitudes thus had to be cultivated. Georg Simmel has noted that "within certain groups, it may ... be a piece of political wisdom to see to it that there may be some enemies in order for the unity of the members to remain effective and for the group to remain conscious of this unity as its vital interest."[78] Frelinghuisen was politically wise.

For several years, Frelinghuisen chose to ignore those who opposed him; in 1723, however, his "political wisdom" led him in a different direction. Looking within his tribal entourage, he suddenly perceived not merely resistance, but three specific demons: Pieter Dumont, Simon Wyckoff, and Hendrik Vroom. Coser has written:

> The inner enemy who is looked for, like the outer enemy who is evoked, may actually exist: he may be a dissenter who has opposed certain aspects of group life or group action and who is considered a potential renegade or heretic. But the inner enemy also may be "found," he may be simply invented, in order to bring about through a common hostility toward him the social solidarity which the group so badly needs.[79]

Dumont, Wyckoff, and Vroom were selected by Frelinghuisen out of a broad range of antagonists. What set these three apart was that they were the first blatantly to snub the local authority structure by traveling together in March of 1723 to New York to share their complaints about Frelinghuisen with Rev. Bernard Freeman. The public status of enemies was conferred on the trio in a series of three citations demanding that they appear before Frelinghuisen and his consistories to explain their actions. Though the stated reason for citing these individuals before the minister and the combined consistories of the four Reformed Churches was supposedly "for the purpose of restoring you, if possible,"[80] little hope of actual restoration was apparent in either the tone or wording of the documents.

> We are not sorry, however, that we have exercised such patience, and permitted you to rage; for now is our longsuffering known, and your folly all the more revealed. We, being assured that your counsel is not from God, knew that he

would not establish it. Therefore we expect, through the gracious aid of God, to use against you the power of the keys which the Lord Jesus has delivered in our hands.[81]

Contrary to the stated purpose of restoration, the real reason for issuing the citations seems to have been the creation and maintenance of an enemy presence. It was definitely not the removal of that presence.

The technique of creating and publicly identifying a group of internal enemies did buy some time for Frelinghuisen and his tribe. The ultimate effect, however, worked against isolation and unanimity. First the New York ministers became involved in the situation and soon after the classis of Amsterdam also intervened. Partially as a result of opposition from these two sources and partially in reaction to changes in the local religious environment, Frelinghuisen's own attitude seems to have begun a slow evolution away from tribalism. As he changed, his congregations changed with him. By the 1740s, Frelinghuisen had come so far that in the revivals associated with Whitefield and the Tennents, he seems almost ecumenical in spirit—a far cry from his tribalistic roots. Frelinghuisen's ability to change speaks highly of the man, but more pointedly it reflects the fact that amidst the pluralistic dynamics of New Jersey all tribes quickly discovered that merely continuing to exist was a formidable and vexing problem.

The Pervasiveness of Tribal Religion

In spite of difficulties, religious tribalism never did die out in the colony, and as late as 1751 it still appeared strong and healthy. In that year, Henry Melchior Muhlenberg recorded the following conversation he had had with a local north Jersey public official.

> The assembleeman . . . said that there was no unity at all among the preachers and they ought, after all, to set a good example to others. I told him that he was asking the impossible; there could be no fellowship between Christ and Belial, between light and darkness, and righteousness and unrighteousness could have no part in each other. From the beginning of the world to the present time there has never been any connection or fellowship between true and false prophets, apostles, shepherds, or teachers. He said that he understood that well enough, but that sometimes preachers of the same denomination held views concerning nonessentials outside of the chief articles of faith about which they quarreled and set the congregations at a bitter strife and enmity among

themselves. I asked him whether he had never read what Paul said: "There must be also heresies among you, that they which are approved may be made manifest among you." He admitted I was right and began to speak of other things.[82]

Neither Muhlenberg nor the "assembleeman" with whom he conversed was a religious tribalist. (Muhlenberg was basically a denominationalist and the "assembleeman" seems to be a genericist of sorts.) Their conversation, however, reveals at least two things about tribal religion. First, by the very subject of the conversation, both speakers acknowledged the prominence of tribalism in the religious behavior of New Jersey colonists. Second, the flow of their conversation indicates how one specific pluralistic style of religion—religious tribalism—could even affect people who were not tribalists. At first the "assembleeman" seemed to expect Muhlenberg to be a tribalist. Later he backed off from that stance and tried to recruit Muhlenburg to his own antitribalistic view, an offer Muhlenburg refused. Either way, and despite the fact that neither conversant was a religious tribalist, it was the reality of tribalism that shaped the conversation. In a truly pluralistic environment there are no impermeable boundaries between different kinds of religious groups. In many subtle ways the histories of all religious groups become intermingled. And tribalism was always part of the mix; it never wholly evaporated from the scene.

THREE

Generic Religion

The New Jersey "assembleeman" mentioned at the close of the last chapter—most likely David DesMarest of Hackensack[1]—held a view of the role and function of religion distinctly different from that of his tribalistic neighbors. DesMarest dropped only a few hints concerning his religious opinions, but the questions and responses indicate that he thought the real distinctions between the different forms of religion he had come across were minor. He also seems to have had a basically negative evaluation of the religious divisions in the colony and he places the blame squarely at the feet of the clergy. Despite this he was not against religion, but he wanted little to do with any "name brand" version of it. This style of religiousness was prominent in the Hackensack area from which DesMarest hailed and it makes sense that he might hold a view congenial to the people he represented.

While DesMarest seems to have had a generic approach to religion he is not the best example of this type of adjustment to religious diversity. His attitude, from what little evidence we have, seems as much antitribalistic as it is positively generic. There is, of course, a certain amount of antitribalism in almost all incidents of generic religion observable in the colony, but generic religion also has its own positive religious roots. It was one way the colonists sought to make their way through the diversity of their environment.

General Characteristics

Generic religion had four basic characteristics: (1) a desire to dissolve the complexity of religious diversity into the simplicity of religion in general; (2) a consumer orientation; (3) a relatively unstructured and accordingly nonexclusivistic social organization; and (4) a dual emphasis on "earthy pietism" and on "life-cycle sacramentalism."

The originating impulse of generic religion was in some ways similar to that which brought forth tribal religion. Both sought to escape the complexity of society by constructing a simpler, more unitary view of their environment; they did so, however, in drastically different ways. Tribal religionists cast their hopes with small-group sameness, while genericists attempted simplistically to ignore the actual facts of difference.

At the heart of tribal religion was the attempt to hold diversity in abeyance by constructing a sociological and intellectual wall around a staked-out domain. Generic religionists, by contrast, almost wallowed in diversity. They could do this because they denied the ultimate meaningfulness of all the peculiar institutional or theological concerns that defined the identities of the various religious groups. This reduced all religions to the status of basically equally marred conduits through which religion in general could be funneled to the people of the land. It sought to flee the problems of diversity by denying that any real or meaningful diversity existed.

While generic religion thus viewed diversity as an imperfect state of affairs, it did not necessarily judge the conditions in the colony negatively. Generic religion was knowingly dependent on diversity for its own origin and continued existence.

The general poverty of the colony was also undoubtedly an encouragement to the growth of generic religion. Quite simply, New Jersey did not have sufficient personal or economic resources to sustain in a pure form the variety of religious groups present. Whether or not recognized by the colonists themselves, religious groups existed in a market situation, in cost competition with one another. In more affluent circumstances, such competition might have resulted in an increased religious specialization like that which characterizes American religion today. New Jersey, however, was a poor rural backwater, and in that context the cost of maintaining the various "name brands" of religion often seemed both wasteful and burdensome. In reaction, a consumer revolt of sorts spurred the emergence of an alternative "generically" packaged religion.

Generic religion existed as a shadow religion. It did not create its own independent organizations but supported itself, in an almost parasitical fashion, on the structures of traditional religious institutions already present. Unlike tribal religion, which was dominated by the clergy and which was presented as a prepackaged whole to be accepted or rejected intact, generic religion represented a lay appropriation of selected items out of a minister's or a religious institution's full repertoire of services. While most ministers were not aware of these patterns of lay discrimination, some ministers were and of these some consciously played to their generic audience. When this occurred, the situation became analogous to contemporary manufacturing conditions when a single company produces both name brand and generically packaged commodities in order to meet the demands of different markets. Whether or not a minister became an active participant in generic religion, however, often had little effect on the strength and endurance of the phenomenon. Laypeople could, with relative ease, selectively appropriate the ministerial services they desired. Institutional organizations were too weak to prevent it.

Generic religion was not merely cheap religion; it had its own inner logic of spirituality. Two concerns were especially prominent: an earthy pietism and a sacramental concern regarding the major passages of life. Earthy pietism refers to a general desire to have the comforts of warmhearted religion applied to the harsh life of subsistence farming in colonial New Jersey. It was pietistic in its demand that religion be emotionally satisfying, but earthy in that such a demand arose at least as much from a this-worldly human orientation as from an otherworldly spiritualized frame of reference. Perhaps the most prominent trait of generic religion, however, was its life-cycle sacramentalism. Generic religionists placed a great emphasis on having all births, deaths, and marriages religiously sanctioned or blessed by an appropriately saintly authority. The official status of the person who performed such acts mattered relatively little, as did the ethical preparedness of the participants. What was more important was that something should be done by someone generally, if not formally, noted for his or her piety.

A. Generic Religion and Peasant Religion

In both earthy pietism and life-cycle sacramentalism, generic religion bears a strong resemblance to peasant religion. Eric R. Wolf states that "peasant religion focuses on the individual and his passage through a series of crucial episodes such as birth, circumcision, passage to adulthood, marriage, death. . . . . Peasant religion must cope with disorder and suffering among specific individuals belonging to a concrete social group." In Wolf's scheme, peasant religion arises out of "first-order"—immediate—concerns of life and appropriately employs "a large number of first-order religious techniques" to deal with those concerns. Because of the concreteness of the problems of life addressed, peasant religion is often "replete with magical crudities" and frequently lacks a developed ethical rationalism.[2]

The resemblance between peasant religion as conceived by Wolf and generic religion as here described is more than merely fortuitous: it could be expected. The early settlers of New Jersey were by and large peasants in their mode of existence. It seems only natural that at least some of them would reflect their peasant orientation in their religion.

While this connection between peasant and generic religion is important, generic religion cannot wholly be equated with peasant religion. It is doubtful, for example, that David DesMarest would have considered himself a peasant. It is also helpful to remember that the characteristics Wolf attributes to peasant religion are not foreign even to our own industrialized world. Edward Shils has reminded contemporary social scientists that nearsighted pragmatism constantly pops up, even in modern societies.

> Sociologists and anthropologists might make it appear as if every man is implicitly a philosopher and a theologian with a coherent image of the cosmos and society and a hierarchy of standards of preference. This is, however, very far from the truth.
>
> Man is much more concerned with what is near at hand, with what is present and concrete, than with what is remote and abstract.[3]

Generic religion as it appeared, while undoubtedly related to the peasant character of life in the colony, can thus not be reduced to peasant religion. It represents, rather, another way Jerseyans adjusted to the diversity around them.

Demography

Case histories revelatory of generic religion are relatively hard to come by. The movement never had a theorist to provide a rationale for it, nor a chronicler to preserve its history. It was essentially an elusive and often unselfaware movement. What is more, it was a "loser" in history, and the "winners" took few pains to preserve its memory. Nevertheless, numerous, if fleeting, examples are contained in the records that remain, and they display a general demographic pattern. Generic religion tended to arise in regions where religious divisions within the total population were relatively equal and multiple. This tendency was exacerbated when such areas were also either sparsely settled (for example, the Atlantic coast region and parts of South New Jersey) or were penumbras around the two influential cities that bordered the colony, New York and Philadelphia. In these latter cases, generic religion took on more of an oppositional attitude toward "official" religion than was the case along the Jersey shore.

A. Southern New Jersey

The type of lay attitude that fostered generic religion is evident in the will of Abraham Porter from rural Portersfield in Gloucester County, who died December 17, 1729. Though his estate was not large enough to match his generosity, Porter ordered his executors to "pay 5 to the Piscable church of Philadelphia, 5 to the minister thereof Dr. Commins, and 5 each to the Piscable Churches of Burlington and Salem, to the Sweed Ministers of Wichacoe and Raccoon Creek and to the Quaker Meetings of Hattenfield and Woodberry Creek."[4] Porter's appreciation of religion was broad: the churches mentioned were the sum of all churches in the area in 1729.

The Swedish Lutherans in Pennsneck provide a group example of generic religion in southern New Jersey and one that developed in apparent opposition to the will of the Lutheran ministers in the Philadelphia area. Until the early eighteenth century, they were served by Lutheran ministers who resided across the Delaware River at Wicacoa and Christiana in Pennsylvania. Because of the difficulties of travel, ministerial visits to the Lutherans on the east shore were few and irregular. Around 1700, a Finn named Peter Shaefer appeared in the region and assumed the position of schoolmaster at Pennsneck. His tenure in this position was short-lived, and soon after arriving, he entered what he called a "deathfast" and "received a revelation that he should arise and wander about at random." The people of Pennsneck importuned Shaefer to stay on as their permanent minister. Shaefer was honored by the request, but left and never did return.[5]

The request that Shaefer remain appears to be more than a mere attempt to fill a vacant ministerial position. Israel Acrelius relates that the "simple people" of Pennsneck "took him for a saint." (Acrelius's own opinion was that Shaefer was insane.) Shaefer appealed to these Lutherans as a holy man, yet Shaefer himself may well have not been a Lutheran. When he first arrived in America, Shaefer had not joined himself to any Lutherans in the area, but had lived instead with a local Quaker magistrate, Edward Whippen. Regardless of any possible religious affiliations, Shaefer's behavior seems to have elicited a broad-based positive reaction. The people of Pennsneck were drawn to him because of his personal characteristics, not because he represented any specific organized religious group.[6]

Shaefer's departure from the area did not signal a return to a more purely Lutheran status quo. Amid a dispute over the right and privilege of the Jersey Lutherans to construct a church building of their own (after they had contributed toward the erection of two churches in Pennsylvania), the people of Pennsneck and Raccoon severed their ties with the Swedish ministers resident in Pennsylvania. To meet their religious needs, they turned to Lars Tollstadius, a possibly ordained Swedish minister, but one who, according to Acrelius, had come to the Delaware Valley "without either passport, authority, or recommendation."[7]

The Pennsylvania ministers were initially angered by Tollstadius's "intrusions" into their region of activity, but they soon came to some sort of agreement that allowed Tollstadius to christen children "in cases of necessity" if he refrained from other "official acts." Tollstadius proved unable so to limit his actions. Within five or six weeks after meeting with the Pennsylvania ministers, he was once again preaching on a regular basis. The Jersey Lutherans apparently preferred Tollstadius's preaching to that of his more fully credentialed rivals from across the river. The few meetings that the Pennsylvania ministers did convene in New Jersey were very sparsely attended.[8]

Very little is known of Tollstadius himself. His reasons for emigration from Sweden are unknown. (Acrelius hints vaguely that they were dishonorable, but apparently had no solid information to that effect.) Tollstadius's opponents called him "restless" and stated that any congregation that supported him "would have no honor and but little advantage from such a minister." Unlike the Pennsylvania Lutheran ministers, the Jersey Lutheran laypeople might not have been interested in honor. Perhaps the "little advantage" of having a resident minister to baptize their infants, marry their sons and daughters, and bury them in old age was sufficient inducement to remain loyal to Tollstadius.[9]

It seems likely that Tollstadius provided his services cheaply, and this undoubtedly would have augmented his appeal. Acrelius states that the Jersey Lutherans had exhausted their financial reserves while assisting the Pennsylvania congregations of Christiana and Wicacoa in the construction of their church buildings. By 1704, however, a new church had been erected at Raccoon by these same Jersey Lutherans without any outside financial assistance. If Tollstadius had been receiving a normal salary, such an expenditure hardly could have been afforded. Most likely Tollstadius received a small stipend from the congregation and augmented it by farming the fifty acres of meadowland owned by the Raccoon church. At the very least, Tollstadius was clearly of a closer kin with his parishioners than were his rival Pennsylvanians. His prospects for a long and well-received ministry were good. Unfortunately, he drowned while crossing the Delaware in May of 1706.[10]

One final note in the history of the Lutherans of South Jersey reiterates the generic theme. Upon Tollstadius's demise, the Raccoon church offered a call to Jonas Auren of Elk River, Maryland. Auren was an ordained Swedish minister who had come to the colony as a cartographer for King Charles XII of Sweden. While in America, he had become convinced of a Saturday observance of the Sabbath and had apparently decided not to return to Sweden. Despite these Sabbatarian opinions, the Raccoon church still "desired him" to be their minister. After conferring with Eric Bjork, the pastor of the Christiana Church, Auren accepted the offer. Finally the Raccoon church had found a pastor willing and able to adapt his ministry to their generic religious needs. Acrelius comments on the amiableness that existed between minister and congregation. He relates, "His Sabbatarian notions he retained to the close of his life, but never thereby created any offense in the congregation."[11]

B. The Atlantic Coast

The Atlantic shore, and especially the Monmouth County portion, was another area in which generic religion was present. Boundaries between religious groups in the Monmouth region generally were muddled. Morgan Edwards related that mixed communion between Baptists and Presbyterians was "in vogue" there.[12] When the Anglican church at Middletown was destroyed in a storm, the Baptists made their meeting house available for Episcopal services.[13] Baptist openness to other religious groups presented a particular problem in 1711, when a violent disagreement among the Baptists of Middletown threatened to undo the church. An informally gathered church council of New Jersey Baptist ministers finally resolved the dispute, but resentment still smoldered beneath the surface. Sensing these remaining tensions, the council felt compelled to remind the church members that they "should keep their places and not wander to other societies."[14] A further example of generic religion in action was provided by Alexander Innes, a "free-lance" Anglican priest who resided in the Monmouth County area for thirteen years. He was never niggardly in the rendering of religious services, and his death in 1713 accordingly was mourned by numerous non-Anglicans of the region as well as by his own parishioners.[15]

C. Northern New Jersey

All the examples so far presented could possibly be construed as the necessary adaptation of the people to the general scarcity of religious ministration available. It is true that generic religion flourished in situations where a clerical presence was noticeably thin, but such regions often existed precisely because the local population simply could not or would not support the expenses commensurate with more regular religious services. It is equally important to note that generic religion did not always spring up in what was otherwise a religious vacuum. In some cases generic forms of religion made their appearance despite the machinations of various antagonistic religious elites. Generic religion was an alternative way of being religious; it was not an inferior one or one that merely filled gaps between the domains of other more organized groups.

Guilium Bartholf

For thirty years, Bartholf was the only resident minister in the entire region of present Bergen and Passaic counties. His institutional affiliation was Dutch Reformed, but his was only a loose ecclesiastical connection. After his ordination, Bartholf never corresponded with any Reformed classis in Holland, and he had little contact with the Reformed ministers in New York. Nelson Burr rightfully describes Bartholf as "practically a free lance."[16]

The majority of the people in Bartholf's parishes can be labeled Dutch and to a greater or lesser degree identified as Dutch Reformed in their religious affiliation. However, the Jersey Dutch were a mixed lot. They were called Dutch because most had arrived in the New World through service in the Dutch West Indian Company, but ethnically many "were of Flemish, Huguenot, Walloon, German, Scandinavian, Polish, and even Hungarian and Italian origin."[17] The nominally Dutch Reformed Bartholf thus served a nominally Dutch Reformed population. For both pastor and people, the simple comforts of religion seem to have been more important than any theological or institutional affiliation or identification.

A. The Context of Bartholf's Early Ministry

Bartholf's rise to prominence came about partially as a result of social disturbances related to Leisler's Rebellion in New York. Responding to the Glorious Revolution that had brought William and Mary to the throne in England, Jacob Leisler seized power in New York in May of 1689 and proclaimed himself governor. Leisler aligned himself against all forces of "Tyranny, Popery, and Slavery" and styled himself a "Protestant hero." His greatest support came from the "common people," and he played to that audience, often castigating the aristocrats of New York as secret "Papists."[18]

The Dutch clergy of the New York area were appalled by Leisler's behavior. They had been gladdened by the accession of their fellow countrymen William and Mary, but Leisler's hubris and seizure of power seemed to them a flaunting of God's ordained structure of authority in the world. These ministers repeatedly preached against the rebellion and its leaders. As a result of these diatribes, many of the Dutch parishioners turned against their ministers, for, as Jacob Leisler Jr. later recounted, "the people, sensible of their just cause, could not endure to hear such sermons."[19]

Leisler's initial success, combined with the disaffection of the laity, weighed heavily on the New York-area ministers Henricus Selyns, Rudolphus Varick, and Godfridus Dellius. In the fall of 1692 they described their sagging fortunes to the classis of Amsterdam:

> Our ministers have been cast under suspicion through slanders against them, while the populace, ever ready for any change, were advised not to contribute for the support of religious services or for ministers' salaries. Choristers and schoolmasters have been encouraged to perform ministerial duties. Members of the Council (of former Governors), who were also mostly Elders of the church, have been saluted by the unheard of titles (for them) of traitors and papists. Church officers and other members have been imprisoned and maltreated, put in irons, and confined to darkness. And not satisfied with doing such things, even the Sanctuary has been attacked with violence and open force.[20]

In this same letter the New York ministers informed their Amsterdam colleagues that the outlying churches of "Bergen, Hackensack, Staten Island, and Harlem have deserted us, yielding to the powers of evil. They say they can live well enough without ministers or sacraments." The ministers concluded with a plea for help and a warning that present conditions in the colony "tend to the destruction of both church and all piety . . . and will turn Christians into savages."[21]

To the relief of the Dutch Reformed clergy, Leisler's Rebellion was short-lived. William and Mary failed to recognize Leisler's authority, and an unsuccessful attack on Montreal, led by Leisler, cost him his popular support. He was executed in mid-1691 by order of the newly arrived Governor Henry Slaughter. Slaughter himself died within a year, and was succeeded by Benjamin Fletcher.

Fletcher's appointment proved a boon to the Dutch clergy. Though conditions themselves took some time to improve, the future looked bright. Writing to the classis of Amsterdam in April of 1693, Rudolphus Varick noted both sides. On the one hand, he regretfully had to report that his salary was still badly in arrears. (He added that in the future, it seemed to him, ministers would have to "live on their own fat.") On the other hand, he was generally encouraged by the direction in which the colony seemed headed:

> Our Governor, a very wise and pious man, has done his duty well towards the assistance of our church, as your Reverence may see from his letter. He has been the chief one to act in my behalf, and has spoken severely to certain ones. He also summoned my Consistory to appear before him in New York. He wrote me a second letter, dated the 10th of February 1692, that I should report to him the names of all deserters from the church, in order to frighten them etc. He has brought it about, that I now receive more of my salary, and that one half of the congregation comes to church.[22]

While generally positive, Varick's letter mentioned one remaining problem: he and the other New York ministers still had not been reconciled with the Hackensack congregation. In New York, the government had assisted in restoring the general authority of Varick and his colleagues, but in New Jersey such assistance was unavailable.

Contrary to the dire predictions of the Dutch dominies in New York, the "Christians" in New Jersey did not exactly turn "savage" after thrusting aside their institutional association with the city ministers. The Hackensack congregation had boasted of being able to "live well enough without ministers or sacraments," but in fact they did not exist long lacking either. Within a year of their break with the New York clergy, the Hackensack congregation had decided to raise one of their own to the pulpit: Guilium Bartholf.

Bartholf was a cooper by trade, and had immigrated to Bergen, New Jersey, from Sluys in North Flanders in 1684. Shortly after settling in Bergen he joined the Dutch Church. When he relocated to Hackensack in 1690, he quickly became active in the local congregation. Since this church had only recently been formed (1687), there was little established leadership, and Bartholf assumed the offices of "lay reader" and "visitor of the sick." It is not known that Bartholf had any special theological training, but the Hackensack congregation found him religiously appealing. Within three years of his arrival in the community, they had chosen him to be their minister.[23]

Bartholf was raised to the pulpit in direct opposition to the New York ministers, who claimed Hackensack as part of their ecclesiastical domain. But this should not be taken as to indicate that most members of the Hackensack Church were religious renegades. They were not, and they took pains to send Bartholf to the Netherlands to be ordained. Varick and the other New York ministers blackened Bartholf's name before the classis of Amsterdam and warned that Bartholf might seek ordination elsewhere—all to no avail. Despite various actions taken by the classis of Amsterdam and the synod of North Holland, the classis of Middleburg near Bartholf's hometown of Sluys ordained him on 16 September 1693.[24]

Before leaving for Holland, Bartholf had already begun to broaden his base of support. The petition he presented at his ordination proceedings at Middleburg was signed by the leaders of the Dutch Church at Aquackenock as well as by the Hackensack congregation. When he returned to New Jersey, Bartholf took seriously the authorization of his ordination papers "to preach on the water and on the land and by the way," and he began to preach at Bergen as well. During the next thirty years, Bartholf's popularity and parish continued to expand. Although he seems to have relinquished Bergen back to the jurisdiction of the New York ministers, he helped organize at least eight other congregations. Until at least 1720, he was the only minister serving the Dutch-speaking population of New Jersey north of the Raritan River and the only minister of any stripe north of the Passaic.[25]

The New York clergy might have had some serious reservations about Bartholf's ministry, but once he had established himself in New Jersey they seem rather quickly to have accepted Bartholf's presence as a fait accompli. As early as November 14, 1694, Henricus Selyns wrote to the classis of Amsterdam:

> As it has not been very practicable in the uncertain and cold weather, to call a meeting of the churches and ministers at Albany or New York, to deliberate over the case of Guilliam Bartholts, (Bartholf,) who has recently arrived from

the other side, and to conclude whether it is best to recognize his ministerial character or not in the service of the Lord, I have remained quiet, and have recommended him to be satisfied and contented with the churches of Acquequenom and Hacquensacq, (Aquackenonck and Hackensack,) and to continue his work begun there, in the fear of the Lord.[26]

Two years later, Selyns indicates that Bartholf had in some measure been accepted as an equal:

> Our number is now full, consisting of five Dutch Reformed Ministers: myself at New York, Dellius at Albany, Nucella at Kingston, Lupardus on Long Island, and Bertholf in New Jersey. The Lord grant that this ministry may prove effectual to the conversion of sinners in this far distant west.[27]

While nominally having accepted Bartholf—and it seems there was little else the New York ministers could have done given the circumstances—no deep or lasting relationships were ever forged between Bartholf and the other Dutch clergy. In the documents that remain, Bartholf's name is more notable by its absence than by its presence. Events of 1698 presaged this pattern. In the process of preparing a call for a second minister to assist the aging Henricus Selyns in New York City, all the Dutch ministers in the New York region, along with their consistories, were asked for their opinion in the matter. The survey was ostensibly limited to only "the neighboring Dutch churches in this Province of New York and Albany," even though Bartholf's churches were as close or closer to New York City than half the other churches mentioned.[28] Furthermore, Bartholf and his consistories seem consciously to have been slighted in this survey of opinion since the Bergen church was included. The church at Bergen may have been specially consulted in this case because it was served on a rotational schedule by the New York ministers. The exclusion of Bartholf's churches, however, can hardly be seen as exceptional. Very quickly this became the usual pattern. The Dutch ministers of New York apparently discovered early on what leaders of the Christian ecumenical movement of the late nineteenth and early twentieth centuries later rediscovered: it is relatively easy to unite under the language of evangelism ("the conversion of sinners in this far distant west"), but much less easy to present a unified front when dealing with practical and institutional issues.

B. Bartholf's Personality and Piety

Little is known about Bartholf's personality or personal motivation. Very few of his own words are recorded, so the historian is dependent for the most part on comments made by the New York ministers, sources that present a somewhat jaded view of Bartholf. Bartholf must have seemed frightening, a "self-created" minister incarnating the same spirit that had previously hindered their work and threatened their safety in the person of the "self-proclaimed" Governor Leisler. Events in Hackensack were seen by the New York clergy as a direct revolt against the classical authority of Amsterdam and against themselves as Amsterdam's representatives. Bartholf as the Hackensack congregation's leader was presented as the worst of the lot, one "violently urging on the revolting party." Varick wrote, "If he succeed there will be more of his kind follow. I have another of the same temper and style of thought under me and then they will make ministers here afraid enough, as already they are."[29]

Many of the New York ministers' statements regarding Bartholf are not personal condemnations of him, but reflect a general concern about the church in the American colonies. They argued against Bartholf's ordination because it divided classical jurisdiction over the area. Godfridus Dellius wrote, "Where such a confusion of tongues exist, the House of God cannot successfully be built." Dellius also thought Bartholf's lack of education should disqualify him from office: "Where such persons, ignorant in more respects than simply concerning the direction of the church-government, are raised to the dignity of the ministerial office, it cannot but bring religion into disrepute."[30] Bartholf's salary was another point of contention. He had accepted his position for only "about one forth" the usual minister's pay. Other ministers in the area found it difficult enough to make ends meet on the standard pay scale. They feared that if Bartholf's salary became the norm, few new pastors could be attracted to the area and local Christians would soon be left shepherdless.[31]

In addition to, and underlying, these ecclesiastical issues, Bartholf's opponents sensed a more profound and theological difference dividing them from their renegade New Jersey colleague. Rudolphus Varick, who claimed a familiarity with Bartholf, wrote to the classis of Amsterdam that Bartholf possessed a "courageous but stubborn spirit." In interpreting Varick's letter, the classis recorded in their proceedings that Bartholf was "a man of very restless spirit" and a person of "schismatic humor." Writing the following year (1694), Godfridus Dellius predicted that if Bartholf proved successful, "soon some marvelous kind of theology will develop here." Henricus Selyns, who declared that his time was "too precious" to allow him to write at length about Bartholf, did take a few moments to inform the classis that Bartholf supposedly had sought ordination in Walchern rather than Amsterdam because he (Bartholf) thought half of the classis of Amsterdam were "not regenerated men."[32]

From the sparse and often hostile sources available, it is difficult to reconstruct with any degree of certainty a picture of Guilium Bartholf, the man. Some scholars, however, have felt no reservation in painting Bartholf as a warmhearted pietist and, as such, a forerunner of T. J. Frelinghuisen. In this process, history has been rewritten and some rather startling conclusions have been derived. James Tanis, the most prominent proponent of this view, has, for example, declared, in the absence of any supporting evidence, that, "Theologically, Bartholf shared much in common with Frelinghuisen, and the two became fast friends." Elsewhere, Tanis cites "the testimony of his [Bartholf's] contemporaries" to the effect that Bartholf's "piety was deep, his judgment and tact superior, his grasp of the Bible clear and strong, his preaching reverent and spiritual, his intercourse with people cordial and magnetic." Unfortunately, this quotation is not attributable to any contemporary of Bartholf. Instead, Tanis has cited the unsubstantiated opinion of Edwin T. Corwin in the *Manual of the Reformed Church in America . . . 1629-1902*, published in 1902. As corroborating evidence, Tanis cites a historical tract prepared in 1910.[33]

Apart from such insupportable overstatements, there is reason to believe that Bartholf had a pietistic bent. His opponents at least once labeled him a "Koelmanist."[34] Jacobus Koelman, from whom Koelmanism derives its name, was a student of Gisbertus Voetius and had for a time been sympathetic to the message of Jean de Labadie. Koelman may also have been a student of English Puritanism.[35] His ideas thus represent an eclectic mix of various influences that broadly could be termed "pietistic." Koelman was also, like Bartholf, a renegade of sorts, who "did not observe the printed forms of prayers or holy days."[36]

Koelman was a pastor of the Reformed Church at Sluys, Bartholf's hometown, from 1662 to 1664, but Bartholf did not formally join the Sluys church until three years after Koelman's ouster.[37] Nonetheless, it is possible that Bartholf imbued certain pietistic ideas either directly from Koelman or from the general religious orientation of the North Flanders region that allowed Koelman's success. Such speculation is reinforced by Bartholf's later decision to seek ordination from the classis of Middleburg (near Sluys), which may have veered toward Koelmanistic sentiments, rather than from Amsterdam.

None of these possibilities amount to a solid case for Bartholf's pietistic orientation. Another line of argument, derived from Timothy L. Smith's observations, provides a fresh approach to Bartholf's theological leanings. Smith postulates that a primary motivation behind the organization of religious groups in colonial America was a "crisis of community" growing out of the mobility of the period. This crisis centered on the need to create "community" in the New World when all previous experience implied that true community was always and only a "natural inheritance, not a human contrivance." Smith postulates that "awe and reverence alone seemed able to generate the mystic force required to knit erstwhile strangers into units of belonging." Furthermore, in groups so gathered, "pietistic sentiments would prevail whatever the beliefs of the members had been before they left Europe." Pietistic passions would naturally arise in these congregations because they were trying to do exactly the same thing as pietists living in Europe—create a new, not traditionally ecclesiastical, religious community out of thin air.[38]

If Smith's reasoning is valid, it seems highly possible that Bartholf was indeed a "pietist" of sorts. Whether or not his youthful experience in Sluys had so predisposed him, his adult experience in the New World could easily have elicited a pietistic type of reaction. This is not a hard-and-fast case by any means, but it seems reasonable and it helpfully points away from a fixation on Bartholf's background as the sole determiner of the shape of his ministry. The environment in which he ministered may well have shaped Bartholf's relations with his parishioners as much as any earlier biographical influences. If we turn to that environment and seek to understand Bartholf's career in northern New Jersey within the context of the general framework of religion that prevailed, his ministry can readily be seen as reflective of generic religious concerns.

C. Bartholf and Generic Religion

Bartholf had founded the original Dutch church at the Raritan around 1699, and later established several other churches in the area. In 1720, he relinquished control over these churches to the newly arrived T. J. Frelinghuisen, but his concern for his former parishioners remained. In an apparent reprimand, Bartholf cautioned Frelinghuisen after observing his mannerisms:

> The congregation at Raritan were very feeble in respect to spiritual things, and that there were danger that Rev. Frelinghuisen, by his harsh conduct, should change the people into Quakers, or Atheists, or Suicides, or Pharisees;—Quakers, because of his talk of praying from the Spirit, and about special illuminations; Atheists, because of his threats in respect to hell and damnation, as though there were no Heaven, and, therefore, no God; Suicides, because he required, before regeneration, despair, which is the path to suicide; and Pharisees, because he descanted on one's ability to perceive his own regeneration, and cause the people to depend, not on God, but on their own opinion of themselves.[39]

The heart of Bartholf's disagreement with Frelinghuisen was that the latter was requiring too much of his parishioners. Bartholf seems to have recognized the normally uncreative nature of peasant religion, and saw his own role as adapting to the limitations and weaknesses of his constituency. Frelinghuisen, on the other hand, while he may have accepted Bartholf's analysis of the spiritual feebleness of his congregation, would have seen such a situation as a problem to be addressed, not as a condition to which he should adjust. The disagreement also reveals the different tenor of each one's ministry. Frelinghuisen "required, before regeneration, despair." Bartholf implied that, in the Jersey clime, hope was a more fitting foundation for religion than was fear.

The short passage from Bartholf's hand indicates his great concern for the people he served. He did not see himself as a ruler over their lives. He admits that he was more than willing to adapt himself to the needs of those within his ministerial care. He was there for his parishioners when they needed him. He baptized their children, married their sons and daughters, and buried them in death. He also brought them a warmhearted message of hope that helped them survive the hardness that characterized life in the largely still wild New Jersey hills. And he provided his services cheaply. All this points in the direction of generic religion.

Bartholf is a complex figure; it is inappropriate to try to summarize his life in terms of any one category of appraisal. He had limits on his own generic activity—for him, Quakers were beyond the pale of respectability and religion. His career is further complicated by the fact that he seems to have risen to prominence as a leader of a quasi-political ecclesiastical faction in the New

York City region during the late seventeenth century. It is doubtful, though, that a temporary political appeal could have carried Bartholf's popularity for thirty years. Theologically, he seems to have been a pietist of sorts; but it is questionable whether the Jersey population was really all that pietistically orientated in a theological sense or that, even if they were, they were informed enough that this would have been determinative of Bartholf's stature in the community. What seems to have most endeared him to his constituents is the importance he placed on the consoling and sacramental functions of religion. Even after the fires of Leisler's Rebellion had cooled, Bartholf's generic approach assured his place among those who had chosen him to minister to them in their pains and joys. Bartholf may not have been a convinced genericist himself, but he proved himself capable of understanding and meeting the needs of his generically oriented parishioners.

Johann Bernhard van Dieren

As Bartholf's long career was coming to a close, a new and more explicit exemplar of generic religion appeared in the Hackensack area: Johann Bernhard van Dieren. Nominally, van Dieren was a Lutheran, but ecclesiastical boundaries meant little to him. Throughout his life, he preached and ministered the sacraments indiscriminately to any group that desired his services. Van Dieren's career presents a different pattern from Bartholf's. Bartholf rose to prominence in a crisis situation; the beginnings of van Dieren's ministry at Hackensack are mundane. Once established in his position, Bartholf's jurisdiction was quickly recognized by his erstwhile opponents; van Dieren never was able firmly to establish himself in a solitary position. Though his support was strong, it was never unchallenged, and ultimately van Dieren was squeezed out of the area.

A. Overview of van Dieren's Career

Johann Bernhard van Dieren arrived in New York City from England sometime around 1721.[40] He was a tailor by trade and in New York he apparently continued to follow that profession. Soon, however, he was claiming to have been sent to the American colonies on a religious mission as well.[41] According to Rev. Michael Knoll, van Dieren stated that "Doctor

Boehm" had sent him to Schoharie "to be tailor and schoolmaster there."[42] This is strange wording for a ministerial commission. Very likely Knoll's reporting of van Dieren's claim contains more than a little sarcasm—Michael Knoll was later to be a bitter foe of van Dieren—but the assertion of a link to Boehme seems to come from van Dieren himself. He apparently brought no commission with him, but may have brought some books from London, possibly even from Boehme himself, thereby giving some credence to his story.[43] In any event, based on that claim, he had by early 1721 established a semipastoral correspondence with the Lutherans at Schoharie and by May was in residence there.[44]

Shortly after van Dieren's arrival in Schoharie, the congregation sent van Dieren to Justus Falkner in New York City to be examined as a prelude to ordination.[45] Falkner's appraisal was less than kind. He wrote of van Dieren, "In him we find great craftiness in place of Christian prudence, great obstinacy in place of Christian resignation, great insolence instead of Christian humble joyfulness. To prove this I will not give myself trouble."[46] Rebuffed by Falkner and still needing to establish his credentials for the church at Schoharie, van Dieren immediately sought ordination at the hands of the Swedish Lutheran ministers on the Delaware. Once again his request was denied, but their evaluation of him was somewhat less harsh.

> As to Bernhard van Dieren I have been able to discover nothing from him except his singular zeal (would that it had been more wisely directed). . . . I only dread that much injury may result . . . if he be unfortunately transferred to administrative affairs for which he has not been fitted. . . . If . . . he be actually a Lutheran I wish . . . he would acquiesce in his [Luther's] words "Await the One who calls thee." . . . Only he is worthy of the ministry who is ordained unwillingly.[47]

Unwilling van Dieren was not, for he soon sought out Anthony Jacob Henkel at New Hanover, Pennsylvania, who, it seems, was willing to ordain him. The validity of this ordination was later questioned by Rev. Wilhelm Christoph Berkenmeyer (Falkner's successor in New York), but at the time it was accepted. Upon his return to Schoharie van Dieren commenced a successful ministry, the people apparently satisfied with him and he with them.[48]

While well received, van Dieren's ministry at Schoharie lasted only a few years. By March of 1724, for unknown reasons, van Dieren was voicing his desire to leave. He did not have another call, but nevertheless he soon did leave, and the Rev. Wilhelm C. Berkenmeyer, who exercised a general authority over the Lutheran congregations of the area, reported that "he went to the Reformed at Tappan and offered to preach the Gospel of Christ unto them, as Christ had commanded." At this juncture a question regarding van Dieren's ordination came to the fore since he, a Lutheran, sought to fill a Reformed pulpit. He was brought before Rev. Vincenius Antonides, the Dutch Reformed minister in Kings County, Long Island, and was asked to produce his license to preach. In response, van Dieren held up a Reformed Bible he had just bought and claimed "that that was his license." Antonides was unimpressed and van Dieren did not settle at Tappan, but from this point on van Dieren seems to have styled himself, on his own authority, "Johann Bernhard van Dieren pastor Ecclie. Jesu Christi et Luthero."[49]

Van Dieren finally settled at Hackensack. His father-in-law, fellow tailor, and firm supporter Johann Michael Schutze lived there, and he had had a call extended to him by one of the "van Boskerkens," permitting him to "occasionally preach in their dwelling houses." In addition to these local activities, it was also reported that "he travels around wherever there may happen to be a church without a pastor, whether Lutheran or Reformed." He obviously impressed the people, for by April 1725 a significant portion of the Hackensack Lutheran congregation had been convinced to call him as their pastor.[50]

Van Dieren's activity in Hackensack placed him in the middle of a complex situation. Two years before, following the death of Justus Falkner in December of 1723, the congregation at New York City had taken it upon themselves to address the Amsterdam consistory requesting that they locate a new pastor for both them and the Lutheran congregations at Albany and Hackensack. The "approaching winter season," however, had prevented them "from notifying the other congregations . . . and likewise from obtaining their consent to the calling of a Nether-Dutch pastor and the carrying out of the promise to pay him." Their haste was occasioned by the imminent departure of Johannes Hannes Sybrand, a sailor and their "fellow brother," for Amsterdam. He, they thought, had gratuitously offered his services to carry their requests to the Amsterdam consistory and, once there, to assist that body in locating a suitable candidate. In Holland, Sybrand and the consistory soon agreed on Wilhelm Christoph Berkenmeyer, but the latter's illness prevented his ordination and subsequent sailing for America until May 1725. During this delay, the congregation at Hackensack, or at least a significant part of it, not having been consulted by the city congregation regarding the call sent to Holland, felt justified in seeking a minister on their own, and they settled on van Dieren. The lengthy delay in Amsterdam's response apparently caused some members of the New York congregation also to lean in van Dieren's direction. Together with the Hackensack members, they notified the Amsterdam consistory of their intention to call van Dieren, but their letter was received after Berkenmeyer's departure.[51]

When Berkenmeyer arrived in New York with Sybrand, instead of finding a unified church joyfully awaiting his arrival, he found a divided church surprised by his appearance. A lengthy dispute over payment for services that erupted between Sybrand and the New York congregation (and in which Berkenmeyer also became entangled) did not help matters. Berkenmeyer, therefore, decided to tread lightly with regard to the van Dieren situation for the time being. He thought it "better not to stir up this matter. I will not condemn any party, neither will I justify any," he wrote to Amsterdam, "but I would gladly see both parties united."[52] By November, however, he was obviously beginning to doubt van Dieren's authority. Letters left by Falkner in the church papers caused him to wonder about the lawfulness of van Dieren's ordination, and he was becoming convinced that van Dieren had not been "called unanimously and by general consent" but had forced his way into the Hackensack church. Despite these doubts, Berkenmeyer continued to recognize van Dieren's basic jurisdiction.[53]

The van Dieren matter seems to have lain quiet for most of 1726 while Berkenmeyer was occupied with the Sybrand dispute and getting acclimated to his new environment. But by May of 1727 he felt secure enough to turn his sights on van Dieren. He penned several letters to the Swedish Lutherans on the Delaware seeking corroboration of the information left by Falkner, and armed with their responding letters, antithetical to van Dieren's cause, Berkenmeyer made his first visit to Hackensack. At the time van Dieren was ministering to some members of the Albany congregation who also supported him.

During his visit to Hackensack, Berkenmeyer found the church council divided. The elders sided with him, but the deacons held loyal to van Dieren. He wanted to present his case against van Dieren to the whole congregation, but van Dieren's supporters would not listen to him. Berkenmeyer later reported that when the "people of the party of the pretender" saw him in the pulpit they simply turned around and "went home again." Undaunted, Berkenmeyer preached on "the evil of disorder." It was decided to administer the Lord's Supper the following Tuesday, but only ten or eleven people received it.[54]

Two weeks later Berkenmeyer was visited in New York by a delegation from the Hackensack church. They requested that he discuss the situation face-to-face with van Dieren. This Berkenmeyer refused to do, "until he [van Dieren] proved himself to be a [lawful] pastor." He further suggested that they, the church council, ought to "forbid van Dieren to minister in the Church" and they should also "keep him out of my congregation up the river" until the matter was settled. The delegation "felt it would be difficult to get the congregation to agree" to this demand, and it was dropped.[55]

At this point van Dieren himself showed up at the meeting. He called Berkenmeyer a liar regarding the accusations he made about the validity of his ordination, and stated that his own motives in the ministry had always been pure. In this awkward position, Berkenmeyer protested once more about speaking directly to van Dieren. Saying debate would do no good, Berkenmeyer recommended that the Swedish consistory be contacted to settle the matter "by exchange of letter." Van Dieren replied that the church council could well enough decide, but the council demurred and a stalemate resulted. At that, van Dieren rose to leave. He extended his hand to Berkenmeyer, but Berkenmeyer ignored this gesture of compromise "since he [van Dieren] had come without being called or desired." Seeing that "nothing was to be accomplished," all those present left.[56]

Berkenmeyer reported in 1728 that van Dieren was still gaining more adherents.[57] But he was also becoming increasingly convinced that the tide was turning. During the years 1728-30, Berkenmeyer worked hard to consolidate his authority over the Hudson Valley. As he did this, the doubts he had sown regarding van Dieren's ordination and the proper formality of his call seemed to take effect. By September of 1730, he could inform Jonas Lidman of Philadelphia that victory was in hand:

> After the members at Hackensack examined the matter of van Dieren more thoroughly, they sent a few of the elders of the congregation to him in order to learn from him whether he would sometime dare to justify his call and actions before the Swedish Consistory. He answered this by saying that he had nothing to do with either the Swedes or the Hackensack members; that he would not stay any longer at his present place even if he should be ordered by a voice from heaven. As such an answer had been anticipated, the same delegates were instructed to forbid him entrance to the parsonage which he had to vacate within two weeks, and to forbid him any longer to enter any church. He accepted this.[58]

As optimistic as this sounds, Berkenmeyer was not one to take things for granted. Part of his plan for consolidating his authority over the Lutheran churches of the Hudson Valley was to restrict the sphere of his immediate pastoral responsibilities to the Loonenburg area. This meant that he needed to find an additional minister to serve the Lutherans of the lower Hudson Valley in and around New York City. It was Berkenmeyer's hope that the Hackensack congregation would join with the New York City congregation in extending a call for this new minister. Not only would this ease Berkenmeyer's personal work load, but he had also come to believe that a "new fraternal relation between New York and Hackensack [was] the only thing . . . that [could] suppress [van Dieren]." Berkenmeyer hoped that the regular presence of a minister at Hackensack and New York would succeed where his seasonal presence and written directives had failed. He had by this time learned, though "altogether too late," that "nothing can be accomplished by letters when dealing with farmers, for they will change their minds."[59] Berkenmeyer's expectation of a quick victory over van Dieren was in vain. Van Dieren's strength in Hackensack was not wavering. Van Dieren did not vacate the parsonage in 1730 (he stayed there until February of 1733) and he continued to preach in the church as well.[60] Not only did van Dieren stay, his position actually seems to have improved. In 1730, he was given a gift of 150 acres of land in Hackensack (apparently as a glebe of sorts). In addition, there were people in Hackensack willing to "cultivate his ground and support him in other ways" so that he might continue to minister both to them and on an occasional basis to the congregations in the northern Hudson Valley.

On one point van Dieren's followers did seem to agree with Berkenmeyer's appraisal of the situation. They were troubled by Berkenmeyer's decision to solicit a new minister for the New York City-Hackensack combined pulpits and seem to have feared that such an appointment would seriously affect the support enjoyed by van Dieren. Shortly after Berkenmeyer sent this call, Johann Schutze departed for Amsterdam himself. Schutze's goal was to stymie Berkenmeyer's plans and validate his son-in-law's authority. He had boasted that he was going to Holland to have Berkenmeyer hanged, but the Amsterdam consistory stood loyally by their man and diplomatically deferred decision on van Dieren's claims.[61] On 9 December 1732, a new minister, Michael Christian Knoll, did arrive in New York.

Van Dieren had begun construction of a mill, and upon Knoll's arrival he seems unilaterally to have decided to release his claim to the Hackensack pulpit. Knoll reported that van Dieren "voluntarily turned over the church and parsonage at Hackensack [to me], saying that he would no longer serve them, so that he and all the Lutherans at Hackensack belong to my call and congregation."[62] Van Dieren's supporters were not as resigned as their leader. In June of 1734, they still hoped for a favorable judgment to come from the Amsterdam consistory regarding van Dieren's standing.[63] That judgment did not come, and later that year van Dieren began to consider a new call from the Lutheran congregation at Tolpenhagen, Pennsylvania.

Until this point Pastor Knoll claimed to have been "seeking friendly relations with van Dieren."[64] But now that van Dieren wanted "to take over another congregation so that he might destroy that one too," Knoll wrote that he needed to "speak up and prevent him from destroying that one too."[65] Knoll accused van Dieren of being "unlearned," "a liar," "a false witness before God," and "entirely lacking the necessary intelligence to share and to apply God's Word." He was also a hypocrite, since he was willing to serve both Lutherans and Reformed; a thief, concerning the glebe land given him; incapable, because of his itinerating, of maintaining his household; and a tyrant.[66]

In response to Knoll's attacks, a placard was posted in Hackensack on Christmas Day 1734:

> That we, the undersigned Elders and Deacons of both Lutheran congregations of Hakkingsack and Remerborch hereby declare Domine Knole to be a liar and a disgrace to the Lutheran congregation and his letter to be a lying letter, until he proves before the Magistrate of Hackinsack what he had written of our Domine van Duhren.[67]

Knoll had overstepped his bounds. Berkenmeyer stated later that "Knoll receives neither love nor respect in New York City because he is not kind enough. After he had violently attacked van Dieren at Hackensack, he was just as violently attacked by van Dieren's followers."[68] The agitation Knoll had stirred up was still strong in August of 1736. Though Berkenmeyer could report that "kindness toward [Knoll] is not decreasing but increasing," he also noted that Knoll constantly had "trouble . . . with van Dieren's followers . . . [and] that he has had to fend and fight in the country and city courts all the time."[69]

While van Dieren's support had apparently deepened in the Hackensack congregation as a result of Knoll's inopportune behavior (the 1734 placard, for example, is the first time the elders of the church are mentioned among his supporters) and had certainly become more vocal, his own resolve seemed to be in the opposite direction. He continued his itinerant ministry, but slackened his efforts at Hackensack. Perhaps, because he was "reluctant to break up his family at Hackensack," he sought to avoid controversy at home and simply led a quiet life there. In any event, his name slowly fades from the records. By 1739 Knoll was able to claim, without apparent opposition, that van Dieren had been driven out of the church.[70]

B. Interpreting van Dieren's Career

Van Dieren's contemporary opponents never did understand the reasons for his success. After years of considering the problem, Berkenmeyer could only conclude in exasperation that "God lets the devil have his way too much."[71] Michael Knoll, always more spiteful than Berkenmeyer, felt that the stupidity of the "simple farmers" who comprised van Dieren's flock was explanation enough: van Dieren, by his craftiness, had duped them.

Attempts to explain individuals like van Dieren have not moved noticeably beyond Berkenmeyer's amazement at God's complacency. While van Dieren himself has not attracted much attention, others whose careers essentially parallel his have usually been grouped by scholars under the same epithets as those thrown at them by their opponents of yore: "pretenders," "vagabond ministers," "interlopers," or "irregular clergy." The motivation of these generically oriented ministers is often questioned, and it is still frequently and derogatorily repeated that they "insinuated" themselves into various congregations. In addition, it has been assumed by many historians that two reasons—"the great shortage of clergymen" and "the absence of effective ecclesiastical supervision"—can wholly account for the success of people like van Dieren.[72]

Van Dieren's career and the strength of his appeal cannot, however, be so easily explained. He was not just filling a void. Although the Hackensack Lutherans consistently sought to avoid choosing between van Dieren and his opponents, when indeed forced to choose, many preferred van Dieren over the regularly ordained and educated clergy. Even after he had agreed to give up the parish, his support continued to grow. It seems fairly obvious that his ministry satisfied, more effectively than that of his fully accredited opponents, a religious need felt by a significant portion of the Hackensack congregation.

What that need was can be put very simply. It was a need to have the comforts of religion applied to the hard life of subsistence farming. This comfort could be found in "good sermons" (i.e., short and practical) and in a resident spiritual leader (one readily available on short notice) who could give religious guidance, blessing, and sanction to the major passages of life. Berkenmeyer and Knoll could certainly meet some of these needs. They, like van Dieren, were willing to travel often and far to administer the Lord's Supper, to baptize, to marry, and to bury those in their charge. But they did not understand the day-to-day trials of their parishioners; this van Dieren did understand. There is no more clear example of the distance between van Dieren's attitude and the attitudes of his antagonists than a letter from Michael Knoll to van Dieren:

> To a man who lives up the river, in the Highlands, right in the woods, and who complained of the cold in winter, you wrote on March 7, anno 1721, as follows:
> "I understand that you had to suffer much from the cold. But console yourself, dear Friend, in the Lord. You doubtless know that if we suffer something for Christ's sake, we shall also partake of His glory. Then joy will follow sadness and coldness will be followed by the warm love of Jesus; then sorrow, complaining, frost and coldness will have an end. Whereas then, the Royal Prince regarded suffering as a joy, let us, who wish to be His servants, for His sake regard as a joy whatever He considers us worthy to suffer." There are 40 mistakes of spelling in 7 lines of High German. Ought you not to have been ashamed thus to flatter lazy shiftless people who live in the woods and who do not want to cut wood, but because of their laziness ruin their body and health, and should you not be ashamed thus to elevate such lazy people to the rank of martyrs? Should you, as an honest man, not have written: Well, since you are lazy and live in the middle of the woods, continue to ruin yourself and your family and to murder your body and health; wait a little and the wrath of God will bring you where it is hot enough and where as the devil's martyr and suicide you will sweat enough.
> Thus you should have written, but Mr. van Dieren you have learned to act in ways that are different from those known to honest theologians.[73]

The poor farmers did not need or want, nor would they long endure, such arrogant pratings as those of Knoll. They would not stand for a minister who pompously dictated how they should live and what they ought to think and feel. Rather, they wanted for a pastor a person who would be responsive to the needs and concerns inherent in their situation, and one who knew how to ease the burdens of their lives with the consolation of religion-in-general.

A Public Affirmation of Religion-in-General

One final historical event can illumine the appeal of generic religion in New Jersey. This story is of a criminal who "got religion" as he stood on the gallows awaiting his execution. On 23 February 1692, Thomas Lutherland was put to death by order of the Salem court. A convicted felon in England, Lutherland had been found guilty of robbing and then bludgeoning to death a local merchant named John Clark. On the day of his execution, the murderer confessed:

> I have been very disobedient to my Parents, a great breaker of Sabbath, which was the cause of my habit of sin. I had rather go to an Ale-house than to any Church. Pray Young People take warning by my shamefull end: keep the Sabbath truly. Go to any Religious Meetings, whether of your own Perswasion or not. The Devil is always at hand to tempt sinners. I have had great Oppression upon my Spirit since I was in this Prison and I thought I should never Repent or Confess, until almighty God softened my hard Heart and gave me Grace to Repent. I beg all good People to joyn in Prayers with me, I have great need of your prayers.[74]

Capital punishment was rare in Quaker-dominated West Jersey, and Lutherland's case was the first in the Salem area. His trial was therefore an event of sorts, and its prominence was reinforced when William Bradford published an account of the proceedings in the following year. Significant simply for its precedent, the confession and execution of Thomas Lutherland also has a revelatory potential with regard to the breadth of appeal of generic religion in New Jersey. Kai Erikson discusses the sociology of deviancy. "Deviant persons often supply an important service to society by patrolling the outer edges of group space and by providing a contrast which gives the rest of the community a source of their own territorial identity." At no time is this territorial identity more strongly reinforced than in the act of public criminal confession. Erikson notes, "To repent is to agree that the moral standards of the community are right and that the sentence of the court is just. . . . In a sense, then, the victim is asked to endorse the action of the court and to share in the judgment against him, to move back into the community as a witness to his own execution."[75]

Standing before the crowd assembled at Salem to witness his death, Lutherland seemed fully aware of his role. Not only did he acknowledge the justice of the court and the moral standards of the community, but he also lectured the crowd on the means of inculcating and preserving godly behavior. He specifically noted how his own "habit of sin" had begun and offered advice on how others could avoid his fate. Lutherland had disobeyed his parents, had broken the Sabbath, and was overly fond of alcohol. He advised "young people" to avoid these sins and particularly recommended a strict observance of the Sabbath.

Of more importance for the discussion of generic religion was Lutherland's emphasis that opportunities for religious assembly should never be missed, "whether of your own Perswasion or not." In his hour of need, the murderer had been given the "Grace to Repent," and in his own view, all religious meetings were beneficial. Facing death, Lutherland minimized differences among religions. In that light, he asked all "good People" (meaning all religious or pious people) to join with him in prayer.

If Lutherland's confession reflected only the fact that one more criminal had "gotten religion" before facing his final trial in God's dock, his words could easily be dismissed. The words of this particular murderer, however, were lifted out of obscurity by the people of New Jersey. They were recorded and published about, and in that process had the approval of society stamped upon the way of life and approach to religion that was reflected in them. As a man, Lutherland was certainly not a religious prophet in any traditional sense of those terms, but in New Jersey his words attained almost that stature in their espousal of a generic approach to religion.

FOUR

Denominational Religion

Denominational religion differs drastically in both style and origin from tribalistic and generic religion. The difference is so great, in fact, that one can almost speak of a quantum leap in accommodation to the diversity of the environment. Denominational religion in New Jersey began with a positive attitude toward the diversity of the colony. The issue in denominational religion was from the beginning how to adapt to diversity, not how to confront it. And this, more than anything else, is what so sharply distinguishes it from the other forms of popular pluralism.

The reason for denominational religion's openness to diversity is obvious—it represented the most honest and logical approach to conditions in the colony. While the emergence of denominational religion was thus in many ways a natural development, its appearance should not be taken for granted. Denominational religion, with its easy acceptance of diversity, flew in the face of one of the most prominent and long-lasting tenets of the Christian religion—single-mindedness in faith. This single-mindedness had put down deep roots in European culture. In the realm of ideas it was represented by a passion for orthodoxy. In the social realm it had found expression in the ideal of Christendom that posited that the only ground for the unity of a people was the uniformity of their faith. This was not an easy heritage to shed. The denominational religionists of New Jersey were by and large all traditionally Christian in their practices and beliefs, and they had no desire to give up any part of that long tradition. But to opt for single-mindedness was not a live alternative. The diversity of the environment made all assertions of single-mindedness sound chimerical as well as presumptuously naive. They did not ring with truth when compared to the colonists' world of experience. Facing up to that social reality, denominationalists in New Jersey set single-mindedness aside. While remaining largely traditional in their Christianity, they ceased to be traditionalists.

The nexus of terms "denomination," "denominational," and "denominationalism" is fraught with ambiguity and carries a heavy baggage of moral and institutional overtones besides. Rather than focusing on the institutional referent of denominationalism (as many others have done), I highlight the general attitude that lies behind and makes possible denominational institutional religious organization. The term is used only in a descriptive sense, with no intention either to praise or condemn the phenomenon.

The idea of denominationalism has always been double-edged. It has been used to emphasize both the dividedness of religion and the sameness of religions. H. Richard Niebuhr took the first approach. In his *The Social Sources of Denominationalism* he denounced denominationalism as "the moral failure of Christianity." He stated that "the denominations are not religious groups with religious purposes, but . . . they represent the accommodation of religion to the caste system."[1]

Diametrically opposed to Niebuhr's negative evaluation is that of Winthrop S. Hudson. Instead of viewing denominationalism as a falling away from a unitive Christian ideal, Hudson saw it "as a basis for ecumenicity." He described denominationalism as a vision of the possibility of Christian unity, without a need for uniformity, that had historically emerged as a reaction to the fragmentation of religion in the early seventeenth-century England.

> Denominationalism is the opposite of sectarianism. The word "denomination" implies that the group referred to is but one member of a larger group, called or denominated by a particular name. The basic contention of the denominational theory of the church is that the true church is not to be identified in any exclusive sense with any particular ecclesiastical institution. The outward forms of worship and organization are at best but differing attempts to give visible expression to the life of the church in the life of the world. No denomination claims to represent the whole church of Christ. No denomination claims that all members of society should be incorporated within its own membership. No denomination claims that the whole of society and the state should submit to its ecclesiastical regulations. Yet all denominations recognize their responsibility for the whole of society and they expect to cooperate in freedom and mutual respect with other denominations in discharging that responsibility."[2]

Both Niebuhr and Hudson evaluated denominationalism in light of their own theological and ecclesiastical sentiments. Their ideological concerns infused their writings with subjective content and appeal. In contrast, more recent literature has typically couched discussions in the emotionally drained language of sociology. Andrew Greeley, for instance, describes denominationalism as "a social organizational adjustment to the fact of religious pluralism."[3]

It would be difficult to argue with Greeley's formulation, but its sociological cleanness ignores psychological components. Without reverting to either Niebuhr's condemnation or Hudson's praise, a definition of denominationalism that retains some subjectivity seems in order. For individuals, like the Jersey colonists, who found themselves in the process of being "denominationalized," the experience was often intensely personal and emotional. Therefore, I emphasize the psychosociological dimensions of denominationalism rather than its institutional aspects.

General Characteristics

A. Competition

Denominational religionists viewed their land of residence as a grand playing field of religious competition. For them, the air of the colony was bracing. It was the way things should be and in many senses it represented the best of all possible worlds. To a denominational way of thinking, religious diversity set the stage for religious competition, and religious competition was the best (if not the only) way to improve one's own religious life. Growth and improvement in one's religious life was essential to denominational religion and to that end a competitive environment was ideal. It provided both a vehicle for the improvement of religious skills as well as ready-made means of measuring one's improvement against other groups.

The idea of competition in relation to denominational religion needs specific definition in order to distinguish it from the idea of conflict, which was central to tribal religion in the colony. According to Robert Park and E. W. Burgess, "Competition is the process through which the distributive and ecological organization of society is created." It is not concerned with power or control but "the distribution of population territorially and vocationally."[4] Conflict, by contrast, is intimately related to control. In this matter Park and Burgess would essentially agree with Lewis Coser's definition of conflict as "a struggle over values and claims to scarce status, power, and resources in which the aims of the opponents are to neutralize, injure, or eliminate their rivals."[5] While the end products of competition and conflict can often look similar, the processes differ markedly. Competitors seek to "outsell" their rivals by improving the quality of their product or by enhancing its appeal through improved packaging, while groups in conflict seek to seize an advantage by eliminating or weakening their opponents. Thus the major thrust of competition is positive development while that of conflict tends to be a reactionary defensiveness.

A helpful contemporary philosophic analogue to the kind of competition operative in colonial New Jersey denominational religion is the notion of "essentially contested concepts" developed by the philosopher W. B. Gaillie.[6] An "essentially contested concept" is one that allows no easy decision about its proper definition. All definitions of such terms necessarily presuppose earlier interpretive frameworks enunciated by some exemplary individual. (Some of the examples that Gaillie provides are terms like "justice" or "democracy.") It is only through a competitive process that the strengths and weaknesses of these different proffered definitions become evident. In colonial New Jersey, denominational religion represented competition over the "essentially contested concept" of "Christianity." Groups and individuals vied with one another to demonstrate the persuasive logic of their own traditions, and in the process pushed each other on to clearer and more creative statements of their own views.

Several correlating traits derive from denominational religion's commitment to competition. First, denominational religionists tended to be optimists. They were optimistic on a personal level—if one is willing to subject oneself to the competitive process it is helpful to believe one has a chance of winning—and on a societal-historical level. As an example of personal optimism, Israel Acrelius serves well. Acrelius resided in New Jersey as provost of the Lutheran churches in the southern half of the colony from 1749 to 1759. Upon his departure he advised all who would come after him to be patient, calm, and persuasive.

> It is necessary to have not only a righteous cause to promote, but also to use mildness and prudence in so doing. The least suspicion should, so soon as it is perceived, be removed by kindness and discretion. People will have liberty not only to think, but also to say what they please. But he who has justice on his side does not need so many words; the majority will protect him. The opposition he meets will soon disappear, and his most violent enemies will become best friends. The Minister who cannot overcome evil with good had better seek a place in another land.[7]

Religion in New Jersey was a voluntary affair. But Acrelius (a staunch Swedish Lutheran) did not sense any threat to religion in that condition of life. Reason, debate, and justice were sufficient both to preserve and to improve the religiosity of the populace.

On a broader historical plane, George Keith (during his "Christian Quaker" phase) represents the type of attitude that prevailed among many denominationalists. Keith suggested that the present was pregnant with a far more glorious future. He envisioned the soon dawning of a millennial-type age and he prophesied that "there are already many whom God hath prepared and is preparing to be the first fruits of the Church, as she cometh out of the wilderness."[8] All denominationalists shared the conviction that the present state of things was not to be taken as the best that could be. Many errors still abounded, and even the best of the options in religion could be improved. But more than believing in the imperfections of the present they believed that the future would be better.

A second correlate to the competitive orientation of denominational religion was a sensitivity concerning religious freedom. Sportsmanlike competition among groups demands a certain fairness of rules. In the realm of religion, fairness of rules means religious freedom, and consistent denominationalists in colonial New Jersey spoke out forthrightly on the subject. One of the most prominent, and one of the most thorough, denominational theorists to address this subject was Jonathan Dickinson, minister of the Congregational-Presbyterian church at Elizabethtown.

Dickinson voiced his support for religious liberty in three different modes. Speaking historically, he denounced the narrow and persecuting sectarianism that had been such a prominent aspect of Christian history up to his own day. In the past, he wrote, "almost every Sect and Party have in their Turns, when they have had the Power in their Hands, used coercive Methods, to bring others to the same Profession with themselves, or as it has been commonly phrased, to the Profession of the orthodox Faith." This type of behavior Christians should condemn and avoid. Speaking prophetically, Dickinson blessed God for bringing into being a new age in which the errors of the past seemed marvelously to have disappeared, and he hoped the spirit of this new age would long endure:

> . . . blessed be God, we are now in an Age of Liberty; an Age, where in the Cause of Liberty has been most excellently defended, by many learned and ingenious Persons against all the Claims of Tyranny and Persecution; that it's hopeful the World will begin to consider themselves as rational Creatures and free Agents, and not so tamely put their Necks under the Yoke for the future.

Finally, speaking from a pragmatic standpoint, Dickinson affirmed for himself and his church that they would give to all "liberty to think for themselves, if they will but allow us the same liberty."[9] For Dickinson, as for all denominationalists, religious toleration was to be given only up to a point. It was a two-way street and if any individual or group refused to reciprocate a proffer of toleration, such toleration could rightfully and properly be withdrawn. After all, competition works only if all play by the same rules.

A third corollary principle to competitiveness found in denominational religion is an attention to numbers and organization. Stated in its most basic form, numbers are important because numbers show who is winning, and organization is important because you have to be organized to count accurately. Denominationally minded people thus tend to form actual "denominations"—defined religious ecclesiastical institutions. Denominationalists in New Jersey also tended to emphasize proselytizing. Conversion (implying incorporation into church membership) was the material means by which denominationalists asserted their vitality. The quality of religious life experienced by group members was always heavily stressed. But quality without quantity was viewed as a contradiction in terms. Logically enough, many of the chief representatives of denominational religion (after 1730 or so) were involved in the various activities of the Great Awakening.

A fourth inherent characteristic of denominational competitiveness was that a certain sense of camaraderie often developed among competing individuals and groups. The logic of this process is easy to follow. Denominationalists may have held different opinions about many things, but they were the same types of people. They may have been on different "teams," but they were all involved in the same "league." Their goal was not to eliminate their rivals, but to push both themselves and their rivals into the more glorious future. The clearest example of this process—and it illustrates just how close antagonists can become—is the legendary friendship of Jonathan Dickinson (pastor of the Congregational church at Elizabethtown) and Edward Vaughan (pastor of the Anglican church in the same town).

The final aspect of denominational religion's competitiveness is the tension that existed in the need to see religious "others" simultaneously as competitors and comrades. While hard to describe, this tension can be illustrated by an incident that took place in Cohansey. "In 1714, eight presbyterians joined this church [i.e., the Cohansey Baptist Church]; the occasion was as follows: Mr. Wightman was invited to preach at Fairfield; but, forgetting his situation, he talked away as if he had been in a Baptist pulpit." Morgan Edwards added the following note to this section of his work. "Since the above was written, I have been informed that but 4 joined the Baptists; and that the other 4 only solicited baptism to ease a scrupulous conscience, and then returned to their own church."[10]

In this incident competition and camaraderie appear mingled with a general confusion about how things should work. Only a strong sense of camaraderie would have prompted the local Presbyterians to invite Wightman to preach to them. Wightman seems to have recognized that fact and acknowledged that in such a situation he should have respected the nature of the platform he had been given (i.e., a *Presbyterian* church). Unfortunately he forgot where he was, and as Edwards so nicely puts it, "he talked away as if he had been in a Baptist pulpit." The Baptist sermon Wightman ended up giving in this Presbyterian church had an awkward result—eight people left the Presbyterian church to align themselves with the Baptists (though four of these people later returned to the Presbyterian fold).

Despite the fact that members had been lost and gained in this incident—usually a touchy subject for churches—no violent antagonism seems to have been generated. And while noteworthy, the event does not seem to have been viewed as abnormal. Edwards's own account reinforces this impression. It is characterized by an emotional detachment and objectivity that makes it read almost like a score card—some you win, some you lose. Edwards's added note iterates the same. He just wanted to report the facts and, being a Baptist himself, he felt an obligation not to exaggerate a Baptist victory.

Denominationalists were competitors. But they sought to be honest. A fudged victory is no victory at all. So it never seems to have crossed Edwards's mind to misrepresent the truth by letting his original story lie. Edwards also seems to imply that bragging was not a helpful art for denominational religionists to master. Despite their competitiveness, all denominationalists conceded that the goal they sought was larger than the answer any one of them had. Though in some senses they were working against one another, in a more profound way they knew themselves to be working together. It is this halfway vision of the world—part friendly, part hostile—that is at the heart of the denominational adjustment to religious diversity.

B. Education and Authority

Authority within denominational groups was conceived in educative, as opposed to dictatorial, terms. It was the task of religious leaders to announce and to explain the distinctives of the group, but it was not one of their prerogatives to demand acquiescence. Agreement with group ideas could only be elicited and encouraged; it could not be demanded.

Put differently, authority in denominational groups was only as good as the publicly presented rationale for its existence. This makes logical sense. Denominationalists had consciously chosen not to use coercion as a means of inculcating religious beliefs and practices. To do so would have been to negate the basis of true religion—religion that sprang from a free decision to serve God and obey his will. Still, denominationalists did not think that stark individualism in religion was the only, necessary, or best alternative. The option they did think best was education into unanimity. It was the minister's task to construct in his sermons a hedge against religious anarchy by enunciating and modeling one distinct vision of religion. That distinct religious vision should not be his personal opinion, but a re-presentation of the worldview grounded in the larger tradition and ecclesiastical structure of which he was a part.

Authority figures had formal status, which is to say that almost all were ordained ministers. Formal credentialing was, however, only an entryway into public religious office; it was not a guarantee of authority. A badge of formal ordination meant that one had tentative standing as a religious authority within a given tradition or ecclesiastical community—one had achieved a certain level of basic training and approval that should allow one to be a good teacher. Real religious authority, however, could be earned only through performance.

In addition to delineating the bounds of religious faith, denominational ministers also wanted to deepen the experience of faith, to bring the members of the group to a state of religious maturity. It was not sufficient for the minister merely to re-present the traditional wisdom and theological beliefs of the group to the group, he needed also to interpret the body of beliefs and values to the congregation and pragmatically apply it to the specific needs of that body. In this regard denominational authority had a certain paternalistic flavor to it. Out of any available set of dogmas, doctrines, and sound advice, the minister had to pick those few items needed by, or appropriate to the maturity level of, a particular congregation—those items designed to push the members of the congregation into deeper levels of religious understanding. There is a parallel here to the way John Dewey would later describe the role of maturity and immaturity in education.

> It is then the business of the educator to see in what direction an experience is heading. There is no point in his being more mature if, instead of using his greater insight to help organize the conditions of the experience of the immature, he throws away his insight. . . .
>
> In this direction he must, if he is an educator, be able to judge what attitudes are actually conducive to continued growth and what are detrimental. He must, in addition, have that sympathetic understanding of individuals as individuals which gives him an idea of what is actually going on in the minds of those who are learning.[11]

A succinct statement of this typically denominational attitude toward the role of the minister is taken from the life of Joseph Morgan. Morgan, who served two congregations in Freehold (one Presbyterian and the other Dutch Reformed), was asked to deliver a sermon on the occasion of Jonathan Dickinson's installation as the Presbyterian minister in Elizabethtown. His chosen topic, appropriately enough, was the rules by which a pastor should conduct his ministry. Morgan sums up the minister's role as follows: "The ministers work is to teach Wholsom Doctrine, such as his hearers need, and apply it as food or Physick according to the need."[12]

There is a similarity between Morgan's advice and the behavior of Guilium Bartholf. The differences are, however, instructive. Bartholf, with generic religionists in general, thought religion needed to be adapted to the limitations and weaknesses of individuals because most people, it was assumed, had very little potential within them for change. Morgan's motivation and goal were just the opposite. He knew that the religious strength of the members of his congregations was limited and weak, but he expected them to change. He expected them to become mature in their religious beliefs and commitments. To put the difference simply, where generic ministers saw only the limitations of their flock, denominationalists recognized in the limitations the potential for real religious growth and development. Because of this difference, the importance assigned to sermons differed drastically in these two groups. For genericists, sermons were intended to comfort and console. For denominationalists, sermons were, as Morgan called them, "Food and Physick" to strengthen the hearers and to make them well. Denominational preachers expected an active response to their sermons, not a passive appropriation of comforting words.

C. Humble Traditionalism

Humble allegiance to tradition functioned on two different levels. Within the denominational group it tended to shift the nature of traditional allegiance from an implicit assumption to an explicit affirmation. In external relations with divergent religious groups and individuals, it demanded a tempering of the jurisdictional claims of tradition.

A good example of the first level is found in the initial remarks Israel Acrelius made to his Swedish Lutheran congregation in the New World. Acrelius was determined to found his enterprise on a solid footing. Accordingly, he informed his parishioners that:

> Although people here had freedom of conscience from men, there was no freedom of conscience with God. His word and commandments were our laws. As regarded external matters and church ordinances, they must be held according to the Swedish church-law, if they were to be and to remain a Swedish church with Swedish Ministers. Without order, no society, no church can stand.[13]

While Acrelius was new to the area, his remarks indicate that he was already somewhat informed about the pluralistic situation. At first glance the Lutheran minister seems to be championing a staunch traditionalism, but a more careful reading indicates a humbler goal. His underlying argument is pragmatic. If his congregation was to maintain its ties to the Church of Sweden from which they could expect a source of trained ministers, they had to follow Swedish church law. They could, of course, choose not to follow Swedish religious traditions, and concerning that possible option Acrelius voiced neither praise nor condemnation. What he did demand was an explicit affirmation from his congregation that they would, by choice, follow the Swedish church law as their church law. Upon that explicit agreement—that explicit ordering of their religious lives—they could build a church that would stand. Without it, they would falter in the sandy soil of diversity.

Acrelius's insistence on the importance of written rules had two somewhat contradictory implications for denominational religion. On the one hand, written rules provide a fixed and stable mooring for religious groups in situations of diversity. An explicit agreement to accept a code of written rules concretizes and to a degree strengthens the authority of tradition. While the writing down of rules and regulations thus advances a sense of traditionalism with a religious group, it also limits tradition. It does so because whenever a code or rule is committed to an authoritative written form, that standard of group identity is opened to a variety of interpretations—i.e., it opens the tradition to a significant degree of internal diversity. Accordingly, the unitive power of the tradition is humbled. (By way of contrast, there is in tribal religion an absolutizing of tradition, made possible by the prominence of individual leaders whose words are definitive.)

The second level of humble traditionalism is also evident in Acrelius's life and ministry. He placed a certain general limitation on all religious traditions. For Acrelius, tradition did not equal truth. Rather, tradition provided an orderly context in which specific groups could approach truth. To phrase it differently, tradition was understood as group specific. Its authority did not extend beyond the group in which it functioned. Seen in this light, the proper attitude toward one another of groups adhering to different traditions should be one of disinterested respect.

Acrelius's behavior toward other religious groups reflects this understanding of things. He had, for example, a cordial yet cautious relationship with the Ephrata community in Pennsylvania. Acrelius was not enamored of the group, but he was convinced that despite their divergent religious paths the people at Ephrata were "well-meaning Christians."[18] This conclusion is beautifully illustrated by the departing conversation Acrelius had with his host at Ephrata, Peter Muller, after an overnight stay:

> I thanked him that he did not dislike me for being of a different way of thinking. I hoped that if we did not see each other any more in this life, we might meet with joy in that place where there should be one fold and one Shepherd; where all controversies in theology would cease; where love should abide forever after all other gifts disappear. He took me in his arms and kissed me, thanked me, and said, "That is a good wish. I hope we shall meet in that place, although we travel different roads. I shall also pray to God for you. Farewell."[14]

Denominationalists in colonial New Jersey were by no means modern ecumenists. Lines of demarcation among groups were part of the essence of the movement. But all denominational groups had a significant degree of openness to communication and interaction with other groups. In many ways, these different groups were moving in the direction of understanding their combined role in society as a "public" (but not established) and diverse Christian church. They were learning how to act in their society combining what Martin Marty calls the "special interiority" the church needs to affirm with the "specific openness" to the world that the "public church" must also embody.[15]

Early Development: 1700-1730

The development of denominationally minded religion in colonial New Jersey can be divided into two periods. The main difference that distinguishes the two periods is a sense of tone. Before 1730, denominational religionists seem still to be groping for a clear way of explaining who they were both to themselves and to others. Accordingly, there is a certain tentativeness to all their arguments and activity. After 1730, denominationalists began to speak and act with more confidence and precision, and by the 1740s this new attitude had crystallized into a real sense of self-assurance. By that time they had developed a clear rationale for their approach to religion and had become convinced that their attitudes and practice represented the only workable long-term approach to the diversity of the colony. One also gets the feeling that denominational religionists had come to believe their own solution to the problem of diversity had the support of the majority of the population.

Denominational religion did not develop as early as tribalistic and generic religion. In part, the lateness of its emergence can be explained by the fact that denominational religion is a more sophisticated approach to diversity—it took longer to incubate. There is also another, more mundane, reason for its late development: basic demographics.

It was not until around 1700 that the population of the colony began to double back on itself. Before 1700, the pattern of settlement was movement to the frontier. People entered the colony from either New York or Philadelphia and made their way inland. Around 1700 these two streams of settlement met in midcolony. After 1700, the option of settling in virgin territory began to decline rapidly. A decision to live in New Jersey came more and more to mean settling among, between, or next to established residents. In that type of setting one needed to learn how to get along amicably with one's neighbors. These were the people with whom you were going to live out your life. And it was in this personal world of face-to-face relation that denominational religion was born.[16]

A. The Cohansey Baptists

A good example of how face-to-face relations could prompt the germination of denominational religion comes from Cohansey in the southern part of the colony. What occurred in this instance was the merging of two formerly separate Baptist congregations. This incident is important for two reasons. First, it presents an early picture of how denominationalists learned to unite with other more or less like-minded groups to form numerically viable local congregations. Second, in the process of coming together the Baptists of Cohansey announced a rationale for accommodation that was to be echoed throughout the history of denominational religion in New Jersey.

The following description of events is recorded by Morgan Edwards.

> In 1710, (continues mr. Kelsay) rev. Timothy Brooks and his company united with this church [the Cohansey baptist church]: they had emigrated hither from Swanzey in Plymouth (now Massachusetts) government, about the year 1687; and had kept a separate society, for 23 years, on account of difference of opinion relative to predestination; singing psalms; laying on of hands, &c.: the uniter was rev. Valentine Wightman, of Groton in Connecticut: the terms of union were, bearance and forebearance.[17]

Two separate Baptist congregations had been founded in the Cohansey area in the late 1680s. One was Irish in origin, springing from immigration from the church at Cloughketin in Tipperary County. The other was of New England derivation, as noted by Edwards. For almost a quarter century these groups had lived together and worshiped apart. But the death in 1709 of Thomas Killingsworth, the Irish Baptist minister, prompted a change. Rather than suffer the difficulties of carrying on in their own strength without ministerial guidance, the Irish Baptists entered into negotiations with their New England Baptist neighbors that eventuated in the union of the two churches.

The decision of these congregations to unite was prompted by necessity, but necessity was often an impetus for denominational religion. What is particularly revealing in this incident is that necessity by itself was not a sufficient reason to unite. In addition to the basic advantage (for the Irish Baptists) of procuring a minister and (for the New England Baptists) of lessening the financial burden of maintaining a separate ministry, these two groups felt a need to agree on a principle by which to unite. That principle was "bearance and forebearance." Its gist seems to have been an agreement about adiaphora in the local context. Each group would bear with the scruples of the other while forbearing any attempt to impose its own scruples on the newly united group. All members of the united church seem to have agreed not to judge any fellow religionist's public behavior on the basis of former (now private) codes of ethics and religiosity, but only on the publicly agreed on rules of their ecclesiastical union. Beginning at Cohansey, the issue of the scope of adiaphora—things not essential—became crucial for all denominationalists in New Jersey. And for all, the principle of "bearance and forbearance" became a watchword.

B. *George Keith as Christian Quaker*

A second example of the genesis of denominational religion comes from the life of George Keith. Keith has already appeared as a representative of both tribal and generic religion. Some explanation of his multiple appearances seems necessary. Perhaps the best explanation derives from Victor Turner's analysis of "liminal" experiences and specifically how such experiences affect a person's conception of self and social role.[18]

A liminal experience is an experience of transition. It is the experience of being between stages of development, levels of status, or communities of belonging, and is often a significant element in religious and cultural rites of passage. During a liminal period an individual is, for a short time, placed outside all typical social roles and expectations. As a result, Turner argues that people undergoing liminal experiences also become aware of a sense of communion with all people in the society, and especially with the "weak." Finally, a person passes through a cultural realm that has few or none of the attributes of the past or coming state. Keith's personal history fits Turner's paradigm. Initially standing as a combative Quaker hero against the non-Quaker domain of the colony, he was soon condemned by those within his own party. Cut loose from his sociological grounding in the Quaker community, he floated freely as a "Christian Quaker" for a number of years before finally docking in the haven of the Anglican Church. This was a "liminal" time for Keith, and during it he enjoyed a period of relatively independent religious creativity. He seems to have experimented with a number of religious options, but felt wholly bound to none.

The year 1693 provides a first example of Keith as a denominational proponent. Angered and hurt by his first religious and then civil condemnation at the hands of the Public Friends of the lower Delaware Valley, Keith responded in *New England's Spirit of Persecution Transmitted to Pennsylvania*. Despite the animosity of the situation and despite Keith's own self-righteous smugness concerning the fact that he had forced the supposedly pacifistic Quakers to reveal a decidedly nonpacifistic hunger for power, he maintained an amazing (for the situation) willingness to count his opponents Christian.

> Albeit we deny them not altogether the name of Christians, because of the publick Profession they make of Christ's Name, yet we may boldly affirm, that they are far from the Perfection of the Christian Religion."[19]

Keith certainly felt little compunction about labeling his opponents religiously inferior to himself. What is surprising is that he still allowed them, indeed conferred on them, the name of Christians. A willingness to admit degrees of religiousness—to allow that individuals and groups of differing religious persuasions could be at one and the same time enemies and friends—represents a first crucial step toward any and all denominationally minded developments in religion.

If Keith could take that first step in such dire straits, one would expect a flowering of those sentiments as soon as he entered a less hostile environment. That is, in fact, exactly what happened. Writing in 1694 to a broader audience and with less vindictive objectives in mind, Keith appears as a model of Christian ecumenicity. Keith began his *Truth Advanced in the Correction of Many Gross and Hurtful Errors* with a "A preface to the Friendly Reader":

> To shun all occasion of giving offense to any Who have the least Tenderness and Sincerity towards God's Truth & Righteousness, I have named none by Name, belonging to any Society of People.

The openness of this introduction, Keith sealed in his conclusions:

> That any visible Society of People, assembling together in visible Gatherings, are come either to that full and perfect Restoration, as was in the best Times of the Church in the Apostle's days, or hath attained, as yet, to all that Glory & Perfection in spiritual Gifts of Knowledge, Virtue, Holiness and Purity of Doctrine, Worship and Discipline, that God hath promised to give unto the Church, after her Return out of the Wilderness state; And that all the Promises of God concerning the Church, her glory, Perfection, and Restoration are fulfilled, doth not yet appear to me, nor many more, though we have great cause to bless God for what he hath already done.[20]

Keith's inclination to recognize the validity of a range of religious opinion and practice surely places him at the forefront of denominational developments in New Jersey. However, such validity was given by Keith only because he sensed it was necessary. Writing in the early 1690s, Keith was convinced that he was living in a religiously revolutionary time. He was an apocalyptist. God, he thought, was acting in history, but his full intentions had not yet been made clear. Keith envisioned a day not far off when the diversity he thought then necessary would be rendered unacceptable in the light of a perfectly restored church. For that reason, while diversity could be accepted as a fait accompli in the present, Keith never took any pains to build bridges among the different religious groups. The religious divisions were real to Keith—he was no genericist—but these divisions were also in his scheme of thinking ultimately temporary.

The thinness of Keith's ecumenical and denominational vision is illustrated by his later life. As his apocalyptic hopes waned, his denominational breadth waned accordingly. A deepening disappointment concerning his earlier vision undoubtedly played a significant part in Keith's turn toward Anglicanism.

C. Joseph Morgan

Turning from the southern extreme of the colony to Monmouth County in the midregion, the embryo of denominational religion is also evident. Joseph Morgan, the Presbyterian minister at Freehold, had from his arrival in the area in 1709 existed in a situation where the development of a denominational mentality may have been all but unavoidable. In Morgan's case, his earlier life also gives evidence of a possible predisposition in that direction.

Morgan's biography indicates a willingness to adapt to the religious dispositions of those he served—at least to adapt within limits. In Freehold, Morgan served conterminously two separate congregations: the one Presbyterian, the other Dutch Reformed. Prior to his immigration to New Jersey he had placed himself in a similar situation. Then residing in New York colony, he had served as minister for two neighboring towns, one predominantly Presbyterian in sympathy, the other independent. Finally, there is some slight evidence that Morgan went so far as to consider, but finally reject, the possibility of conforming to the Church of England when one of these two churches (the one at Bedford) contemplated returning to communion with that church.[21]

Whatever his previous predilections, in New Jersey Morgan acted as a convinced, if somewhat broad-minded, loyal Presbyterian. He attended three-quarters of the meetings of the Presbyterian synod of Philadelphia between 1717 and 1735, and was a staunch defender of Calvinist orthodoxy in the face of a perceived encroaching Arminianism. Of the latter, he wrote that Arminianism "under the specious pretext of indicating God's benevolence and encouraging virtue . . . privately strikes the work of regenerating under the fifth rib, and is usually followed by Socinianism and that by Deism."[22]

Morgan may have been convinced of his own theological opinions, but several practical considerations combined to complicate his understanding of religion and the religious life. First, Morgan seems committed to the idea that the New Testament commandment to love your neighbor as yourself was a rule of life to be taken seriously and literally. No allegiance to a theology or ecclesiastical body could override this all-encompassing injunction. Such a commitment weighed against narrowness in religion. It did so not because of any necessary disjunction between compassion and religious dogmatism, but because any opening of oneself in such an indiscriminate manner to those outside one's own religious communion creates cracks in the social environment that envelops and protects one's religious beliefs and commitments. Those cracks need not lead to a dissolution or weakening of particular and narrow religious ideals, but in Morgan's case they seem to have had that effect.[23]

A second complicating factor was that, through contact with other religious groups, Morgan—partly because he served two different groups and partly because of his ethical ideals—became convinced that true religion existed outside his own particular religious tradition. In his words, he became aware that "noted men for Piety" existed in other "perswasions" than his own.[24]

Finally, Morgan began to recognize that all the various religious distinctions and quarrels that existed in the world were clearly secondary to a more fundamental division of humanity, that between religious and irreligious humankind. This reality was especially brought home to him as a result of his mission preaching along the Atlantic coast. In 1725 he lamented conditions in this territory:

> I could tell . . . of Places where I have gone to Preach (without any Prospect of a Reward in this World) & that, in some of them for more than Thirty times; till I have been discouraged and given over, more than once, for want of Hearers.[25]

Differences among the various Christian groups in the colony had to look minor compared to the abject lack of interest in things religious on the part of these people.

Morgan was not a systematic theologian, but he felt some need to organize and unify his diverse religious thoughts, experiences, and behavior. His most extended attempt at this task was completed early in his ministry and was couched in the form of an allegory.

The *History of the Kingdom of Basaruah* (published in 1715) represents the most developed statement of denominational thinking in New Jersey before 1730. A synopsis of Morgan's allegorical history runs as follows: The land of Basaruah (which the author states "lies toward the North of America") was originally the most perfect and delightful land in all the world. The citizens of Basaruah, however, disregarded their blessed state and listened to the lies of their neighbors "the Ruhoths." They began to feed upon the forbidden and poisonous fruits of "Ambition and Self-dependence" and soon became blinded by their diet. They lost touch with the "Pleasant Country" where their king lived. Though the king sent edict after edict, and finally even sent his own son to woo his people back to him, few responded. The way back to the "Pleasant Country" had become difficult. Because of the disastrous course of events, all land routes to the king's land were blocked. Only by crossing the great river Palingenesis (the Greek term "rebirth") that flowed to the Burning Lake could inhabitants of Basaruah arrive at the king's land.[26]

The general outline is transparently a recitation of Christian sacred history. But as Morgan fills in the details, a number of interesting points emerge. The first is that several islands exist in the river Palingenesis. Morgan notes that many people who set out to reach the king's land by crossing the river (i.e., seeking heaven through conversion) arrive on these islands and mistake them for the far shore, their true goal. His description of these islands is interesting and, for an understanding of denominational religion, instructive.

> There was also the Island of a Visible Profession (which many took to be the good land it self) and the Island of Zeal against other Opinions (which satisfied some) and the Island of Confidence of being Right: Here dwelt such as look only at the outside.
>
> There was adjoyning to this, another, called zeal unrequired, or zeal above what is written, some call it, A being Righteous overmuch; They are usually well-meaning who come upon it, but their Labour brings little Profit, and by spending their time here, they hinder Labour which might be to advantage elsewhere.[27]

Many individuals have asserted that zeal is an insufficient test of religious truth. But Morgan's point is different. For him, overzealousness indicated a *lack* of true faith. The fanatic—the "true believer"—is deluded: his faith is a sham of self-conceit. Not surety of faith but humility was the primal virtue in Morgan's scheme.

In a later section of his history, Morgan raises another issue pertinent to his denominational viewpoint. That issue "concern[ed] the great strifes and Divisions about the Interpretation of the Proclamation." In Basaruah, as in Christendom, the good news of the king's provision for salvation through conversion had constantly to be proclaimed. As time progressed, however (and just as in Christendom), different proclaimers appeared to be offering different terms of compliance. Morgan explained how this had happened in Basaruah with an obvious and only thinly veiled application to the real world:

> They all held some Truth, and something good; For otherwise they could have gained none to their Party; but they improved the Good which they held, to the utter overturning another Good necessary (in its place) to their Happiness, like Poison in good food.
>
> They were like several Men going to view a great piece of Land, One comes to one part of it, and sees all good clear Land, and goes and reports the Land to be such; another comes to another part and finds all good Wood Land, and reports accordingly; A third comes to another part, and finds all good Meadow Land, and reports accordingly; A fourth goes and views it all over, and reports it as it is; so all these report what they have seen, and every one is sure he is in the Right, and that all the rest are wrong, and will not be convinced, for he has seen it, and knows it; And so they accuse one another of lying, and bringing up a false Report of the Land.[28]

While Morgan could explain how these differences had emerged, he had no easy explanation of why God had allowed such developments. If nothing else, diversity had at least "put many upon study" and study was always a good thing. But falling back on his Calvinistic faith, Morgan admitted that ultimately God alone knew the reason for such confusion. In the light of human wisdom, the results of the situation could only be deemed baneful. "The unhappy Effects were many."

> First, Thus many were led aside and strengthened in their natural Adverseness to that which the King required. . . .
>
> 2ndly, The People being strengthened in their Adverseness, and learned to believe and rely upon a False way, and abhor the true way, and think they know the right way, and being strengthened with Learning and Arguments against the

> Right way, they were in a far worse Condition than if they never heard the Proclamation at all.
> 3rdly. this Occasioned abundance of Strife, Debate, Contention, Hatred, Lying and Slandering. . . .
> 4thly. there were so many Ways, and every one had so much to say, that many well-meaning People who had a desire to go over the River, knew not which way to take; and this Confusion caused some to return to the Country of Heathenism again, and never think to go over at all.
> Some having seen so many Ways, and hearing what every one alleged against all the rest, and finding so many real or pretended Evils in them, thought they were all wrong, and so set up some new ways to avoid all the objections against the other Ways, and so made the Confusion yet greater.[29]

While Morgan could not fully comprehend the wisdom of God that allowed religious diversity, he was fairly certain of how one should conduct one's life in the midst of such a religious maze. Morgan's answer was pietistic and positive—distinctly different from the negative approach of the Baptists of Cohansey who sought to expand tolerance by enlarging the realm of unessentials. Morgan's denominational liberality was founded on a commitment to a vague but palpable shared "substance" of religion that was loved and recognized by all who had truly experienced it.

> Thus there were a Multitude of Opinions and Societies; and even those that took up the right meaning of the Proclamation, in the substance of it, differed, in many circumstantial things, and such as had not improved their knowledge by going over to the Good Land, looked so much at these Circumstances, that they would condemn those that differed from them, and not hold communion with them; But such as loved the substance, heartily loved all in whom they saw it.[30]

While seeming to border on becoming a genericist, Morgan never took that step. For him, differences of religious opinion were not necessarily perversions of, or encrustations on, religion-in-general. Rather, they reflected the finitude of human understanding. Differing religious traditions deserved allegiance; they were the only means by which to arrive at the substance of religion. That substance could never be apprehended or approached in itself. Christian humility thus demanded that respect be given to those with whom one disagreed, even if no unity would ever be reached.

D. The "Complainers" Against Frelinghuisen

A final example of early denominational developments is set in yet another region of the colony and emerged from a dynamic process different and distinct from the others. It is found in the *Complaint Against Frelinghuisen* and represents the religious orientation of Frelinghuisen's opponents. Frelinghuisen's opponents did not state their case in the clearest fashion. But they deserve attention here because they constructed their argument in a decidedly denominational style. Further, if this incident can be understood in denominational terms, it means we must temper frequently repeated assertions by historians that Frelinghuisen's opponents were either captive to a "dead orthodoxy" or bound by an autocratic conservatism.

Theodorus Jacobus Frelinghuisen arrived in New Jersey from Holland in 1720 to assume charge of the Dutch Reformed churches of the Raritan Valley. Within the next few years, a number of his parishioners became convinced that their minister was, in certain respects, unorthodox. They were bothered by his sermons, but more than that they objected to his frequent divergences from the fixed liturgical practices of the Dutch Reformed Church and to his apparent claim to be able infallibly to recognize the truly converted.

For some time these disaffected members lived under Frelinghuisen's ministry in silent protest, but in 1723 Pieter Dumont, Simon Wykoff, and Hendrik Vroom took their complaints to the Rev. Bernard Freeman on Long Island. Frelinghuisen was appalled by this act; he perceived it as a direct attack on his authority. Frelinghuisen and his newly appointed consistories summoned the three individuals involved to appear before them. When they ignored Frelinghuisen's instructions, the consistory promptly excommunicated them. In response to this excommunication, the aggrieved members published (with considerable assistance from the New York City minister, Henricus Boel) their *Complaint Against Frelinghuisen*.

The primary argument of the *Complaint*, repeated over and over again with slightly different emphases, was that Frelinghuisen had no authority over those whom he had excommunicated, because as early as his first summons he had identified the group as a "seceded congregation." If they truly were a seceded congregation—a separate and distinct religious society of their own—Frelinghuisen had no right to judge them. As formulated by the "complainers," the issue was one of religious jurisdiction.[31]

The complainers argued that divisions among religious groups ought to be the result of individual choice and should never be forced. They objected to

Frelinghuisen's attempt to "stir up the people, against us and our society who remain aloof from them." Such activity was an implicit denial of religious liberty. Frelinghuisen's opponents went farther. They voiced their discontent with Frelinghuisen's labeling of them as "leaders" of the dissenting group, asserting that even within their group authority was exercised in accordance with religious liberty.

> We three, well knowing that everything in God's Church must be done decently and in order, seek in the name of all, to promote the good cause, without exalting ourselves, in the assumption of authority, above any other well-meaning persons of our assembly, or in the least degree forcing them; than which we rather desire that they should only exercise their religious liberty.[32]

In typical denominational fashion, Frelinghuisen's opponents were willing to state the exact principles by which they defined their group.

> It is and shall continue to be our sincere desire "with divine assistance to maintain the pure doctrine and discipline of the true Reformed Dutch Church, established by the National Synod of Dorcrecht, and in accordance with the ordinances of the Church of Holland."[33]

And they boldly stated that they would gladly allow Frelinghuisen his jurisdiction, if he would cease from interfering in theirs.

One final point about Frelinghuisen's opponents is that while they wanted to keep religious jurisdictions clear, they did not want to cut off communication with all other religious groups. In direct opposition to Frelinghuisen's assertions, they voiced their right "for any member of our four special congregations to correspond in reference to ecclesiastical matters with the pastor of another congregation."[34]

Frelinghuisen's opponents seem to have been operating within some kind of denominational religious framework. This is not to imply that the disturbances at the Raritan associated with Frelinghuisen can all neatly be encapsulated in a footnote to denominational religion. Theological issues and long-standing disagreements concerning the nature of piety and the Christian life certainly played their part, as did Frelinghuisen's tribalistic instincts. The dynamics of the situations also changed dramatically several times during the extended controversy. However, in the face of repeated assertions by historians concerning the supposed dead orthodoxy and/or autocratic conservatism of Frelinghuisen's opponents, it is necessary to emphasize the general denominational approach to religious diversity that was at the heart of the complaints they brought against the Dutch dominie.[35]

After 1730

Around the year 1730 the tone of denominational religion in New Jersey changed. Earlier exploratory and hopeful attitudes were replaced by a more systematic and optimistic spirit of confidence. No particular event stands out as the catalyst for this change, but one helpful insight is suggested by the historical philosophy of José Ortega y Gasset. Struggling to understand the halting and uneven development of ideas in history, Ortega turns to the idea of generations as an interpretive device. Ideas, he opines, are not held by individuals, but by generations of individuals. Ortega likens these generations to the "caravans" in which people move along through history. These generational caravans are not airtight—Ortega admits there is some amount of communication between generations—but, he asserts, "the belonging to a generation is an existential mode which affects all fields and imprints its ineradicable stamp on each member."[36]

Ortega suggests that a given generation lasts about thirty years. If his speculations are correct, a new generation of denominationalists should have been coming to the fore around 1730. And this is precisely when a new crop of denominationalists does seem to emerge. Ortega's philosophy cannot explain all that is new in denominationalism after 1730—much of the change in spirit was a result of long-term social changes. However, Ortega's historical approach does help explain why this change did not occur earlier. A generation that had already broken with the past as much as had the first generation of denominationalists was very likely not capable of much more change. Further developments in denominational thinking had to wait for a second generation.

Second-generation denominationalists built their world on top of the work of the previous generation. They were not groundbreakers as much as systematizers. Their task was to codify and consolidate the gains of their forebears and they did this on three different levels. Theologically, second-generation denominationalists raised the status of religious diversity from an occasional subject (one problem among many to be discussed) to a foundational element in the structure of their thought. Concerning explicit rules of behavior within and among groups, later denominationalists tried to regularize and codify in a broad and institutional manner patterns of behavior that had earlier originated in the free play of compromise and accommodation on the local level. And finally, with regard to the general spirit of the movement, later denominationalists seem to have developed a confident sense of etiquette—a knack for knowing how to act denominationally even in the absence of standardized rules.

A. The Theology of Mature Denominationalism

Among the many denominationalists in New Jersey, Jonathan Dickinson stands out as the theological genius of the movement. His contemporaries recognized his talents, and the eulogy of the Rev. John Pierson of Woodbridge has preserved their evaluation of Dickinson:

> In controversy his Dexterity was of such remarkable Eminence: his Strength and Courage so peculiar and distinguishing, as to be observed and acknowledged by all. . . . And yet he was not of a litigious Disposition, but a truly pacific Temper, and could sacrifice any Thing but Truth and Duty for Peace.[37]

Dickinson had been raised as a Puritan of the Puritans. His family's roots in the New World dated back three generations, and soon after assuming his position in Elizabethtown he married Joanna Melyen, daughter of the former minister and descendant of one of the original members of the Elizabethtown association. For all practical considerations, Dickinson's early life makes him look more like a candidate for tribal religion than denominational. But upon his arrival at Elizabethtown, Dickinson discovered that he had inherited a peculiar situation. A unique string of events had recently conspired to break down the tribal barriers between the Congregational-Presbyterian and Anglican congregations. The cordiality that had developed between the Anglican and Presbyterian populations of the town before his arrival seems to have demanded of Dickinson a rethinking of his youthful prejudices.

The result of this rethinking process was no mere acquiescence to the situation. Dickinson moved beyond a minimum of necessary adjustment. He established a deep and lasting friendship with his Anglican rival, the Rev. Edward Vaughan. (A friendship that was maintained even when in 1724 Dickinson lashed out against the "great apostasy" at Yale where a group of Congregational leaders had "announced their intention to seek Anglican orders in England."[38]) On a more objective level, Dickinson developed a system of theology and anthropology that very neatly and nicely accounted for religious diversity, and he also outlined a practical program of action that could be adapted by any religious group that found itself in a pluralistic situation.

At the heart of Dickinson's understanding of the nature of religious diversity was a basic conviction about the being of God and the order of the creation. According to Dickinson, God had willed religious diversity into the very nature of the creation. The potential for diversity—indeed the unavoidability of diversity—was inherent in human nature and its actual flowering was guaranteed by God's own divine nature.

> It must also be observed that every Person, and every religious Society, have the same Title to suppose themselves in the Right and to stedfastly adhere to their own Sentiments whatever they be. For tho' there certainly is from the Nature of Things an infinite Difference between Truth and Error, and infinite Danger of Damnable Delusions: which should prompt us to the most serious and Solemn Search after the Mind and Will of God in his Word; Yet it is impossible for any Man to have greater evidence of any Doctrinal Truth, than the full and firm Persuasion of his own Mind. And every one that has attained this Persuasion, how different soever from other Men, or how different soever from the Truth, has all the Assurance that he can have, or that any Body else can have of Being in the Right; and is therefore utterly uncapable, without new Conviction, of thinking otherwise than he does.[39]

In the past, Christians had failed to recognize this ineradicable basis of diversity. They had commonly fought, for the sake of truth, to eliminate all false opinions from the societies they dominated. "For above fourteen hundred years past," Dickinson asserts, Christians in Europe had through a policy of coercive unanimity sought to institute religious purity. But such a solution was in reality no solution; it denied in principle the God that Christians affirmed by faith:

> The Fountain of Peace and Love, can never be supposed to be the Author or Encourager of Cruelty or Barbarity, or to establish his Interests in the World upon the Ruins of all Humanity, Kindness and Compassion. This were not only to violate the Laws of Nature and to subvert the great Design of the Gospel which is to bring us into an Estate of Peace with God and one another . . . [40]

According to Dickinson, it was not the job of the church to seek forcefully to eliminate diversity from the world. It could not be done and God himself disallowed the attempt. Rather, the task of Christians was to act Christianly—to embody the virtues of divine love and patience:

> This also leads us to observe, the Necessity of mutual Forbearance, Kindness, and Charity towards one another, notwithstanding our different Speculations in doctrinal Points. For I have no more Cause to be displeased with another, for his different Opinions, than he has to be displeased with me. 'Tis as much out of his Power, as out of mine to help thinking as he does.[41]

Dickinson did add a qualifying clause to this discussion. Forbearance could be extended only to those who had not "been criminally negligent in seeking of the Truth." This opens a door to a wholesale reinstatement of coercive establishmentarian policies. Nonetheless, the primary and clearest point Dickinson seems to be making is that religious belief not only ought not, but cannot, be coerced. As a result, religious diversity appears as the natural and untampered state of human society. Dickinson's great advance in this matter is that he grounded the fact of diversity in the essential structure of things, not in the vagaries of historical accident. By shifting the theoretical basis from a temporary to an enduring foundation, Dickinson also reversed the usual problem of Jersey denominationalists. Previously, Jerseyans had sought to build a theory of denominationalism that would justify their already present emotions and patterns of behavior. For Dickinson, the problem of practice proved more "thorny" than that of theory. If diversity was inevitable, and by God's fiat humanly uneradicable, on what basis could one make valid distinctions among religious groups or establish limits of association?[42]

Dickinson's answer was given in three points. First, religious divisions and associations were practical in nature, not absolute. Second, the principles upon which any group welcomed or excluded individuals ought to be clearly and publicly delineated by that group. And third, the jurisdictional claims of each group so formed ought to be respected by other similarly formed groups. Dickinson's own words amplify each point.

> This introduces the thorny Question, how far Christian Communion in all sacred Ordinances should be extended? To which we Answer, It should extend to all, that we can charitably suppose to be real Christians. . . . That is, all that are united in what they suppose the Essentials of Christianity, should unite in partaking of all the privileges of it, and not fall out by the Way for they are Brethren. . . . But then on the other Hand, we can't admit those to Communion in sealing Ordinances, whose Errors we suppose inconsistent with the Grace and Favour of God. . . . It is true that we are not infallible in our

Judgment, Christ may own them at the last, whom we now disown. But yet we have nothing but our own Persuasion, to guide us in this affair. If the best light we have, represents them uncapable of a State of Grace, we must act according to it.

. . . every Society must judge for themselves in this Matter; so ought they to take the best Means to be acquainted with their Principles, who offer themselves to the Exercise of their sacred Trust, and with what Apprehensions these entertain, what they believe to be the essential Doctrines of the Gospel. . . . Every Christian Society is upon an equal Level of Liberty, and has equal Claim to Power and Authority. For if Christ has given his Authority to any Church, he has given it to every Church, without Difference.[43]

Dickinson was by far the clearest and most logical apologist for denominational religion in colonial New Jersey, but his work does not stand alone. Dickinson's approach was not so much verbally repeated as it was acted out on different stages and in different locations throughout the colony. Rather than repeating Dickinson's theological affirmations, other denominational groups expressed their affinity with Dickinson's view in their codification of group rules of conduct.

B. Rules of Conduct

Not all denominationalists developed a full-blown theology like Dickinson. Some denominationalists (typically Baptists) instead formulated rules of conduct that only implicitly reflect a Dickinsonian-denominational approach to religious diversity. On example of this is *A Confession of Faith . . . Adopted by the Baptist Association met at Philadelphia September 25, 1742*. This confession was not drafted by the Philadelphia Baptists Association; rather, it was adopted from the English Baptists "in London and the country," with the addition of only two other articles. While the doctrinal statement thus cannot be used uncritically as a portrait of Baptist sensibilities in the New Jersey-Pennsylvania area, it does give some insight into those sentiments. Of particular interest is a section of the preface where the Baptists affirmed:

There is one thing more which we sincerely profess, and earnestly desire credence in, viz. that Contention is most remote from our Design in all that we have in this matter: And we hope, the Liberty of an ingenuous unfolding our Principles, and opening our Hearts unto our Brethren, with Scripture-grounds on Which our Faith and Practice will by none of them be either denied to us, or taken ill from us. Our whole design is accomplished if we may obtain that Justice, as to be measured in our Principles, and Practice, and the judgement of both by others, according to what we have now Published: which the Lord (whose Eyes are as a flame of Fire) knoweth to be the Doctrine, which with our Hearts we most firmly believe, and sincerely endeavor to conform our Lives to.[44]

It was the Baptists' intention clearly to lay out their distinctives in order that others would be enlightened by them and that they themselves would have an internal standard of belief and practice. The overall thrust seems pragmatic: they believed that religious bodies, their own included, needed rules of governance. The document contains no hint of any tribalist claim for absolute superiority or any agenda for interreligious warfare. Instead, an implicit assumption regarding the jurisdictional limits of their assertions pervades all.

Behind all denominational talk of jurisdictions and rules of conduct lay a deep-seated concern with boundaries. This was Dickinson's "thorny question." Ideas were important in defining boundaries, but ideas alone were insufficient. Somehow social structures needed to be developed that would allow denominationalists to maintain a distinctive sense of identity while simultaneously remaining open to and tolerant of people with divergent religious ideas and practices.

One of the best places to observe the process of codifying and regularizing denominational rules of conduct is in the correspondence of individual Baptist churches with the Philadelphia Baptist Association (which included churches in New Jersey). This association was formed in 1707, but did not meet regularly until the mid-1720s. The Philadelphia Baptist Association had little real power in local church affairs beyond the giving of advice. Local congregations sometimes heeded and sometimes ignored the proffered wisdom. But as the eighteenth century progressed, more and more local Baptists did turn to the association for counsel. The organization came to function as a clearinghouse of ideas, and its decisions slowly took on the form of a collection of precedents. As the keeper of this code of approved behavior, the association took on an image as the "official" interpreters of the collection.[45]

It is instructive to return to the story of the Cohansey church. The original congealing of this congregation from two separate Baptist congregations did not mark the culmination of denominational developments in this church. In 1730, they addressed a query to the Philadelphia Baptist Association seeking advice concerning a difficult issue. The nature of their problem illustrates the breadth to which the limits of bearance and forbearance had been stretched.

> In case a member of a regular church separate himself on the account of the seventh day, and join himself to those that hold the same for a Sabbath, when, at the same time, the church he was a member of allowed, if it was to him a matter of conscience, he might observe it, and keep his place as a member, and they would respect him as they need to do; yet, nevertheless, he goes away, and presumes to be a leader among the aforesaid seventhday people. What must the church do in such a case in order to discharge their duty?
>
> The Association replied: Resolved, That it is the duty of such a church, in as moderate a way and manner as they can, to disown such a member, so as he may not be looked upon to be a member with them on any account.[46]

Loathe to cut any Baptist off from their fellowship, the Cohansey Baptist Church had nevertheless been pushed to the brink of its tolerance by one seventh-day observant delinquent member. The fact that they had forborne as much as they apparently had seems remarkable for the time. Their inquiry to the association only underlines the hesitancy with which they broached the question of actively excluding any Baptist from their society. The association's reply is instructive in its own right. Implied in their resolve is the fact that the tolerant spirit that informed the behavior of Cohansey's Baptists was a widespread phenomenon.

Ten years later the Cohansey church sent a query to the association asking about the obverse problem—who should be included. The particular incident dealt with the need for individuals baptized as infants to be rebaptized as adults upon request for membership in the local congregation.

> Whether a pious person, of the number of Pedo-Baptists, who forbears to have his own children sprinkled, may be admitted in to our communion without being baptized? And doth not the refusing admittance to such a one, discover want of charity in a church so refusing?

The association answered this inquiry "all in the negative."

> 1. It is not for want of charity that we thus answer. Our practice shows the contrary; for we baptize none but such as, on the judgement of charity, have grace, being unbaptized; but it is because we find, in the commission, that no unbaptized persons are to be admitted into church communion.
> 2. Because it is the church's duty to maintain the ordinances as they are delivered to us in scripture . . .
> 3. Because we cannot see it agreeable, in any respect, for the procuring that unity, unfeigned love, and undisturbed peace, which is required, and ought to be in and among Christian communities.[47]

The twin concerns of denominational religion for tolerance and distinctives are evident. The local congregation at Cohansey felt the need for a flexible tolerance more strongly than did the association. They, after all, were dealing with a known person, a friend. Still, they were sensitive enough about rules and distinctives to bring their concerns to the association. The association, in turn, though obviously more concerned about rules of order and Baptist distinctives, seems clearly to have understood the pangs of the local situation. The members of the association took care to defend their decision in terms sympathetic to the wording of the original request for advice. Denominational religion demands "unfeigned love" and "undisturbed peace" and, because of that, no effluence of unreflective tolerance should be allowed that at a later date might result in the need to feign love or disturb the internal peace of the church.

A second regional glimpse into denominational developments is provided by a series of questions addressed to the Philadelphia Baptist Association by the church of Middletown, New Jersey. In 1734 this church was without a minister and wrote the association for advice regarding the range of speakers the members of the church might have available to them. There seems to have been some dissension in this congregation about this matter, and the association was undoubtedly consulted with the hopes of adjudicating the issue through the aid of an outside authority.

> Several queries from Middleton come to the Association, viz.—
> 1. Whether we may accept and take in a minister of a different persuasion at our appointed meetings. Answered in the negative; unless the church see cause, upon some particular occasions. 2. Whether it may not be more convenient for us to keep up our meetings, as usual, by reading the Scriptures, singing of psalms, and prayer, than to admit men of different persuasions? Answered in the affirmative. 3. Whether it be justifiable for our members to neglect our own appointed meetings, and at their pleasure go to hear those differing in judgement from us? Answered in the negative.[48]

In Cohansey the question was one of membership; in Middletown, it was how to carry on worship and instruction in the absence of a resident minister. Three options presented themselves to the Baptists of Middletown: (1) they could bring into their meetings preachers of "different persuasions"; (2) they could continue at best they could without any ministerial leadership; or (3) they could go to other churches for worship and instruction.

In the wisdom of the association, the second option was the only normative answer. Boundaries had to be protected. No Baptist group should indiscriminately open itself to ministerial intrusions from the outside or allow its members to wander to other religious instructors at will. While reaffirming the normative importance of boundaries, the association also indicated that the walls of the group should not be impervious to outsiders. On "some particular occasions" it might indeed be right to invite ministers of "different persuasions" into the Middletown Baptist pulpit, but not at their "appointed meetings"—their regular meetings for worship.

As in the case with Cohansey, the baptists of Middletown seem more willing to tolerate communication and cross-fertilization between religious groups than was the Philadelphia Baptist Association. Again, the difference seems to be one of familiarity. The Middletown Baptists knew the preachers they might want to invite to address them or to whom they might want to listen. But they were willing to second-guess themselves. They were willing to appeal to the advice of the association because they had come to trust the wisdom of accumulated experience embodied in the association. The Baptists of Middletown had learned that relations with other religious groups had to be defined by codified rules as much as (if not more than) by the immediate sense of the situation. In this regard their reaction differs significantly from the reactions of most earlier denominationalists. Earlier denominationalists tended to allow the exigencies of the immediate situation to determine the lineaments of compromise and cooperation. The importance of rules of precedence and appeals to outside objectivity (as embodied in the Philadelphia Baptist Association) increased as denominationalism progressed through the eighteenth century.

One final incident from the annals of the Philadelphia Baptist Association, this one from 1752, illustrates how far some local congregations thought tolerance should be pushed. It also underlines the importance placed on theological, as well as sociological, boundaries of churches by the association. The query in this case came from Kingwood.

> Whether a person denying unconditional election, the doctrine of original sin, and the final perseverance of the saints, and striving to affect as many as he can, may have full communion with the church?

Given the generally strong Calvinistic orientation of the Baptist churches in New Jersey, one wonders why the church of Kingwood felt it necessary to consult the association on this manner. A clue is given in the association's response:

> ... we adopt, and would that all the churches belonging to the Baptist Association be well grounded in accordance to our Confession of faith and catechism, and cannot allow that any are true members of our church who deny the said principles, be their conversation outward what it will.[49]

Most likely the person referred to in the query was a person of exemplary "outward conversation." In its response to this situation, the association indicated that piety was an insufficient test of faith and an inappropriate measure of the breadth of Baptist fellowship. What was important for membership was the adopted "Confession." Christian fellowship of some sort might still be possible with people who disagreed with that "Confession," but such fellowship could not be sanctioned within Baptist institutional structures. Once again the importance of clear, visible, and institutionally defined boundaries was asserted. This was the only hedge against degeneration into religious anarchy.

The Power and Prevalence of Denominational Etiquette

Denominational discussions of rules of religious conduct dealt mainly with how to keep within boundaries. One of the most significant characteristics of denominational religion, however, was the crossing of boundaries. Colonial denominationalists in New Jersey never addressed this topic head-on. Allowable patterns of behavior were hinted at, but little more. This type of indirect discussion was illustrated in the oblique reference by the Philadelphia Baptist Association (in its answer to the query from Middletown) regarding the allowability of having ministers of "different persuasions" preach to Baptists only on "particular occasions," not at regularly scheduled meetings.

In the place of articulated rules on the subject, a sense of etiquette developed that provided an informal but very real guide for behavior. This operated on a range of levels, but one of the clearest situations in which to observe the practice of denominational etiquette was the stage of public debate.

As denominational religion gained in strength, Baptist and Presbyterian groups seemed to gravitate toward the forefront of the movement (or at least they became the most outspoken on the subject). In that light, a debate held in 1742 at Cape May between a Baptist (Rev. Abel Morgan) and a Presbyterian (Rev. Samuel Finley) concerning the mode of Christian baptism is revealing. The main point of debate is relatively uninteresting (it concerns the pros and cons of paedo-baptism), with each side amassing Scripture texts for their position while disputing the meaning of the texts assembled against them. Near the end of the discussion, however, a curious point arose.

To seal his argument, Finley charged that the argument of his Baptist opponent would "exclude and unchristian all other Protestant Churches on the Account of this Mode [of baptism]."[50] Finley's charge struck like a blow below the belt. It was out of place and impertinent, not only because each group was, by that time, implicitly committed to a denominational view of religion, but also because the very situation of which he was a part (i.e., heated yet congenial debate) denied Finley's charge.

Abel Morgan sensed the inappropriateness of Finley's remarks and jumped on the issue:

> What an odd way has Mr. F. of representing things! When did he ever hear any of us say that there were no Christians in other Denominations? . . . Does a Society unchristian all others with whom it cannot or doth not hold Communion. If so the Presbyterian Society unchristians all other Communions with whom it cannot or does not hold Communion. 'Tis then high Time for Mr. F. to look around him, and answer for himself.[51]

It seems from Morgan's remarks that he and the audience deemed a denominational understanding of religion the only proper base for religious discussion. The vehemence with which he castigated Finley for his accusations indicates a sense of outrage understandable only within such a context. While miffed at the situation, Morgan actually may have gained ground in the argument. By the very act of lodging charges of antidenominational religious behavior against his fellow Christian, Finley indicated that he himself harbored antidenominational attitudes in his heart.

This same sense of etiquette is observable elsewhere. Perhaps the most succinct statement of it was penned by Griffin Jenkins in *A Brief Vindication of the Purchassors Against the Propritors, in A Christian Manner*, published in 1746. Jenkins states bluntly:

> What is it to be Episcopal, Presbyterians, Congregationals, etc. Our Religion lies not, much less our Perfection, in these or any other Opinions, and Form of

Government. I doubt not but there are Saints in all these Forms, yet withal I believe and affirm that none of these Forms makes them saints. . . .
. . . For Oh how good and pleasant a thing it is for Bretheran to dwell together in Unity; let us not be like Ephraim & Judah to Envy and Vex one another; but love one another with pure love Fervently.[52]

One last incident reveals even more than the above how broadly dispersed a denominational sense of etiquette had become in the colony. The description is taken from the itinerarium of Alexander Hamilton (an account of his travels through the American colonies in the year 1744) and the event itself is set in the town of Kingston located just a little north and east of Princeton.

After breakfast, as I sat in the porch, there arrived a wagon with some company. There were in it two Irishman, a Scotsman, and a Jew. The Jew's name was Abraham Du-bois, a French man by birth. He spoke such bad English that I could scarce understand him. . . .

This Jew and the company that were with him begun a dispute about sacred history. He insisted much upon the books of Moses and the authority of the Old Testament. He asked the Scotsman in particular if he believed the Old Testament. He replied that now a days there were few Old Testament people, all having become *New Light men*, "for," says he, "among the Christians, one wife is sufficient for one man, but your Old Testament fornicators were allowed a plurality of wives and as many concubines as they could afford to maintain." The Jew made no answer to this nonsensicall reply but began very wisely to settle what day of the week it was and what time of that day that God began the creation of the world. He asserted that it was upon the day that the Christians call Sunday, and that when the light first appeared, it was in the west, and therefor it was in the evening that the creation was begun. "Had that day no morning then?" replyed the Scotsman with a sneer. To which the Jew answered that there had been no dawn or sun rising that day because the sun was not yet created to run his diurnall course, but that a glorious stream of light suddenly appeared by the mandate of God in the west. "I never heard of an evening without a morning in my life before," replied his antagonist, "and it is nonsence to suppose such a thing." "Cannot black exist," said the Jew, "without its opposite white?" "It may be so," said the Scotsman, "but why does your countryman Moses say 'and the evening and the morning were the first day?' " The Jew answered that the evening was there first mentioned because the work was begun upon the evening, att which the Scotsman swore that the words were misplaced by the translators, which pert reply put an end to the dispute.

After a deal of such stuff about the Jewish sabbath and such like subjects, the waggon and company departed.[53]

This dialogue, while it shows both a good deal of tolerance and a fair dose of humor, is also a serious debate. Neither of the participants may have been well versed in the doctrines and beliefs of his respective group, but each was ready and willing to defend his beliefs. In the end, however, no one cursed the other or damned the other to eternal perdition. They simply dropped the conversation and got on with their traveling. These conversationalists might not have been the most refined in their denominational manners, but it is important to point out that this exchange was also not simply a Christian dialogue. This was a conversation between a Christian and a Jew held along denominational lines of etiquette.

All of these events point toward an important change regarding denominational religion that took place around 1740. After this date, the denominational religious mode of interaction between members of different religious persuasions seems to become the standard mode of operation. During the 1740s denominational religionists seem increasingly to have felt little need to argue for their position. Prior to this time, denominational religion had almost always been couched in apologetic terms. After the 1740s, denominationalism spoke with the authority that comes from representing a dominant viewpoint.

FIVE

New Jersey's Public Piety of Neighborliness

Over and above private and diffuse pluralistic developments, the colonists of New Jersey also constructed a public and focused framework within which religious diversity could meaningfully be comprehended. What was most significant in this process was not the mere identification of a unifying "central zone" of society (for this is a necessary task of all societies), but the fact that this center of society came to be defined in distinctly pluralistic terms.[1] This public center of pluralism emerged slowly, and for those involved the process rarely seemed either simple or clear. Such would be expected, however, for these colonists were involved in a fundamental reordering of their society. They were not merely deciding among available options, but making a corporate exploration of new ways of thinking and acting.

The public solution to the problem of pluralism as it was finally worked out can best be described as a commitment to neighborliness. Neighborliness recognized differences among people and groups. But it recognized only relative differences, not absolute ones. Viewed through the spectacles of neighborliness, New Jersey's population was not a motley mix of sinners and saints, but a melange of ordinary people, each of whom was part sinner and part saint. Underlying all relative differences, neighborliness also posited a basic unity of the population—a human unity inherent in the created order itself—that called all to cooperate for the common good.

Public Piety Defined

The public adjustment to religious pluralism amounted to a restructuring of existing public piety. The term "public piety" is a rough equivalent of the phrase "civil religion." In the way I use "public piety," however, it is different from "civil religion" in that public piety connotes a more fluid and unstructured version of social organization and group understanding than that typically implied by the idea of a civil religion.

Public piety is a widely held system of beliefs, values, and attitudes that expresses the inherently understood and accepted religious or quasi-religious underpinnings of a given social order. It provides a yardstick that sets minimum standards of acceptable public behavior and also points to the ultimate ideals desired by a society. The content of public piety is revealed in public discourse. During the colonial period, the two most obvious examples were speeches and proclamations made by public figures acting in their official capacities and the pronouncements of ministers who corporately constituted a religious elite.

Public piety rarely exists in the form of a logically coherent set of politico-religious axioms or beliefs. Rather, it is a loose collection of emotive, as well as rational, values and ideals akin to what Wilhelm Dilthey called the "common mood" of a nation or society. The various strands of thought and value that make up public piety exist as symbols, providing unifying images around which the members of a society can align themselves. In sum, public piety represents the sometimes unexpressed but always assumed goals, ground rules, and expectations of social interaction. It is the unifying glue that holds a people together amid the confusion that is part of every human collectivity.

Like all social constructions of reality, public piety is subject to change. Emil Durkheim spoke of this in terms of the conflict between the ideals of the past and those of the future.

> It is undoubtedly true that it [society] hesitates over the manner in which it ought to conceive itself; it feels itself drawn in divergent directions. But these conflicts which break forth are not between the ideal and reality, but between two different ideals, that of yesterday and that of to-day, that which has the authority of tradition and that which has the hope of the future.[2]

In most traditional societies these changes are almost invisible. In New Jersey, however, changes in public piety are observable. Colonial New Jersey was largely a traditional society, but it was also a colonial society. In all colonial societies, the task of defining a center—a public piety—is made difficult by the need to balance the claims of two competing social realities. For Jerseyans, one of these realities was the relatively well-defined social myths, norms, and ideologies of England, the "mother" country (in Durkheim's terms the ideal of the past). The other reality was the historical and sociological distinctives of the colony itself (Durkheim's "hope of the future").

The historically related interplay of these two realities produced in colonial New Jersey a sort of zero-sum game of influence. As the prominence of distinctively English forms of public piety waned, the strength of an emerging indigenous sense of public piety increased. Three phases of development naturally presented themselves in this process. During a first phase, English forms of public piety predominated. During a second phase, an alternative form of public piety emerged alongside this initial English model. There was a tendency not to recognize the newness of this alternative form of public piety. This is logical enough in that the settlers of New Jersey were traditional people and did not expect or seek change. Finally, however, the colonists did recognize the distinctiveness of their own view of things and when this happened a third period of development began. As this new "indigenous" sense of public piety slowly became the view of the majority of the population, the central theme that emerged was the idea of neighborliness. In contrast to the English model that had first been present in the colony—a model that assumed a significant degree of social uniformity—this indigenized New Jersey understanding of itself was rooted in the diversity of the colony.

Civil religion, even in its most intense forms, is sometimes hard to document because it is typically more a part of the ethos of a community (the unspoken code of identity) than it is a part of the conscious and articulated morality of the culture. The following discussion of New Jersey's public piety has a distinctly impressionistic feel to it because of this. A search for the public piety of the colony will largely consist of collecting hints. Civil religion never leaves the clear "fossil" record in historical documents that institutional religion does.

The English Model of Public Piety

English citizens who immigrated to New Jersey all brought with them one variant form or another of traditional English public piety. This national religious self-awareness was simply part of who they were. They were English and, even though removed from England by several thousand miles of ocean, they intended to remain English. The public piety of England had an appeal beyond mere national chauvinism. It promised divine protection, and it seemed ancient and unchanging (even if it was not).

A. Public Piety and English History

By the close of the sixteenth century, most Englishmen had come to believe God had specially chosen their nation above others. Whether Anglican or Puritan, all conceived of their nation as elect in God's sight, preserved and protected throughout history by God's grace. The clearest recitation of this vision is the *Actes and Monumentes* of John Foxe (1563). Its most blatant expression, however, is John Aylmer's oft-repeated assertion that "God is an Englishman."

Aylmer's nationalistic hubris may represent, as Maurice Powicke suggests, the sanctification (or perhaps more accurately, the deification) of a "very insular and English" national consciousness.[3] More likely, it reflects a means of coping with the need to provide a new foundation for English society after Henry VIII's break with the Roman church. The English Reformation, by cutting the nation off from its previous papal, apostolic, and divine sanction, created "a dramatic need for a new authority" that did not "rely upon anything but England's own sovereign past."[4] The idea of England as "The Elect Nation" provided a solid basis for just such an authority.

This vision of God and English history provides the plot for Foxe's *Actes and Monuments*. The nationalistic importance of this book is indicated by the fact that it was often placed on public display in Anglican churches alongside the Bible. In Foxe's account of church history, he links a long succession of English rulers whom he claims owed their authority directly to divine appointment. He then attempts to show how these monarchs prospered or not depending on whether "they heeded their vocation to defend the faith and the people in the faith, or suffered themselves to be misled by false counsellors, or overborne by misbelieving usurpers and invaders."[5] The same sense of national call and mission informs the title "Defender of the Faith" assumed by Henry VIII. This was not a lightly worn title of the monarch, nor was it one easily ignored by the people. Ensconced in the accolade was England's ultimate, and elemental, hedge against social, moral, and historical chaos.

The concept of "The Elect Nation" led by the "Defender of the Faith" became, in fact, the founding myth of post-Reformation English society. Once enunciated, this paradigm was read back into history. The event that had spawned its development was quickly reinterpreted so that the Reformation came to be seen not as a hiatus in the country's spiritual life, but as the "vindication of the divine authority of the English past."[6] The people, however, were soon to push the origins of God's special favor on their land even farther back in history. God's choice of England as "The Elect Nation" had not originated in remembered time; it was a part of God's eternal providential will for the world. In the language of Mircea Eliade, England had been chosen of God *in illo tempore*[7]—in original time, before the beginning of the world. The eternal providence of God thus was seen as working through history, not over against history. And logically enough, the people came to believe that the commands of God, reflecting his providential will, could "in no way be discontinuous with the way things were."[8]

English piety, thus construed, tended to promote social passivity toward the political order. This was especially the case after the Restoration of the Crown in 1660. In the person of the monarch and in the structure of society, God's will had become incarnate. The explosive revolutionary potential of the concept of election—so forcefully exploited by the Puritans during the early and mid-seventeenth century—was for the most part, and for most Englishmen, effectively kept in check after 1660 by being wedded to a particular and unquestioning understanding of how the nation's existence fit into God's providential scheme. In this view of things, history was not seen in terms of degeneration and revival (a favorite Puritan scheme of interpretation), but as a series of "deliverances" of the nation by God from the hands of its internal and external enemies. English piety was thus more priestly than prophetic. It sought to maintain in purity what had been given by God as a gift. It did not seek to redirect and purify the present order to accord more fully with some idealistic vision. Uniformity and obedience, growing out of a spirit of thankfulness to God for having continually preserved the nation, became shibboleths in this rendering of reality. English public piety was never totalitarian. Uniformity was encouraged, but not with threats of death. And certain forms of dissent were allowed, though obviously none was encouraged. To force things more than this would have been to make impossible a proper obedience to God, one that was not feigned and one that sprang from a truly thankful heart.

B. *The English Model in New Jersey*

This form of public piety seems to have been readily and naturally brought to the new world by English colonists. It is evident in Carteret's calling of the first New Jersey Assembly "for the making and Constituting such wholesome

Lawes as shall be most needful and Necessary for . . . the maintayning of a religious Community and ciuil society one with the other as becometh Christians."[9] It is also evident in the proclamations of days of Thanksgiving by the General Assembly in 1676 and 1679.[10] The move toward an informal establishment of religion that occurred during the 1680s is further evidence that Jerseyans were basically operating out of an English vision of public piety. Records from the early years are sparse, however, and direct and blatant evidence of the prominence of English forms of public piety is thin. Still, the very sparsity of these records in some way validates the assertion that the traditional English model of public piety did define the operational expectations of colonists. Social self-conceptions like public piety are often noted only when they are breached, and no evidence indicates a turning away from the assumptions that colonists would have naturally brought with them.

One later example indicates that the presence of a traditionally English model of public piety was an enduring reality. On 7 March 1722, Governor William Burnet addressed the opening session of the first New Jersey assembly elected since his arrival in the colony. Given this "happy opportunity" of learning the sentiments of the country through these newly elected officials, he "in the most publick manner" felt obliged to "fully inform" them of his own views. His speech was short, but one-quarter of it was devoted to an elucidation of the type of public piety he thought proper for the colony. He concluded his speech as follows:

> To this remarkable deliverance [the accession of King George I] by an overriding hand of providence, you owe the preservation of your laws and liberties, the secure enjoyment of your property, and a free exercise of religion, according to the dictates of your conscience. These invaluable blessings are so visible among us, and the misery of countries where tyranny and persecution prevail so well known, that I need not mention them, to raise in your minds the highest sense of your obligations to serve God, honor the King, and love your country.[11]

Within the general structure of English public piety, the address by Governor Burnet is easily comprehended. God's latest "deliverance" of England from its enemies' snares (beginning with the Glorious Revolution and ending with the accession of George I) should, he informed the assembly "raise in your minds the highest sense of your obligation to serve God, honor the king, and love your country." All has been guided "by an overriding hand of providence." The only proper response was to love the nation upon which

God continued to pour his love, and willingly, even joyfully, to submit to God's will through obedience to his representative, the king.

In response to Burnet's address, the assembly stumbled over itself to agree. "We gladly embrace this opportunity," they intoned, "to assure your excellency, that our sentiments and those we represent are one and the same, cheerfully to demonstrate our loyalty to our sovereign King George." Further, they hoped the governor would excuse them for "falling short of words to express our thankful acknowledgements to God Almighty and those under him, who have been instruments in working deliverance to that glorious nation to which we belong." Finally, they begged Burnet "to believe the sincerity of their thoughts" and "their duty, gratitude and obedience" to their sovereign. Burnet accepted the assembly's response as "a peculiar honor to me to be thus justified in all my conduct by the publick act of the whole legislature" and assured all present that he would "study to keep a conscience void of offence towards God and towards man."[12]

Political language, of course, can rarely be taken at face value. When it addresses concerns of public piety, it should sometimes be even more suspect. In the example at hand, this is manifestly the case. The assembly Burnet addressed in 1722 was not the first New Jersey assembly with which he had had to deal. Soon after his arrival he had prorogued the then sitting body of representatives because, as colonial historian Samuel Smith says, they (the assembly and the governor) did not "very well agree" with each other.[13] Burnet himself says they had had "a wrong notion of each other."[14] After new elections had been ordered and a new assembly gathered, each side returned somewhat chastened and educated and ready to make peace. The gush of conciliatory language that resulted in this situation could hardly be expected clearly to delineate the differences of spirit that remained. Each side was scrambling for a middle ground and the verbal formulas of agreement obfuscate divisions as much as they reveal a longing for unanimity. Without any doubt, however, this encounter attests to the fact that many Jerseyans still found England's public piety a powerful and attractive means of understanding themselves.

The Waning of English Piety

As attractive as the English model of public piety was to many colonists, it finally proved unexportable. It did so partly because the ethnic diversity of

New Jersey's population demanded a broader base and partly because of simple logistics (the difficulties of travel and communication between England and the colony). Most important and fundamental, however, English public piety was incongruent with the conditions that were shaping the development of the colony. The societal needs of New Jersey that demanded a publicly religious answer were not the same as those of England. English themes of public piety were prominent during the first fifty years of the colony's history. In the eighteenth century, however, this support increasingly became limited to the circle of individuals immediately surrounding the royally appointed governor.

While many colonial Jerseyans were religiously and ethnically English and could thus identify with England's history and mission in the world, many were not. By the end of the seventeenth century, representatives from at least nine different religious groups and as many or more cultural groups could be found in the colony: there were Quakers, Baptists, Puritan Congregationalists, the Reformed Church, Lutherans, Anglicans, Presbyterians, Keithian Quakers, and a smattering of sectarian groups. The ethnic diversity included in its kaleidoscopic range immigrants of English, Dutch, Swedish, Finnish, French Huguenot, Flemish, Walloon, Scandinavian, New England, Scotch, Irish, and Scotch-Irish heritage. Few of these groups had any natural propensity to adopt the English model as their own. Some groups held visions of public piety at distinct odds with the English model.

For colonists of English origin the picture is different, but the result is similar. Even they did not have unimpeded access to England's social myths. A tension evident in England between "court and country"—between hierarchical and localistic claims of authority—was exacerbated in the New World. (The term "country" here is basically synonymous with what we now call "county," and "court" is a synonym for the monarchy.) Loyalties and identity associated with "country," were, in England, as tenacious and significant as any fixed on the Crown and nation. The explosive tensions that existed between these two definitions of loyalty are obvious in the role they played in the so-called Puritan Revolution of the 1640s.[15] When "court" and "country" were separated by three thousand miles of ocean, the potential for a violent conflict between competing groups was minimal. In the same light, however, it was almost inevitable that the national half of this dichotomous self-understanding would wither. New Jersey was not England, and as the life of the colony took on more and more of its own independent and distinct flavor, purely English forms of public piety began to lose their attractiveness.

A. The "Ordinariness" of New Jersey's Early History

The central factor in the waning of English forms of public piety was the ordinariness of New Jersey. There simply were no obvious examples of divine intervention in the history of the colony. While the idea of God's "remarkable deliverances"—his miraculous intervention in the history of the nation—had stood at the center of English public piety, New Jersey's history was flat. Rather than anything "remarkable," a distinct pale of ordinariness hung in the Jersey air.

The early history of New Jersey needs to be seen in light of the date of its founding. By the 1660s English colonization had become an "ordinary" enterprise. The restoration of the English monarchy in 1660 marked a new phase for both England and North America, and the early development of New Jersey public piety must be understood in this context. As order was reinstituted in Great Britain, the fires of religious and political dissatisfaction, which earlier had fueled a substantial portion of New World immigration, cooled. As they did, the pool of potential immigrants from which each colony could draw recruits shrank commensurately.

As colonization became a more ordinary and a more competitive enterprise, both new and established colonies were forced to state their distinctives and rationales for existence in order to attract settlers. The *Concession and Agreement* of 1664 represents one type of literature growing out of this situation. It is a legal document enumerating the liberties and rights each settler would enjoy. The assumption behind this approach to recruitment was that the facts, plainly and simply stated, would promote the speedy planting of the province. This assumption, however, proved false, and a second literary genre emerged: the blatantly promotional tract. Few concerns were taken for granted by these pamphleteers in their attempt to woo settlers. Because of this, these pamphlets are extremely helpful in uncovering both the attractions of immigration and the hesitancies would-be settlers had about it. They detail the intellectual and emotional composition of the seventeenth-century immigrant mentality. And in that process they reveal, in the attitudes of the settlers, what would become the groundwork of the future public piety of each colony.

The best-known and apparently one of the most successful tracts is *The Model of the Government of the Province of East New Jersey in America* drawn up by George Scott of Pitlochie, and published in Edinburgh in 1685. The major problem that Scott felt obligated to discuss was the tendency of people to remain where they had been born. "I must confess," he admits, "there is in the generality of Mankind a natural inclination to love the Land of their own Nativity beyond other places." Yet, he continues, referring to a demographic history of North America he had just finished outlining, "we see, it hath been frequently so ordered in Providence, that severals, upon different motives, have been brought to quit their Native Soyl, and inclined to make choice of strange and remote Countries for their habitation."[16]

Scott, as an active promoter of colonization, could not, however, be content merely to prove by precedent the allowability of immigration. He also had to offer a positive argument why one should do so. Scott took two tacks in this task. The first was economic and political. "In our civil state," he contended, "a few Men flourish" while "the rest wax weak, and languish as wanting room and means to nourish." The obvious solution to this problem was to establish new colonies. This work, he said, would at the same time "tend to the Honour and advantage of our nation in General" by relieving tensions at home, and would also provide an avenue to prosperity for those who actually relocated. Scott suggested, "The Spirits and Hearts of Men are kept in better Temper by spreading wide . . . and shifting into empty lands enforceth Men to Frugality and quickeneth invention."[17]

For the concerns of public piety, Scott's second line of argument is more instructive. He reminded his readers that God had issued a command to Adam "to replenish the Earth and subdue it. Gen. 1.26." For Scott, this had the force of a "perpetual law" of colonization for all mankind, as long as "Men and any void places of the Earth continue."[18] While few of Scott's contemporaries would have argued directly against this divine decree to fill the earth, many thought the work of planting colonies represented an "extraordinary" means of compliance. In this light, they argued that any decision to immigrate demanded "an extraordinary warrant, such as Abraham had from God, to call him out of Mesopotamia to Canaan." Scott's reply to such caviling was immediate and to the point:

> I must grant Abraham's undertaking was in many things extraordinary, and therefore needed an immediate direction from God; he was to go alone with his Family and Brethren, to such a certain place far distant, possest already by the Canaanites who were to be expelled, that land was to be wholly appropriate to himself and his Issue, he was not to plant it at present, but only to Sojourn in it, and walk through it for a time: Now none of these circumstances fit our ordinary colonies.[19]

In 1685 when Scott wrote his tract, New Jersey represented leftover land—empty space remaining between other already well-established English colonies. It was not a wilderness that readily attracted isolationistic sects. Nor was it a virgin territory that beckoned budding entrepreneurs. Rather, the type of colonists attracted to New Jersey were ordinary folk. This is evident in the letters Scott appended to his *Model*, letters included for the purpose of illustrating the kinds of people the colony had already attracted and still needed. One letter can represent the tone of all. In 1684 John Reid sent a letter to a friend in Edinburgh describing the colony:

> Here is no outward want, especially of provisions, and if people were industrious they might have cloaths also within themselves; by the report of all, its the best of all the Neighbouring Collonies, it is very wholesome, pleasant, and a fertill land . . . I know nothing wanting here, except that good Tradesman, and good Husbandmen, and Labourers are scarce.[20]

B. The Religious "Ordinariness" of the Colony

New Jersey was not only ordinary in its business aspect. It was also a religiously ordinary place. At first glance this might seem surprising. After all, the point has often been made that the earliest settlements in East New Jersey were Puritan and thus they had to be religiously zealous in demeanor.[21] But even in Newark, the most strongly Puritan of the East New Jersey towns, religious enthusiasm seems to have evaporated quickly. As early as 1679 complaints were brought to the town meeting that there were "grown Persons, as well as Boys, . . . misbehav[ing] themselves on the Lord's Day in the time of Public Service, both in the Meeting House and Without."[22] In 1681 the town fathers had to pass a motion to prevent "the disorderly Meeting of Young People at unseasonable times" and to coerce the cooperation of the families of these people who had apparently allowed such behavior to go on unchecked at their homes.[23] Even in Newark religious zeal was abating. By 1684, the general tenor of religion in East New Jersey as a whole was such that John Barclay and Arthur Forbes could report to their fellow proprietors still resident in England that while "there be people of several sorts of religion" present in the colony, there were "but few very zealous."[24]

Across the land in West Jersey a similar situation seems to have prevailed. William Penn's attitude is indicative. Penn was not averse to seeing the New

World as a place for religious zeal and purity. With regard to Pennsylvania, in fact, he stated that he hoped the colony would be a Quaker "Zion," an example before "the Eyes of the Inhabitants of the Lands." When speaking about New Jersey, however, Penn was quick to caution potential Quaker settlers that "the body of friends, as a religious society of people" was not necessarily behind the scheme. He cautioned all would-be immigrants to consider their decision carefully, "lest an unwarrantable forwardness should act or hurry any besides or beyond the wisdom and counsel of the lord."[25]

Colonial New Jersey was not a land of zealotry—either on a personal, group, or societal level. It was an ordinary country for ordinary people. Few believed it was God's special turf in any way other than through some vicarious participation in England's national sense of being chosen, and a good number of colonists didn't even believe that. (Some tribalistic groups may well have thought their niche of the world was special in God's eyes, but these groups would not have conceived the colony as a whole to be specially chosen by God.) The public documents indicate that an English sense of things lingered in New Jersey (at least among social elites) well into the eighteenth century; however, it is also clear that the conditions that would ultimately cause this English model of public piety to wither were in place before 1700.

The Rise of an Indigenous Public Piety

As the strength of English public piety waned a foundation was simultaneously being laid for the building of an alternative indigenous sense of public piety. The primary impetus was the need Jerseyans felt to understand their "ordinary" land in some kind of religious manner. The colonists were not modern secularists and they did not want, nor did they expect, the state to be a "naked public square."[26] On the other hand, there were certain solutions that were simply not live options. Most important, conditions in the colony mitigated against the erection of any formal and dogmatic religious establishment. Whatever solutions Jerseyans might propose as a way of religiously construing the meaning of their common life, they had to be relatively noninstitutional in form and theologically nondogmatic in their particulars.

Taken as a whole, the settlers may not have been overly zealous in their religious concerns, but this does not mean they were quietistic or separatistic in their religious or civil comportment. Almost without exception, those who entered the colony came from situations in which religious and political structures had been co-joined. More important, almost all (except the Quakers) had been members of churchly, as opposed to sectarian, religious groups. As such, they assumed—even if for no other reason than folk memory—that the civil and the religious ordering of society should be at least parallel, if not connected. Relatively few were content to accept the particularity of their own community of faith as a sufficiently wide realm in which to locate their total self-identity, and fewer still were convinced that the common life of society was religiously neutral or meaningless.

The base on which this emerging indigenous sense of public piety was built was the habitual linkage established between religious diversity and a commitment to public peaceableness among the groups. The colony was from its inception marked by religious diversity and from the times of the earliest proprietors the leaders had insisted that the various groups publicly get along with one another. The original proprietors had foreseen the possibility of friction developing between the groups they were seeking to attract. In order to circumvent, or at least minimize, actual conflict, they fenced in their allowance of religious liberty with a hedge of social order and in doing so they unwittingly began a process that would end in the construction of a new sense of public piety. The *Concession and Agreement* of 1664 states:

> All and every such person and persons may from time to time and at all times, freely and fully have and enjoy his and their judgments and consciences in matters of religion throughout the said Province, they behaving themselves peaceably and quietly, and not using this liberty to licentiousness, nor to the civil injury, or outward disturbance of others.[27]

Within this framework, the early settlers were legally bound only to tolerate each other. However, this merely legal sense of tolerance easily metamorphosed into a more internalized community rule. The colonists very quickly seemed to make peaceableness a publicly commended virtue. Breaches of behavior were seen more as social offenses than as legally punishable crimes. A shared soil, a common governmental jurisdiction, and a similar commitment to public order together soon also forced an opening of communication among groups. The resultant modicum of agreement represented the necessary foundation for the development of a distinctive New Jersey definition of public piety.

An indigenous public piety took some time to develop. For ease of description this process can be divided into two periods. A first phase began with the founding of the colony and continued until roughly 1700. Most developments during this period occurred in West New Jersey. The result of this process was a distinctive melding of concerns for morality and public civility. A second phase began after the turn of the century, when Jerseyans discovered that their own vision of public piety was different from the traditional English model. Before 1700, the colonists had been unconsciously developing their own understanding of the religiousness of the public order—often using the language of English piety in an only slightly altered form to express their emerging convictions. After 1700, this process of articulating a distinctly New Jersey public piety became increasingly a self-conscious task and one worked out in conscious contrast to the English model, which still found some support.

A. First Formulations

During the first period of development certain elements that would later prove central to New Jersey's full-fledged public piety began to coalesce, but Jerseyans showed little awareness of the fact that these formative aspects diverged in the slightest from English ways of conceiving the issue. Attempts to comprehend the pluralism of the colony were couched in terms basically borrowed from, or at least compatible with, English forms. While no conscious attempt was being made to constitute an independent societal self-understanding, the process of picking and choosing only some items from the overall scheme of English public piety nonetheless amounted to an initial and practical reconceiving of the fundamental base of New Jersey society.

Two separate concerns formed the center of public piety during its initial phase of development. One was a demand that all colonists make an honest commitment to peaceful coexistence with all religious groups. This represents an internalization and personalization of what had formerly been merely a legal injunction. The second concern was that God's moral standards should, at least minimally, be maintained so that God's judgment on the land would be avoided and his "ordinary" blessings assured. ("Ordinary" blessings refers to the basic and general prosperity God would grant the region, and this stands in contrast to the "remarkable" blessings that were so central to English public piety and that typically had to do with God's special protection of the country from foreign invasion, internal revolt, and national apostasy.)

The increasing prominence of these two concerns is especially evident in West New Jersey. West New Jersey was founded as a combined commercial venture and as a haven for persecuted Quakers. Its original constitution accordingly allowed for a wide and pragmatic freedom of religion. *The Concessions and Agreements of the Proprietors, Freeholders, and Inhabitants of the Province of West New Jersey, in America*, formulated in 1676, stated "that no men, nor numbers of men upon earth hath power or authority to rule over men's consciences in religious matters."[28] In this vision, religion was seen as solely and wholly an individual matter. By 1686, however, when certain new "fundamental agreements" were made, this individualistic element had slipped in prestige, and social concerns had risen. Liberty of conscience in religious matters in this latter document was to be accorded only to those who agreed to "live peaceably and quietly."[29]

Disturbance of Quaker meetings by religious "ranters" who claimed liberty under provisions of the original *Concessions and Agreements* may have abetted this change of spirit.[30] Another factor was also at work, however—the "improvement" of the colony. This is revealed in a law passed by the West Jersey General Assembly in 1683, which limited immigration only to those who could give written proof that they had lived their lives "soberly and honestly to the best of their knowledge." All people of "prophane, loose, and idle, and scandolous" lives were to be prevented from settling among those people already in the colony "who (for the generality of them) fear[ed] God, and [were] painful and industrious, in the promoting and improving the said Province."[31]

The picture was rounded out a decade later (1694) when in a preface to a bill, "Discouraging Whoredom and Adultery," the rationale for the legislation was described in terms of concern for the whole colony. The West Jersey assembly theologized that it was because of "heinous transgressions" such as these that "God Almighty afflicts a land." It was therefore only reasonable that for the good of the colony as a whole (as well as for the spiritual assistance of any individuals who might be prone to sin) such offense against God be wiped from the face of the land.

In all these examples it is basic morality that is being announced or enforced, not any sectarian religious beliefs or practices. That focus is significant, for underneath the attention to public morality, a concern for peaceableness is implied. These laws were not simply announcing moral limits; they were also designed to eliminate potential tensions among groups that might arise out of breaches of "common" decency. And it is this wedding of peaceableness with morality that constitutes the distinctiveness of New Jersey's developing indigenous public piety.

Perhaps the clearest and most succinct statement of the public piety of this period comes from a proclamation by Governor Jeremiah Basse (of West New Jersey) concerning "the Suppression of Vice and Immorality," issued in 1698.

> It being very necessary for the good and prosperity of this Province that our principle care be in obedience to the laws of God and the wholesome laws of this Province to endeavor as much as in us lyeth the exterpation of all sorts of looseness and phophanities and to unite and Join in the fear and love of God and of one another that by the religious and vertuous carriage and behavior of every one in his respective station and calling all heats and animosities and dissentions may vanish and the blessing of Almighty God's accompany our honest and lawfull endeavours.[32]

Basse's main point is that if the individual members of society would obey God's moral dictates and join together, leaving off "all heats and animosities and dissentions," the blessings of heaven would surely fall on the land. Woven together in his vision are all the strands of thought evident in the examples cited. The "heinousness" in God's sight of all "looseness and prophanities" in living is implied just below the surface of this plea, but Basse has given a positive tone to his warning. It is not so much the affliction of God that he fears as it is his hope that the people of New Jersey might be able to expect the blessing of God on the land.

Basse is an especially appropriate spokesperson for this developing sense of public piety as it existed at the end of the century. He is so because other events in his life indicate that he had little awareness that his remarks were out of line with the English model. Within a few years of issuing this call for a sort of familial community Basse was arguing in a different context.

> Without government, no society or number of men can long be cemented, much less flourish and increase; without the censures of the Church are duly and impartially administered how shall either virtue be encouraged or vice in all its forms be detected and punished? The authors and perpetrators of some crimes may be too great for the Civil government to take hold of in these parts of the world, that might soon be corrected by the Ecclesiastical Governor; we need such an Ecclesiastical Governor that dare reprove and censure any that infringe the just Laws and Constitution of the Church; let us have such a Bishop as St. Ambrose, and we shall soon have such Governors as Theodosius.[33]

Basse basically argued that the colony needed to have an established church like that of England. It is difficult to understand how the sort of formal religious overseeing of the colony he proposed could have been reconciled with his earlier remarks. Perhaps Basse had some way to bring together these two seemingly divergent sets of ideas. Perhaps he did not feel the tension between them. In any event, Basse's flip-flopping Janus-like behavior is a good indication of the transition the entire colony was in at the turn of the century. The arrival of Lord Cornbury would soon wake the colony from this amphibious existence.

B. The Clash with English Public Piety

As New Jersey public piety coalesced, friction developed between it and the more purely English public piety that also found representation in the colony. The colonists were not consciously trying to construct an alternative public piety; however, an awareness of the actual differences between their own and the English conceptions of public piety was slowly forced on them.

One particular incident reveals this widening gap. In May of 1707, the assembly delivered a remonstrance to Governor Lord Cornbury. This document contained several grievances against the governor, and one of these directly addressed the issue of the relationship between the moral orderliness of society and God's judgment. Two women, it seems, had been indicted for murder—one for poisoning her husband and one for killing her child—and both had been granted reprieves by the governor. The assembly viewed such action as unacceptable in terms of public sensibilities and, more important, dangerous to the prosperity of the colony. They reminded Cornbury that "the Blood of these Innocents crys aloud for Vengeance, and just Heaven will not fail to pour it down upon our already miserable Country, if they are not made to suffer according to their demerits."[34]

Cornbury's response to this remonstrance reveals a disjuncture between his English understanding of public piety and that of the assembly. He asserts that his "Power of Pardoning or Reprieving, after Condemnation, the Subjects of this Province, her Majesty has been pleased to entrust me with, and I am in no wise accountable to any person or number of persons whatsoever, for what I do in these matters, except to the Queens Majesty alone." The governor's only self-perceived duty in this case was whether or not he had acted within his royally prescribed limits of power. If so, he could be accused of no wrong, for his power was sanctioned by God through the monarchy. As for God's vengeance being poured down on the country, Cornbury had this to say:

> I am of opinion, that nothing has hindered the Vengeance of just Heaven from falling on this Province long ago, but the infinite Mercy, Goodness, Longsuffering and Forbearance of Almighty God, who has been abundantly provoked by the repeated crying sins of a perverse Generation among us, and more especially by the dangerous and abominable Doctrines, and the wicked Lives and Practices of a number of People, some of whom under the pretended Name of Christians, have dared to deny the very essence and being of the saviour of the World.[35]

Only God's long-suffering providence had spared the colony, he said, from the just deserts of the people's religious sins. Implied in his answer is the belief that New Jersey had been sheltered from God's wrath primarily because of its status as a royal English colony—that is, by the fact of its participation, even if only to a minor degree, in England's "elect" designation before God.

Shortly after Cornbury's arrival in North America, Colonel Robert Quary wrote to the Lords of Trade remarking that "it is the expectation of all that his Excellency My Lord Cornbury will reconcile all these differences [in New Jersey]—unite all interests, settle 'em on a sure foundation—make 'em all easy and happy."[36] Cornbury's response to the assembly's remonstrance of 1707 is indicative of how well he did, in fact, unite all interests in the colony. This unity was formed, however, not behind him but against him. More than any other single factor, Lord Cornbury's tenure as governor provided the stimulus Jerseyans needed to begin the process of consciously constructing public piety.

Neighborliness: The Mature Public Piety

Early in the eighteenth century Jerseyans began to realize that traditional English models did not fit their own situation and that they needed to construct their own sense of public piety. They spoke variously of the need for "unit[ing] in love," for arriving at a "sincere and hearty agreement among ourselves," and for "dwell[ing] together in unity."[37] The concept that captures best their longings, however, is the idea of "neighborliness." This became the central image of the colony's public piety and it provided a focus around which religious diversity could be comprehended and made meaningful. The idea of neighborliness assumed that differences would always exist, but it simultaneously posited that a basic unity was present in the very nature of the created order. In its fully developed form, New Jersey's public faith rested on two basic tenets: (1) a vision of God as the parent of all members of the society and as the creator who had implanted a need for human cooperation into the very structure of the world, and (2) an affirmation that the doctrinal claims of specific religious groups should in no way contravene the religious-social ethics of the colony's public faith.

Public political figures were the first to elucidate the themes that formed the core of this new understanding. In short order, however, the ministers began to enlarge on the theme and flesh out its logical corollaries.

A. Political Expression

One of the clearest early political expressions of New Jersey's maturing sense of public piety comes from Jeremiah Basse. Earlier he had seemed confused over the direction he thought the colony should take. Now he spoke in a more single-minded fashion. In an impassioned speech delivered to the united New Jersey Assembly on 15 January 1716, he sermonized:

> Here is the source and rise of all our misfortunes, our divisions, heats, discords, and animosities. We are using one another as the heathen did the primitive Christians, dressing each other up in the skins of wolves and bears, and then beating them as such. Would to God, Mr. Speaker, we could each of us learn to look upon another to be better than himself, to let that charity, which is the golden bond that connects heaven and earth together, (and without which the most splendid gifts, natural or acquired endowments, are but as the sounding brass and tinkling cymbal,) govern both our lives and actions. We complain, Mr. Speaker, of bad crops, blasts, mildews, and sometimes of epidemical distempers raging amongst us. It is no wonder if our common Parent sends these scourges, that by these means he might teach us to love one another. Let us then take that advice, which his Excellency once gave the representative body of this Province; let us leave disputes to the laws, and injuries to the avenger of them; let each one weed the rancor out of his own heart. Let each of us look upon parties and divisions as a common enemy, a common evil, and use our utmost endeavors to quench that fire that has hitherto so raged in this Province, that it has more or less affected all persons, all relations, our bodies, our reputations, and our estates. Let us unite in love, and then, how inexpressibly beautiful would such a union be?[38]

Using this speech as a primary text, four themes of New Jersey's maturing public piety can be isolated. First, public piety was implicitly future-oriented. Basse portrayed both the past and the present as unacceptably discordant and over and over stressed the need to learn new and better ways of acting. No exhortations to return to the time-worn patterns of a sacral history appear in Basse's speech. The piety he proclaimed was critical and prophetic, as opposed to England's priestly deification of its history.

A second element was that public piety was ethically grounded not in law but in an extralegal (supralegal) sense of morality: love. This differed, in separate ways, both from English emphasis on obedience and earlier New Jersey emphasis on the moral orderliness of society. Regarding England, the contrast is basic and disjunctive, and can be illustrated from Basse's own life. In 1714 he rhetorically asked, out of an English perspective, how "without the censures of the Church are duly and impartially administered . . . should either virtue be encouraged or vice in all its forms detected and punished?"[39] In 1716 he responded to his own query by asserting that a union in love would be sufficient to correct all social ills. Basse's call to unite in love seems to grow out of a fusing of the two most prominent elements of the earlier period of development of the colony's public piety. The dual emphasis on social peaceableness and legalistic morality was replaced by a single concept that defined each of these elements in terms of the other. Peaceableness was reconceived as God's minimal moral standard, and, as a now divine moral injunction, the demand of peaceableness was rephrased from the negative (leave each other alone) to the positive (love each other).

A third major feature was the conception of God. Basse referred to God as "our common Parent." God was presented not in divisive imagery as the protector and defender of a certain tribe or nation, but in unifying terms as the single and shared transcendent source of all human life.

The fourth and broader theme of New Jersey's public piety is that it was to be "horizontal" as opposed to hierarchical. It placed all members of society on the same level. This emphasis derived from and united the previous three. The future-orientedness of public piety dismissed the importance of the past on which all hierarchical visions of social life are based. A universal call to unite in love placed all members of the society under a single ethical code. And God's common parentage of all provided a metaphysical basis for these egalitarian sentiments. New Jersey's developing public piety did not necessarily amount to a democratic faith, but it was clearly moving in that direction.

B. Clerical Expressions

While Basse's address of 1716 outlined the main themes of New Jersey's public piety it was left to others to enlarge on these ideas. One of the first to do so at length was the Presbyterian minister Joseph Morgan. As early as 1725 Morgan had begun to think about the problem of social relations in the colony: "when instead of Praying for Grace, men Pray against each other ... it is time for Zion's Children to Mourn and Weep." Here Basse's injunction to love each other is transposed back into the negative (don't pray against each other), but Morgan also issued some advice concerning the positive bonds that should hold the community together: "Beg of him to pity your Neighbors who know no need of pity from any, and desire none to help them, and think to deal honestly with their Neighbors, is enough to save them."[40]

For Morgan, as for Basse, neighborliness was not simply a virtue one ought to incorporate into one's life; it was the only proper way of acting because an ethic of neighborliness was structured into the very essence of the world. Basse grounded this conviction in a transcendent vision of God as the "common Parent" of all members of the society. Morgan offered a more divinely imminent metaphysical warrant for his beliefs. He argued that neighborliness is a necessary virtue for living well in this world because God has woven such a demand into the basic structures of human existence.

> Riches is commonly taken for a Plenty of the Necessaries for the Support of Human Life: And if every Man would seek the Good of others, as truly and sincerely, as men ought to seek their own; there would be no Occasion for any Man to have his Riches or Estate to himself. For every man would labour sincerely in his calling for the Good of the Whole. . . . Thus all Men would have Plenty, and Contentions would be taken away.
>
> It is an approved Way, Acts IV, 32. Sin is the only Hinderance: For now, since men love none but themselves, such a thing would be vain to talk of; few men would labour faithfully, and all things would come short, so that there is a Necessity that each man be the proper Owner of what his Industry raises. And Covetousness (which is Idolatry) must be the Support of the World, and the Misery of it both. Each man coveting to make himself rich carries on the Publick Good: For Men cannot gain Riches and use 'em, except they help others by it. Thus God in his wisdom and Mercy turns our Wickedness to publick Benefit, or the World could not stand.
>
> Riches are given for Publick Good, and it is not in the Skill of the most covetous and envious Man to make it otherwise. It must be put to the use it was

made for. He cannot swallow it all into his own Belly. Others must have a part with him, or he cannot gain or keep his Riches.[41]

Morgan's idea of society as a God-ordained interdependent and interpersonal organization—a neighborly network—was quickly adopted by other clergy. One of the most prominent spokesmen for this position was Griffin Jenkins, author of *A Brief Vindication of the Purchassors Against the Propritors, in A Christian Manner* (1746). This work was presented as a general public and Christian defense of those who had engaged in the land riots of the previous few years. The cause of these riots was the seizure by the proprietors of a significant portion of improved land from individuals who did not hold proper legal title. The situation was exacerbated by the fact that most of these settlers had thought their deeds proper and legal. While this was the immediate reason for Jenkins's work, it was not the riots but his own vision of the colony's public piety that provided the foundation for his argument. He very quickly moved beyond the economic issues involved to more particularly religious concerns.

In reviewing the events, Jenkins considered all parties to the disturbances blameworthy, but felt that the proprietors had instigated the troubles and thus had a greater sin.

> I think it is a plain Cause to all Men, that it was Covetousness brought in these Proprietors, as you call them, into the Plantations of these poor People. If there was not some desirable Entertainment for the Flesh you would never seek these Improvements. Let Conscience speak, and I dare say it will accuse . . . let the God of Reason argue the Cause, and your Conscience awakened, and you must Confess that you was in Fault.[42]

Like Basse and Morgan before him, Jenkins argued that an ethic of neighborliness was inherent in nature itself. It was "the God of Reason" who judged the proprietors, not a God revealed only to a special people or group.

Jenkins went on to explain how the proprietors, not listening to this "God of Reason," had gone "to some ministers and told them their Grief and desired them to Preach a Sermon for their Defense." Apparently these ministers did preach several sermons in support of legal authority and proprietary rights. Predictably ill-received by the people, the sermons prompted the author of the *Vindication* to comment:

If the Word of God is to be Preached, it is to be done in a more civil manner then so, if ministers makes Parties he builds with one and pull's down with another; which makes me think that such Preaching is not agreeable to God's will. . . . And methinks that such preaching was nothing else but a Mocking of God's Word, which is very plain if rightly considered, for who can think, that great Jehovah, will hear such Prayers and Preaching when there is Strife and Contention, and I am sorry that I must tell those Ministers that the Spirit of Blindness was upon them, or else methinks that they might perceive the Nature of things better.[43]

Regarding the "Nature of things," Jenkins had some rather pointed observations to make to these clergy. He cautioned all regarding the place and importance of religious zeal in relation to the colony's neighborly ethic: "Think not thy self discharged from the Duty of Righteousness toward thy Neighbor by any extraordinary measure of pretended Zeal and Piety towards God." He went on to iterate that "our Lord and Master Jesus Christ gave us a precept in Matt. XXII, 39 that we should love our Neighbors as our Selves, and by this Precept should Men find whether they are Christ's Disciples or not."[44]

Two final incidents nicely illustrate the way public piety cut away the divisive power of religious diversity. The first example reveals something of how interpersonal relations were affected. Samuel Smith was an ardent Quaker, but also a good historian. He wrote of those he both liked and disliked. One person he must have disliked on a personal level was John Barclay. Barclay was the brother of the Quaker apologist Robert Barclay, but while resident in New Jersey he had left the Society of Friends to become an Anglican. In Smith's eyes John Barclay must have been a renegade, a traitor to the true faith. Whatever personal animosity may have separated the men, however, Smith wrote of Barclay with respect. His final evaluation of Barclay's life is contained in the short eulogy he paid him in his history of the colony: "He bore the character of a good neighbor."[45] This is precisely what the colonists had come to expect from their peers—little more and no less.

Though the date is somewhat late, an event of the 1780s beautifully illustrates the interreligious group dynamics of neighborliness. Morgan Edwards records that the Haightstown Baptist Church consisted of two branches. The main church originally had been settled in Cranbury but was relocated to Haightstown in 1785. A second branch centered at the Crossroads in Nottingham Township. No meetinghouse was erected in this location for some time, but when it was, it seems to have been done under some form of duress. Edwards states, "This meeting-house was built in 1788, chiefly by mess. Nutt and Eldridge; the latter gave the lot; and the other exerted himself to build the house; neither of which, perhaps, would have been done, had the presbyterians been as good neighbors as they might be."[46]

Under the ministry of Peter Wilson, the Cross-roads Baptist congregation had grown considerably and apparently at the expense of its now unfriendly counterpart: nearly half of the church members of 1789 had "been brought up in the presbyterian way."[47] Unable to keep their own by persuasion, the Presbyterians took more drastic action, denying the Baptists the use of their building, which apparently they had previously shared. In other times or different places, such behavior might have been deemed normal. In New Jersey it singed moral sensibilities; it was at odds with prevailing community expectations.

C. Public Piety and Political Critique

Public piety had attained sufficient strength by the mid-eighteenth century to serve as a base for the critique of religious elites. Religious elites, however, are relatively safe targets; they have little real power in society. A sign of the increasing strength of the model of public piety is that in the 1740s this vision of society became one foundation for the political critique of the government.

In 1745, Governor Lewis Morris greeted the New Jersey Assembly with a speech that the members of that body considered unnecessarily condescending and bitter. In response to the governor's diatribe, the assembly issued a critique of his arrogance and justification for their own behavior:

> We have liberty by our constitution to act freely and speak freely while we do it with decency and good manners. . . . We are a nation known for its liberty. With liberty knowledge will increase, and although but a small portion of it may fall to our share, with that we are as happy as we are content, and by it we are taught that we are as fit to use our own understandings in the conducting of our human affairs, as they are whose reasoning we cannot be convinced is better than our own.[48]

The assembly's response to Morris implicitly appeals to the sense of neighborliness that stood at the center of New Jersey's mature public piety. Jerseyans were coming to believe that if society was conceived in neighborly terms, a logical conclusion was that neighbors, as collectively represented in the assembly, were rightfully the final determiners of public policy.

A willingness on the part of the assembly to correct the governor was not new. As early as 1707, the assembly had brought a *Remonstrance* against Governor Cornbury. But that was an exceptional act. During Morris's time in office the propensity of the assembly to instruct the governor regarding decorum in office became almost typical. In 1746, for example, the assembly took the occasion of a request for the financial support of the government and for aid in establishing order in areas where rioting had occurred to instruct the governor regarding the character of the colony.

> The people of New Jersey have always been of the opinion, that sincere and hearty agreement amongst ourselves is at all times desirable, and now in a time of war with our foreign enemies, and when a most unaccountable rebellion is stirred up and carried on in our Mother country, by a Popish Pretender and his abandoned faction, against our rightful and lawful Sovereign King George the Second, we think such an agreement absolutely necessary, as well for his Majesty's interests as our safety, which we esteem to be inseparable: And notwithstanding any thing that may have been suggested to the contrary concerning us, we have so good an agreement subsisting among ourselves, as we hope will at all times discourage every thing of a contrary tendency, and that nothing less than what we conceive to be the true interest of his Majesty, and the people of this colony, shall ever prevail on us to enter into a controversy with any other branch of the Legislature. And we hope they will heartily join with us in removing every grievance that may be likely to promote it, so that a perfect union amongst all the branches of the legislature may be thereby established upon a solid and lasting foundation.[49]

This way of thinking was not necessarily independence-minded or antimonarchical; however, it is a far cry from the hierarchical model of traditional English public piety. The king was still seen as the most powerful and prominent governmental figure and one to be taken fully into account in all public decisions. But the Crown (and the governor as the Crown's representative in the colony) was in many ways seen merely as a first among equals, a noteworthy neighbor. What was important was the common good—the "true interest" of *both* the colony and the king. And the assembly made it clear that if any lack of agreement did exist, it was not the fault of the colonists. The residents enjoyed a "sincere and hearty" agreement among themselves. Unneighborly tensions came from elsewhere.

Governor Morris seems, at the time of these incidents, not yet to have understood or agreed with New Jersey's sense of public piety. By the end of his life, however, he had apparently modified his views. His will stands as a testament both to the character of the man and to the strength of New Jersey's developed model of public piety.

> I forbid . . . any man to be paid for preaching a funeral sermon over me: Those who survive me, will commend or blame my conduct in life as they think fit, and I am not for paying of any man for doing of either; but if any man, whether churchman or differenter, in or not in priest's orders, is inclined to say anything on that occasion, he may, if my executors think fit to admit him to do it.[50]

For a final evaluation of his life Morris did not turn to the church of his youth, the church he had once desired to see established as the religion of the colony. Nor did he limit remarks at his grave to those who would laud him out of loyalty or duty. Rather, he sought the unsolicited judgments of his neighbors. In doing so, he affirmed that in mid-eighteenth-century New Jersey few other evaluations were as important. It is a long jump from a person's testament to actual public behavior. Rhetoric does not always match reality. Still, it is highly significant that Morris's final remarks are so compatible with New Jersey's public piety. The members of the assemblies with which Morris fought could only have felt confirmed in their earlier opinions by the governor's last words.

A Rustic Enlightenment

Despite the many differences between English and New Jersey forms of public piety, certain similarities developed over time. English public piety, like New Jersey's, was dynamic. It did not freeze in its mid-seventeenth-century form, but continued to develop, and the direction of that development narrowed to a certain degree the gap that had separated the two.

Changes in English public piety basically occurred in conjunction with, and as a result of, the first stirrings of the Enlightenment. The English Enlightenment represented, at least in its early phase, a move away from the "extraordinariness" that had characterized the insular public piety of the country. This reflects the overall thrust of the Enlightenment in Europe, which amounted to a powerful (and in retrospect a largely successful) attempt to replace Christianity as the public faith with a more truncated and reason-based set of beliefs. The Enlightenment was in many ways not an antireligious movement, but an alternative religious movement.

This was especially the case in England. Both Isaac Newton and John Locke, the two pillars of early Enlightenment thought, were devout Christians. However, both also tended to sever the spiritual from the temporal realm of society—two aspects of society that had previously been seen as organically linked. Locke, in particular, thought that religion was an inner persuasion of the mind and could not be regulated. For him, the idea of an established church did not make much sense. Both of these thinkers also saw God's activity in the world more in terms of regularity than special intervention. And these two attitudes worked corrosively against England's earlier claims to hold special national religious status with the deity.

One other characteristic of Enlightenment thought in general was its internationalism. Increasingly frequent contact between differing peoples spawned an awareness of the provinciality of all purely nationalistic visions of reality. It was becoming apparent that God might not, after all, be English. As the Englishness of God evaporated, a reasonable and loving divine father figure came into view. Very quickly this image of God was severed not only from its link with England, but also from any particularistic expression of religion. Pure religion came to be seen as basically ethical in impulse, not theological. No "priestcraft" could conjure up this true essence of religion; in fact, true religion did not even need to be taught. What God required of all individuals was very simple, reasonable, and clear—it was, in fact, "natural religion." In this scheme, religious tribalism was negated, lost in one's duty to and ties with one's fellow humanity.

It would be impractical to argue that the development of public piety in colonial New Jersey was somehow the result of the European Enlightenment. What is evident, however, is that by following their own path, the colonists seemed to have arrived at a set of public conclusions fairly similar to those of the English Enlightenment. Most colonists were uneducated farmers, and public piety was never seen as severed from the active participation of God in the events of humanity either as private individuals or corporately in society. Nonetheless, the colony's "ordinary" beginnings and its multicultural population tended to push the development of its public piety in the same direction as that in which Enlightenment thought had moved England's. In the case of New Jersey, however, public piety, instead of becoming internationalistic and rationally ethical, became provincial and neighborly.

This neighborly public piety, rustic yet enlightened, served as a center for religious pluralism. This was similar to the role Enlightenment thought was coming to play in the context of European religious and nationalistic diversity. The colony's public piety contained an implicit demand that the churches get along. This was legally enforced during the early history; later, it was internalized. More important, public piety, as least in its fully developed stage, unified the colony by essentially becoming a ubiquitous second religious commitment, held by all (or almost all) members of the society along with (and sometimes over against) their own more traditional and institutional religious affiliations.

Religion in the colony had essentially been divided into two forms. On one level stood the traditional and institutional religious affiliations, and on another was a shared and public piety that amounted to a common religious faith. Religions were by law and habit increasingly relegated to the private sector of society, while a distinguishable public piety—or common societal religious faith—slowly evolved in the public realm to fill the vacuum left by this exodus.

This common faith or public piety was rarely in direct conflict with the various religions—all Christian—present in the colony. Actually, it was overwhelmingly "Christian" in its imagery, ideals, and ideas. (Aaron Leaming and Jacob Spicer, in a preface to their celebrated collection of the laws of the colony published in 1751, even went so far as to call the colony a Christian society.[51]) While "Christian," this public faith was by no means synonymous with Christianity. Rather, it represented a highly abbreviated and decidedly universalized appropriation of the symbols and ideas of the Christian religion that had been restructured into a separate and distinguishable form of religious public piety. This sense of public piety never evolved into a full-fledged civil religion. It remained throughout the colonial period less well organized and less visible than the label civil religion implies. But as the common faith it provided a much needed focus for the religious pluralism of the colony.

Conclusion

In the preface to *Settlement and Unsettlement in Early America*, Kenneth Lockridge asserts, "It is the job of the colonial historian to give coherence to incoherence in order that Americans may understand themselves better."[1] My final task is to do just that—to relate a coherent picture of religion in New Jersey to the larger American colonial scene "in order that Americans may understand themselves better." To that end I very briefly compare the structure of religious pluralism in New Jersey with the structures of religion in the other twelve colonies and the American nation. No attempt is made to analyze independently the actual structures of religion in all the colonies. The task at hand is, instead, one of summarizing in a somewhat impressionistic manner current scholarly opinion about the nature of religion in these colonies.

This comparative section follows the standard pattern of dividing the colonies on the basis of their religious makeup. The Puritan colonies of New England are discussed first, then the southern colonies where Anglican establishments of religion were the rule, and finally—with more detail to each specific colony—those colonies where colonywide religious establishments were lacking and where religious diversity was more or less the norm (New York, Rhode Island, and Pennsylvania). Methodologically, this study describes the structure of religion in each of these colonies or groups of colonies according to the threefold scheme already applied to New Jersey (diversity, diffuse pluralism, focused pluralism).

New England law had little truck with religious diversity or with the liberty that would have made such diversity possible. (In the region, religious liberty was interpreted in terms of giving all who disagreed the freedom to stay away. If this was not done voluntarily, such freedom could be forced on an individual through banishment.) Nonetheless the Puritan colonies of New England were far from blissfully homogeneous in their religious makeup. Even during the earliest years of settlement, the population represented a good mix of "saints" and "strangers."[2] The diversity of opinion that smoldered beneath the surface was not always visible, but occasionally, as in the Antinomian controversy or the events surrounding the expulsion of Roger Williams from Massachusetts Bay, it did break into the open.[3] Thus, while religious diversity of a sort was certainly present in New England's Holy Commonwealths, the diversity was distinctly limited. Diversity of any and all types was legally discouraged in the region, and what diversity did appear covered only a very narrow spectrum of opinion and practice.

These generalizations are fairly obvious with regard to the seventeenth century, but they are not limited to that period. Throughout the eighteenth century, and despite the disruptions of the Great Awakening, this pattern remained basically the same. All forms of dissent were consistently and strenuously resisted by the governing elite. And while a smattering of Anglicans and even fewer Quakers could be found in the region by the close of the colonial period, most religious groups still reflected their Puritan origins and sentiments. Religious diversity grew primarily as a result of "in-house" religious disputes. But while New Englanders may have fought one another over religious concerns, few dissenters ever wholly defected from the general Puritan orientation of religion.[4]

If religious diversity was of a narrow scope in New England, religious pluralism was almost nonexistent. Without the push of diversity, there was no reason to move in that direction. Of course, exceptions could be uncovered. Boston, for example, was a commercial city and experienced the diversity that trade brings to a town. With that diversity, certain forms of diffuse religious pluralism must have developed. But in this aspect and many others, Boston was always different from the rest of the region, and its exception does not disprove the rule.[5]

Regarding focused religious pluralism the picture seems even clearer—it did not exist. In fact, the actual state of affairs might accurately be described as hostile to religious pluralism. The central myths of New England Puritan society were structured around ideals of religious purity. As the colonial period progressed, definitions of the nature of that purity may have broadened somewhat, but the ideal itself seems to have lasted even into the early national period. As the large picture of religion in New England is surveyed, it becomes clear that religious pluralism represented only a minor, and then a discordant, theme. The real dynamics of religion revolved around the story of how a Puritan elite, with the aid of a significant portion of the population, tried to build and maintain a Puritan establishment of religion. Diversity entered this story only in the form of dissent, and the response of the Puritan oligarchy to this dissent rarely, if ever, went beyond the most necessary limits of toleration.

The southern colonies reflect a structure of religion significantly different from that of New England, but in the South as in the North the presence of a religious establishment short-circuited the development of pluralism, especially pluralism of a focused type. At first glance, many of the southern colonies seem to represent fertile ground from which pluralism could have sprung. Anglican establishments were generally weak, and religious diversity was distinctly more prominent and more valued in the South than in New England. Early in the colonial period, groups of Puritans, Catholics, and Quakers settled alongside Anglican neighbors. This diversity was further broadened with the massive, forced importation of African slaves in the late seventeenth and early eighteenth centuries. In the second quarter of the eighteenth century, there was a steady influx of Presbyterians and Baptists. The sheer numbers of these diverse groups became so great that only in Virginia were Anglicans able to maintain a majority of the population.

While the scope of diversity in the South was large, a simple recitation of statistics is deceiving. Non-Anglican groups tended to settle in clusters, both with their own group and together with other dissenting groups. For instance, Albemarle Sound in North Carolina developed early into a haven for a mixture of Quakers, Baptists, Presbyterians, and Puritan dissenters. The backcountry piedmont later became a safe territory for Scotch-Irish Presbyterians and a host of other dissenting groups.

Thus, demographic isolation along with the presence of an Anglican establishment tended to discourage the growth of pluralism. Some forms of diffuse pluralism undoubtedly did develop among the dissenting portion of the population, for they lived in areas where a de facto religious diversity simply displaced all establishmentarian pretensions and power. Within the more predominantly Anglican regions of the South, however, no real pluralism ever developed. In those areas where the general vision of life held by the elites prevailed, Anglicanism became an integral aspect of the total hierarchical social structure. The Anglican Church was controlled by the southern gentry, and they conceived its raison d'être largely in terms of social control. Donald G. Mathews has described the situation.

Churchmen believed that the church's primary mission in the New World was to bring all inhabitants—Indians, Africans, Europeans—under the rule of religion as outlined in the Thirty-Nine Articles and the Book of Common Prayer. If they had stopped there, they might have been more successful in America; but they did not. They identified their church with the perpetuation of a hierarchical social system. This in itself would not have doomed their future communicants to minority status if churchmen had not been so concerned with the definition and maintenance of the upper order. But almost everything about the church prevented its eliciting meaningful participation in common devotion and Christian equality. The organization of the local church was itself a constant reminder of social distinctions, as the wealthy sat in their private pews musing about how they should run the church and dispense the social services of the parish. From the pulpit, a careful, lifeless preaching informed parishioners about proper behavior, appropriate attitudes, and a comely sense of deference to social convention.[6]

The real dynamics of religion in the South concerned how religion and the hierarchal social order ought to be related, and non-Anglican diversity was discussed only in terms of dissent. Thus, pluralism in the South, as in the New England colonies, was a minor theme at best. Several differences between the situation in the South and in New England, however, should be noted. First, the southern establishments of religion were Anglican rather that Puritan, and therefore never experienced the need to mollify their claims of power under the threat of English interference. Second, the overall social structure in the South was much more hierarchical than that of New England, leading to a heightened consciousness of social levels. Third, governmental power in the South was less localistic than in New England. All of these factors combined to make dissent in the South probably even less acceptable than it was in New England. As Mathews phrases it, "Religious dissent was looked upon not as a mere difference of opinion, but as a challenge to authority and therefore a disruption of community."[7]

Mathews goes on to state that the result of this way of viewing things was the development of "an adversary relationship between churchmen and the lower-class people that was impossible to overcome."[8] This attitude was so thoroughly ingrained that even as late as the last decade of the colonial period, by which time most of the gentry had become basically deistic and should thus have been somewhat more open-minded about religious diversity, dissent was still understood by all parties involved much more in terms of revolt than of mere difference.[9] While such an adversarial relation may be a first step toward pluralism, the general picture of religion in the colonial South was far from the type of pluralistic structure evident in New Jersey.

Much more similar to New Jersey than either New England or the South were Pennsylvania, New York, and Rhode Island. Of these three, New York represents the most complex situation. The colony needs to be divided in two to understand the religious dynamics at work. One set of generalizations can be drawn for New York City, another for the more rural remainder of the colony.

New York City was founded on and existed almost exclusively for the purposes of trade, and from its earliest years the demands of commerce determined the religious structure of the city. One element of the structure was diversity. This fact was frequently bemoaned both by the first Dutch dominies and by the early governors. This religious concern notwithstanding, both the Dutch West India Company and estates general knew that the enforcement of purity in religion could only depress profits in trade. Seeking to please all involved, the government took a middle road, one that had already proved useful in the homeland. In the words of George L. Smith, the Dutch developed a policy of "connivance" with regard to religious diversity. That is, the law remained fairly adamant in its support of an established Dutch Reformed church and in its disallowance of dissenting meetings, but in practice most transgressions of these statutes were overlooked. The result was a rather bald and acknowledged hypocrisy that avowed support for a public uniformity of religion but at the same time refused to enforce laws that would transfer that ideal into reality. By the time the English conquered the region in the early 1660s, this policy of connivance was so thoroughly assumed by the residents and was working so well that it was retained essentially intact. Local countywide religious establishments were determined by majority vote, but religious dissent was everywhere quietly allowed.[10]

Under the protective umbrella of connivance, religious diversity expanded almost unimpeded in New York City. Pluralistic developments naturally ensued. These were usually a diffuse, rather than a focused, pluralism, however, and the reason lies once again in the city's policy of connivance. The blatant and accepted hypocrisy of connivance amounted to a negation of any attempt to form a focused pluralism. Diversity had been tolerated by publicly ignoring it; to bring the question into the fore would have jeopardized the equilibrium by inaugurating a potentially disruptive debate about the nature, scope, and purpose of a religious establishment.[11] Such an argument, besides being socially disruptive, would have been antithetical to the dominant commercial interests. Therefore, pluralism remained a highly prominent aspect of the religious structure, but in a diffuse form limited to private relations among religious groups and individuals.

A different dynamic prevailed in the more rural sections of New York, but it also was one that stymied the emergence of a focused form of religious pluralism. A segregated pattern of countrywide religious establishments developed as a result of the law that called for a vote to decide which local church should be publicly funded. The checkerboard pattern was reinforced by the nature of land settlement. Immigrants, especially those who were non-English-speaking, tended to locate in isolated cultural enclaves. The resulting cultural and ethnic diversity was much greater than in either New England or the South, but it was diversity on a local level, which was often minimal.

The lack of local diversity restricted the growth of pluralism in the rural areas of New York, and the forms of diffuse pluralism that did develop tended to be more traditional than those, for instance, in New Jersey. Rural pluralism in New York frequently followed Old World precedents such as the building of union Reformed-Lutheran churches. The transfer of these practices to the New World setting may have reflected the development of diffuse pluralism, but they remained predominantly local affairs. Colonywide focused pluralism was distinctly inhibited by the legal and sociological structure of the colony's diversity.[12]

In Rhode Island, as in New York, diffuse religious pluralism was widespread, but focused religious pluralism was almost nonexistent. Though the pattern was similar, Rhode Island's pluralism developed from a very different set of circumstances. Instead of being founded for purposes of trade, Rhode Island was founded on the vision of one individual, Roger Williams. Expelled from Massachusetts Bay, Williams attempted to erect in the wilds of Narragansett Bay a civil order based on an uncompromised ideal of "soul-liberty."[13]

Rhode Island was founded as a conscious experiment in religious liberty and with a corresponding assumption that such liberty would entail religious diversity. Very early in its history, the colony became known as the "latrine" of New England. A host of dissenting groups and individuals, almost all English, poured into the colony. Some staunch Puritans arrived to practice their personal religious regimentation, as well as several schismatic sectaries (mostly Baptist), Quakers, Catholics, and even Jews. Diffuse pluralism flourished.

While the colony had a center in the founding vision of Roger Williams and had a vigorous range of diffuse pluralism, it proved impossible to unite these two elements into a focused form of religious pluralism. Williams's ideal for the relationship of religion and society was essentially antithetical to focused pluralism. Williams believed church and state—religion and society—were utterly different realms of being. Religion was private and personal; society was public and pragmatic. Furthermore, Williams's views attracted individuals who shared his disjunctive doctrine, and the colony was populated primarily by sectarian groups that eschewed all desire religiously to control, or often to participate in, the public realm. The mix of religious groups resulted in diffuse pluralism, but focused forms of religious pluralism were not only proscribed by Williams but also unappealing to the type of people attracted to the land.

The development of religious pluralism from diffuse to focused forms was inhibited in New York by a commercially oriented policy of connivance with religious liberty and in Rhode Island by a founding ideology that encouraged the privatization of religion. In Pennsylvania, religious pluralism was prevented from developing into a focused form primarily by a sort of social and ideological schizophrenia.

William Penn not only allowed diversity legally in the colony, he seemed to go out of his way to encourage it. So while English Quakers abounded in the early years, numerous German-speaking groups, Welsh, Swedes, Dutch, and Scots were also present. Penn's welcoming of these varied groups stemmed not only from a pragmatic desire to populate the land quickly, but also from his ideological commitment to religious diversity. If any colony represented a potential hothouse for religious pluralism of all sorts, Pennsylvania was it.

Curiously enough, Pennsylvania was very slow to develop a focused form of pluralism. The cause for this was at least three disjunctive themes that ran through the colony's history. First, Penn himself seemed unable to decide whether the venture ought to be conceived primarily in commercial or agricultural terms. He sold the scheme to Quaker entrepreneurs by emphasizing the potential for trade, but longed to see Philadelphia become a "greene country town" directed toward the needs of a farming majority.[14] Second, the disorderly realities of the settlement process conflicted with Penn's orderly and utopian proposals for rational and communal town planting. Penn envisioned a landscape dotted with neat, rectangular, symmetrical townships; however, the people sprawled ragtag over the land, forming "complex, open-country neighborhoods without certain edges or centers."[15] Finally, and most important, Penn's desire to ensure that the colony remain a distinctly Quaker Zion before the eyes of a watching world conflicted with his commitment to an essentially unrestricted ideal of religious liberty.[16]

These three tendencies all encouraged a distinct splintering of Pennsylvania society, thereby discouraging the growth of focused religious pluralism. By dividing the colonists simultaneously along several axes—traders versus farmers, people versus proprietors, and Quakers versus non-Quakers—all three combined to create a general air of distrust and hostility. The public realm of society simply could not entertain any truly pluralistic suggestions: the presence of too many bitterly opposed factions would not allow it. This generally negative attitude toward a focused religious pluralism was reinforced in turn by the apathy of the largely sectarian population.

Religious dynamics in Pennsylvania did undergo a change as the colonial period drew to a close. Between 1725 and 1755, the religious character of immigrants shifted drastically, becoming almost wholly churchly in orientation—primarily Presbyterian, Lutheran, and Reformed.[17] All of these churchly oriented religionists expected public life to be religiously meaningful. In addition, the Quaker leadership finally acceded to pressure to defend militarily the province in violation of their pacifistic ideals. They surrendered control of the government and ended forever any Quaker claim of hegemony in the area, reducing the Society of Friends to the status of one among many religious organizations.[18] These two developments set the stage for a rapid growth of focused religious pluralism similar to the "public religion" advocated by Benjamin Franklin.[19] Significantly, this occurred only after Pennsylvania's religious and political landscape came to resemble that which had characterized New Jersey's from at least 1700.

The Shape of Things to Come

It seems clear that New Jersey stood alone during the colonial period in its early diversity and development of a two-tiered structure of religious pluralism. This structure rested on a real and broad religious diversity, which was layered over by a range of localistic, diffuse pluralistic adjustments, and culminated in a focused pluralistic religious vision that could comprehend the whole and arbitrate between the constituent groups. This framework was in many ways haphazard and incomplete, but it definitely existed, and, what is more, it worked.

What took place in New Jersey cannot serve as a paradigm for developments elsewhere. However, given the degree to which New Jersey has been neglected in traditional histories of religion in America, it seems appropriate to end this study with a rather bold claim. New Jersey's style of religious pluralism in many ways prefigured the shape of things to come in the American nation more clearly than any other colony. William Penn called his colonial enterprise a "holy experiment" and Rhode Islanders called theirs a "lively experiment." Unlike those two colonies, which have often been cited as precursors of American religious pluralism, New Jersey was an "unprov'd experiment." Jerseyans entered their particular religious foray not knowing either how it would or how it should turn out. They had no prepackaged ideology to guide them, or any religious establishment against which to revolt. Their experiment, in other words, was a real experiment like the American one that was to follow.

I do not claim that the structures of religious pluralism in colonial New Jersey are identical with those in the American nation or that somehow the seed of later developments was planted in New Jersey. (These claims cannot validly be made for any other colony either.) Rather, I suggest only that there is a strong resemblance between the dynamics and developments of religious pluralism in colonial New Jersey and dynamics and developments of religious pluralism in the later American nation. New Jersey may have little or no causal significance regarding the shape of religious diversity in the nation, and the nation's adjustment to religious pluralism certainly represents a larger and more complex story than the narrative of events in the colony. Nonetheless, the study of religious pluralism in colonial New Jersey is foundationally significant, for it was in that small backwater colony that the issues of religious diversity were first faced in the way we have chosen to face them ever since—without an official ideology and yet seriously. The colonists of New Jersey groped their ways to various private and public adjustments to pluralism. No solution was seen as final and the experiment was always "unprov'd." And in that way New Jersey precurses the "unprov'd experiment" that is America itself.

Notes

INTRODUCTION

1. Samuel Smith, *The History of the Colony of Nova-Caesaria, or New Jersey* (Burlington, N.J.: James Parker, 1765; reprint ed., New York: Arno Press, 1972), p. viii.
2. See Catherine L. Albanese, *America: Religions and Religion* (Belmont, Calif.: Wadsworth Publishing Company, 1981) for a good analysis of American religion organized in this two-leveled manner.
3. Examples are James Lemon, *The Best Poor Man's Country: A Geographical Study of Early Southeastern Pennsylvania* (Baltimore: The Johns Hopkins Press; reprint ed., New York: W. W. Norton and Company, 1976); J. William Frost, *The Quaker Family in Colonial America: A Portrait of the Society of Friends* (New York: St. Martin's Press, 1973); Peter O. Wacker, *Land and People: A Cultural Geography of Preindustrial New Jersey* (New Brunswick: Rutgers University Press, 1975); Stephanie Grauman Wolf, *Urban Village: Population, Community and Family Structure in Germantown, Pennsylvania, 1683-1800* (Princeton: Princeton University Press, 1976); F. Ernest Stoeffler, ed., *Continental Pietism and Early American Christianity* (Grand Rapids, Mich.: William B. Eerdmans Publishing Company, 1976); William W. Zuckerman, ed., *Friends and Neighbors: Group Life in America's First Plural Society* (Philadelphia: Temple University Press, 1982).
4. For a good study of the literary dimension of historical writing see Hayden White, *Metahistory: The Historical Imagination in Nineteenth-Century Europe* (Baltimore: The Johns Hopkins University Press, 1973).
5. See especially the prefaces to Perry Miller's *The New England Mind: The Seventeenth Century* (New York: Macmillan Company, 1939; reprint ed., Boston: Beacon Press, 1961) and *The New England Mind: From Colony to Province* (Cambridge: Harvard University Press, 1953; reprint ed., Boston: Beacon Press, 1961). Some contemporary scholars have continued to employ the imagery of a natural historical laboratory in their work (for example, Wacker, *Land and People*, p. xvii), but generally it has fallen into disrepute. For a critique see Zuckerman, *Friends and Neighbors*, pp. 8-11.
6. Nelson Burr, "The Religious History of New Jersey Before 1702," *Proceedings of the New Jersey Historical Society* 56 (October 1938): 256.
7. Ibid., p. 259.
8. Ibid., p. 263.

9. Thomas Jefferson Wertenbaker, *The Founding of American Civilization: The Middle Colonies* (New York: Charles Scribner's Sons, 1938; reprint ed., New York: Cooper Square Publishers, 1963), p. 349.
10. Ibid., pp. 95, 178-79.
11. Leonard J. Trinterud, *The Forming of an American Tradition: A Re-examination of Colonial Presbyterianism* (1949; reprint ed., New York: Arno Press; Philadelphia: Westminster Press, 1970); Nelson Burr, *The Anglican Church in New Jersey* (Philadelphia: The Church Historical Society, 1954.
12. Wallace N. Jamison, *Religion in New Jersey: A Brief History* (Princeton: D. Van Nostrand Company, 1964), pp. 5-6.
13. Ibid., pp. 2-4.
14. Ibid., p. 5.
15. Ibid., p. ix.
16. Ibid., p. 1.
17. Ibid., p. 55.
18. Wacker, *Land and People*, pp. 410-11.
19. Peter L. Berger, *The Sacred Canopy: Elements of a Sociological Theory of Religion* (Garden City, N.Y.: Doubleday and Company, Anchor Books, 1969), p. 175.
20. Clifford Geertz, *The Interpretation of Cultures* (New York: Basic Books, 1973), p. 127.
21. Ibid., p. 90.
22. A similar distinction, but one that fails to discriminate between pluralism and diversity, has been made by William Neuman in *American Pluralism: A Study of Minority Groups and Social Theory* (New York: Harper and Row, 1973), pp. 54-58.
23. For a detailed definition and discussion of the concept of "civil religion" see Robert N. Bellah and Phillip Hammond, *Varieties of Civil Religion* (San Francisco: Harper and Row, 1980).
24. See, for example, Burr, *The Anglican Church in New Jersey*; Jon Butler, *Power, Authority, and the Origins of American Denominational Order: The English Churches in the Delaware Valley 1680-1730* (Philadelphia: American Philosophical Society, 1978); Gerald F. DeJong, *The Dutch Reformed Church in the American Colonies* (Grand Rapids, Mich.: William B. Eerdmans Publishing Co., 1978); and, Norman H. Maring, *The Baptists in New Jersey: A Study in Transition* (Valley Forge, Pa.: Judson Press, 1964).
25. Bernard Berenson, *Aesthetics and History* (New York: Pantheon Books, 1948; reprint ed., Garden City, New York: Doubleday and Company, 1954), pp. 40-41.

CHAPTER ONE

1. Richard Hooker, *The Works of Mr. Richard Hooker*, ed. John Keble, 3 vols. (Oxford: The Clarendon Press, 1874), 1:285.
2. Quoted in Owen Chadwick, *The Secularization of the European Mind in the Nineteenth Century* (New York: Cambridge University Press, 1975), p. 28.
3. Michael Kammen, *People of Paradox* (New York: Oxford University Press, 1972), p. 30.
4. The details of this complex situation are discussed in Edwin P. Tanner, *The Province of New Jersey 1666-1738* (New York: Columbia University, 1908), pp. 81-96, 125-38.
5. "The Secret Instructions as to Religion, to Col. R. Nicolls, Etc., in Reference to New England; and New Netherlands, if Conquered," 23 April 1664, *Ecclesiastical Records of the State of New York*, 7 vols., (Albany: New York State printer, 1901-1916), 1:544-45 (hereafter cited as *Records*).
6. John E. Pomfret, *Colonial New Jersey* (New York: Charles Scribner's Sons, 1973) p. 8.
7. For details and complete references see Fredrick J. Zwierlein, *Religion in New Netherlands* (Rochester, N.Y.: John P. Smith Printing Company, 1910), especially pp. 136-86.
8. Ibid., p. 182.
9. "The Conditions for New Planters, in the Territories of his Royal Highness the Duke of York," quoted in Harry C. Ellison, *Church of the Founding Fathers of New Jersey: A History [of] First Presbyterian Church Elizabeth, New Jersey 1664-1964* (Cornish, Maine: Carbrook Press, 1964), p. 8.
10. For the Dutch injunction see John E. Pomfret, *The Province of East New Jersey* (Princeton: Princeton University Press, 1962), p. 13. For Nicolls's requirement, see Ellison, *Church of the Founding Fathers*, p. 7.
11. Ellison, *Church of the Founding Fathers*, p. 16.
12. Application for Elizabethtown Grant, 30 September 1664, *Archives of the State of New Jersey*, First Series, 48 vols. (Newark, 1880-1949), 1:16 (hereafter cited as *N.J.A.*).
13. Pomfret, *East New Jersey*, p. 38.
14. Wertenbaker, *The Middle Colonies*, p. 132.
15. *The Concession and Agreement of the Lords Proprietors of the Province of New Caesarea, or New Jersey, to and with all and every The Adventurers and all such as shall settle or plant there*, 10 February 1664, in Aaron Leaming and Jacob Spicer, eds., *The Grants, Concession, and Original Constitutions of the Province of New Jersey* (Philadelphia: W. Bradford, 1751; reprint ed., Somerville, N.J.: Honeyman and Company, 1881), p. 14 (hereafter cited as *Grants*).
16. Ibid., p. 25.
17. *N.J.A.*, 1:57.
18. John C. Miller, *This New Man, the American* (St. Louis: McGraw-Hill Book Company, 1974), p. 156.

19. "Propositions Agreed Upon by the Committee in the Name and Behalfe of the Companie to be Presented to the Much Honored Governor of the New Netherlands," 18 November 1661, *Records*, 1:510-12.
20. Pomfret, *East New Jersey*, p. 49.
21. Ibid., pp. 49-50.
22. See Charles M. Andrews, *The Colonial Period of American History*, 4 vols. (New Haven: Yale Univiversity Press, 1934-38), 2:188.
23. *Records of the Town of Newark, 1666-1836* (Newark: The New Jersey Historical Society, 1864), p. 2.
24. Ibid., p. 4.
25. Governor Carteret to the Patentees of Middletown and Shrewsbury, 28 May 1672, *N.J.A.*, 1:88.
26. Benjamin C. Taylor, ed., *Annals of the Classis of Bergen* (New York: Board of the Dutch Reformed Church, 1857), pp. 55-56.
27. See Pomfret, *East New Jersey*, pp. 56-81.
28. *A Declaration of the true Intent and Meaning of us the Lords Proprietors, and Explanation of there Concessions made to the Adventurers and Planters of New Caesarea or New Jersey*, 6 Dec. 1672, *Grants*, p. 33.
29. "Minutes of the Council of New Netherland," 29 September 1673, *N.J.A.*, 1:135.
30. *The Concessions and Agreements of the Proprietors, Freeholders and Inhabitants of the Province of West New Jersey, in America*, 3 March 1676, *Grants*, p. 394.
31. Samuel Purchas, *Microcosmus or The Historie of Man* (London, 1619; reprint ed., New York: Da Capo Press, 1969), p. 604.
32. Proclamation calling the first Assembly, *N.J.A.*, 1:57.
33. *Grants*, pp. 98-99, 106-7.
34. Ibid., p. 124.
35. *Grants*, pp. 237-38.
36. "Record of the Governor and Councill In East Jersie," 19 April 1686, *N.J.A.* 13:158.
37. Ibid.
38. Ibid.
39. Pomfret, *Colonial New Jersey*, p. 49.
40. Ibid.
41. "Record of the Governor and Councill In East Jersie," 19 April 1686, *N.J.A.* 13:158.
42. "The Fundamental Constitutions for the Province of East New Jersey in America," 1683, *Grants*, p. 162.
43. Pomfret, *Colonial New Jersey*, p. 45.
44. Ibid.
45. Ibid.
46. *Grants*, p. 425.
47. Pomfret, *Colonial New Jersey*, p. 46.
48. *Grants*, pp. 460-77.
49. Ibid., p. 477.

50. Ibid., p. 519.
51. Ibid., pp. 394, 519.
52. Ibid., pp. 548-49.
53. Ibid., p. 372.
54. "Record of the Governor and Councill in East Jersie," 4 March 1708, *N.J.A.*, 13:310.
55. Ibid., 13 Dec. 1710, 13:429.
56. "The Memorial of the Proprietors of the Province of East New Jersey in America," *Grants*, p. 590.
57. "The humble Memorial of the Proprietors of the Province of East and West Jersey in America," 12 August 1701, *Grants*, p. 602.
58. "Instructions for our Right Trusty and well beloved Edward Lord Cornbury," 16 November 1702, *Grants*, pp. 633, 638-40.
59. Richard Hofstadter, *America at 1750* (New York: Alfred A. Knopf, 1971; reprint ed., New York: Random House, Vintage Books, 1973), p. 200.
60. Charles II to James, Duke of York, "Patent of New York, New Jersey and Territories thereon depending," *Grants*, p. 5.
61. *The Concessions and Agreement*, *Grants*, p. 14.
62. Governor Cornbury to the Lords of Trade, 4 November 1704, *N.J.A.* 3:66.
63. "Instructions for . . . [Lord] Cornbury," *Grants*, p. 633.
64. "Address of Lieutenant Governor [Sunderland] and Council of New Jersey to [Gov.] Lord Lovelace, relating to the Proceedings of the Assembly," 29 July 1708, *N.J.A.*, 13:413.
65. Ibid., p. 414.
66. "Representation from the Lieutenant Governor and Council of New Jersey to the Queen, relating to the proceedings of the Quakers in that Province," 2 November 1709, *N.J.A.*, 13:472.
67. "Record of the Governor and Councill in East Jersie," 11 March 1713, *N.J.A.*, 13:541.
68. Governor Montgomerie to the Lords of Trade, 20 April 1729, *N.J.A.*, 5:234-35.
69. The Lords of Trade to Governor Montgomerie, 9 July 1729, *N.J.A.*, 5:248.
70. Lewis Morris, *The Papers of Lewis Morris, Governor of the Province of New Jersey, from 1738 to 1746* (New York: New Jersey Historical Society, 1852), pp. 117-18.
71. Smith, *History*, p. 419.
72. Ibid.
73. Morgan Edwards, *Materials Towards a History of the Baptists in New Jersey* (Philadelphia: Thomas Dodson, 1792), p. 41.
74. Smith, *History*, p. 417.
75. *Grants*, p. i.
76. Montesquieu, *The Spirit of the Laws*, trans. Thomas Nugent, 2 vols. (New York: Hafner, 1949), 2:52.

CHAPTER TWO

1. Berger, *The Sacred Canopy*, pp. 16-17.
2. See Mircea Eliade, *The Sacred and the Profane*, trans. Willard R. Trask (New York: Harcourt, Brace and World, 1959), especially pp. 29-67.
3. Larry R. Gerlach, *Prologue to Independence: New Jersey in the Coming of the American Revolution* (New Brunswick: Rutgers University Press, 1976), p. 12.
4. See, for example, Claude S. Fischer, *To Dwell Among Friends: Personal Networks in Town and City* (Chicago: University of Chicago Press, 1982).
5. Herman Harmelinck III, William W. Coventry, and Sharon Thomas Scholten, *The Reformed Church in New Jersey* (n.p.: Synod of New Jersey, 1969), p. 7.
6. Wacker, *Land and People*, p. 121.
7. See Brian K. Roberts, *Rural Settlement in Britain* (Hamden, Conn.: Archon Books, 1977), p. 92.
8. Carl Christopherson Springer to John Thelin, 31 May 1693, quoted in Israel Acrelius, *A History of New Sweden*, trans. William M. Reynolds (Philadelphia: The Historical Society of Pennsylvania, 1874), pp. 187, 189.
9. Robert Redfield, *The Little Community* (Chicago: University of Chicago Press, 1960), p. 6.
10. Quoted in Edward Whiting Fox, *History in Geographic Perspective* (New York: W. W. Norton and Company, 1971), p. 14.
11. Wacker, *Land and People*, p. 150.
12. The phrase is Harold Isaacs's. See his *Idols of the Tribe* (New York: Harper and Row, 1975), p. 1.
13. Acrelius, *New Sweden*, p. 187.
14. Lewis A. Coser, *The Functions of Social Conflict* (New York: The Free Press, 1956), p. 8.
15. Francis Makamie, *An Answer to George Keith's Libel Against a Catechism Published by Francis Makamie* (Boston, 1694), p. i.
16. Rev. John Talbot to Mr. Gillingham, 10 April 1703, quoted in George Morgan Hills, *History of the Church in Burlington, New Jersey* (Trenton: W. S. Sharp, 1876), p. 34.
17. George Keith, *The Heresie and Hatred Which was falsly Charged upon the Innocent Justly returned upon the Guilty* (Philadelphia: William Bradford, 1693), p. 14.
18. Ibid.
19. Rev. Seth Fletcher to Rev. Increase Mather, 25 March 1681, in Ellison, *Church of the Founding Fathers*, pp. 19-20.
20. John Willsford, *A Brief Exhortation to all who profess the Truth* (Philadelphia: William Bradford, 1691), pp. 2-3.
21. Ibid., p. 2.
22. *Records of the Town of Newark*, p. 1.
23. Ibid., p. 4.
24. Mary Douglas, *Purity and Danger* (New York: Frederick A. Praeger, 1966), p. 2.

25. Hills, *History of the Church in Burlington*, p. 34.
26. Makamie, *An Answer to George Keith's Libel*, p. i.
27. Society of Friends, *A General Epistle given forth by the People of the Lord, called Quakers, That all may know we own none to be of our Fellowship, or to be reckoned or numbered with us, but such as . . . keep faithfully to his Heavenly Power* (Philadelphia: William Bradford, 1686), pp. 1, 6.
28. Letter of Rev. Edward Vaughn, 4 December 1709, quoted in W. Northey Jones, *The History of St. Peter's Church in Perth Amboy, New Jersey* (n.p., 1924), p. 35.
29. Coser, *Social Conflict*, p. 70.
30. The phrase is Eric Hoffer's. See *The True Believer* (New York: Harper, 1951; reprint ed., New York: Mentor Books, 1958).
31. Coser, *Social Conflict*, p. 70.
32. *N.J.A.*, 4:214-15.
33. Governor Hunter to the Lords of Trade, 25 July 1715, *N.J.A.*, 4:213-14.
34. "Deposition of Georg Willocks, relating to the conversations had with the Reverend John Talbot," 21 May 1717, *N.J.A.*, 4:303-4.
35. Quoted in William A Whitehead, *Contributions to the Early History of Perth Amboy* (New York: D. Appleton and Company, 1856), p. 216, n. 14.
36. See, for example, Governor Belcher to the committee of the West Jersey Society, 27 June 1748, *N.J.A.*, 7:146 and Governor Belcher to Colonel Alford, 15 June 1751, *N.J.A.*, 7:579-80.
37. Quoted in Coser, *Social Conflict*, p. 43.
38. Whitehead, *Perth Amboy*, p. 216, n. 14.
39. Berger, *The Sacred Canopy*, p. 31.
40. Max Weber, *The Sociology of Religion*, trans. Ephraim Fischoff (Boston: Beacon Press, [1922] 1963), p. 30.
41. Richard Sennett, *Authority* (New York: Alfred A. Knopf, 1980).
42. For Newark see Alexander MacWhorter, *A Century Sermon* (Newark: W. Tuttle and Company, 1807), pp. 17-18; for Woodbridge see Whitehead, *Perth Amboy*, p. 391.
43. Sennett, *Authority*, pp. 16-17.
44. Rev. Michael C. Knoll to Rev. Wilhelm C. Berkenmeyer, 21 February 1735, in *Lutheran Church in New York and New Jersey: Lutheran Records in the Ministerial Archives of the Staatarchiv, Hamburg, Germany*, trans. Simon Hart and Harry J. Kreider (Ann Arbor: The United Lutheran Synod of New York and New England, 1962) p. 65, (hereafter cited as *L.C.N.Y.N.J.*); and Rev. Johann A. Wolf to Rev. Michael C. Knoll, 4 May 1735, ibid., p. 83.
45. Ernst Troeltsch, *The Social Teaching of the Christian Churches*, 2 vols., trans. Olive Wyon (New York: The Macmillan Company, 1931; reprint ed., New York: Harper and Row, Harper Torchbooks, 1960), 1:331.
46. Society of Friends, *A Testimony and Caution to such as do make a Profession of Truth, who are in scorn called Quakers, and more especially such who profess to be Ministers of the Gospel of Peace, That they should not be concerned in Worldly Government* (Philadelphia: William Bradford, 1693), pp. 1-2.

47. For accounts of the Keithian schism, see Jon Butler, "Gospel Order Improved: The Keithian Schism and the Exercise of Quaker Ministerial Authority in Pennsylvania," *William and Mary Quarterly*, 3rd series, 31 (July 1974): 431-52; Ethyn Williams Kirby, *George Keith 1638-1716* (New York: D. Appleton-Century Company, 1942); Gary Nash, *Quakers and Politics: Pennsylvania, 1681-1726* (Princeton: Princeton University Press, 1968).
48. Butler, "Gospel Order Improved," p. 446.
49. Ibid., p. 445.
50. Kirby, *George Keith*, p. 83.
51. Frost, *The Quaker Family in America*, pp. 218-19.
52. See Leon Festinger, *A Theory of Cognitive Dissonance* (Stanford: Stanford University Press, 1957).
53. Ellison, *Church of the Founding Fathers*, pp. 33-34.
54. From the records of St. John's Church, Elizabethtown, New Jersey, quoted in ibid., p. 34.
55. Ibid.
56. Samuel A. Clark, *The History of St. John's Church, Elizabethtown, New Jersey* (New York: Thomas N. Stanford, 1857), pp. 55-56.
57. Jones, *St. Peter's Church*, p. 50.
58. Henricus Boel, *Boel's Complaint Against Frelinghuisen*, trans. and ed. Joseph Anthony Loux Jr. (Rensselaer, N.Y.: Reformed Church Historical Society, 1979), p. 34.
59. See, in addition to Wertenbaker, *The Middle Colonies*, Sydney E. Ahlstrom, *A Religious History of the American People* (New Haven: Yale University Press, 1973) and Charles H. Maxson, *The Great Awakening in the Middle Colonies* (Chicago: University of Chicago Press, 1920).
60. See Herman Harmelink III, "Another Look at Frelinghuisen and His 'Awakening,' " *Church History* 37 (December 1968) 423-28. Harmelink concludes: "Was there an awakening or simply a disaffection? Tradition claims an awakening: the available facts indicate only a disaffection."
61. For the views of Joseph Morgan see Joseph Morgan, *The History of the Kingdom of Basaruah*, ed. Richard Schlatter (Cambridge: Harvard University Press, 1946). For evidence of the conflict between Frelinghuisen and Morgan see Boel, *Complaint*.
62. Boel, *Complaint*, p. 30.
63. James Tanis, *Dutch Calvinistic Pietism in the Middle Colonies* (The Hague: Martinus Nijhoff, 1967), p. 36.
64. Boel, *Complaint*, p. 177.
65. Ibid., p. 142.
66. Ibid., p. 137.
67. Ibid., p. 67.
68. Ibid., p. 70.
69. Ibid., pp. 49, 51.
70. Berger, *The Sacred Canopy*, p. 50.

71. Boel, *Complaint*, p. 66.
72. Ibid., p. 74.
73. Ibid.
74. Ibid., pp. 72-73.
75. Ibid., p. 140.
76. Ibid., p. 74.
77. Ibid., pp. 123-25.
78. Quoted in Coser, *Social Conflict*, p. 104.
79. Ibid., p. 107.
80. Boel, *Complaint*, p. 49.
81. Ibid., p. 51.
82. Henry Melchior Muhlenberg, *The Journals of Henry Melchior Muhlenberg*, trans. and ed. Theodore G. Tappert and John W. Doberstein, 3 vols. (Philadelphia: The Evangelical Ministerium of Pennsylvania and Adjacent States, 1942), 1:296.

CHAPTER THREE

1. See Muhlenberg, *Journals*, p. 296n.
2. Eric R. Wolf, *Peasants* (Englewood Cliffs, N.J.: Prentice-Hall, 1977), pp. 100-106.
3. Edward Shils, *Center and Periphery: Essays in Macrosociology* (Chicago: University of Chicago Press, 1975) p. 111.
4. *N.J.A.*, 28:371.
5. Acrelius, *New Sweden*, p. 316.
6. Ibid.
7. Ibid., p. 212.
8. Ibid., p. 318.
9. Ibid., pp. 317-18.
10. Ibid. At the time of his drowning, Tollstadius was transporting a plowshare, apparently for his own use, across the river.
11. Ibid., pp. 319-21.
12. Edwards, *Baptists in New Jersey*, p. 15.
13. Ibid.
14. Ibid.
15. Burr, *Anglican Church*, p. 14.
16. Burr, "New Jersey before 1702," p. 175.
17. Wacker, *Land and People*, p. 164.
18. Miller, *This New Man*, p. 273. The most complete treatment of these events and their impact on religion in the area can be found in Randall Balmer, *A Perfect Babel of Confusion: Dutch Religion and English Culture in the Middle Colonies* (New York: Oxford University Press, 1989).
19. From the account of Jacob Leisler, Jr., regarding the events of 1 September 1692 to 31 October 1695, *Records*, 2:1131.

20. Revs. Henricus Selyns, Rudolphus Varick, and Godfridus Dellius to the Classis of Amsterdam, 21 October 1692, *Records*, 2:1042.
21. Ibid., 2:1043.
22. Rev. Rudolphus Varick to the Classis of Amsterdam, 3 May 1694, *Records*, 2:1051.
23. Adrian C. Leiby, *The United Churches of Hackensack and Schraalenburgh, New Jersey, 1686-1822* (River Edge, N.J.: Bergen County Historical Society, 1976), p. 17.
24. Rev. Rudolphus Varick to the Classis of Amsterdam, 3 May 1694, *Records*, 2:1051; "Minutes of the Classis of Middleburg," 2, 3, and 16 September 1693, *Records*, 2:1072-73; and "Acts of the Classis of Amsterdam," 3 May 1694, *Records*, 2:1100.
25. "Acts of the Classis of Middleburg," 16 September 1693, *Records*, 2:1073; and Rev. Henricus Selyns to the Classis of Amsterdam, 14 November 1694, *Records*, 2:1107. The churches founded principally by Bartholf are Raritan (Somerville), N.J.; Tappan, N.Y.; Tarrytown, N.Y.; Port Richmond, Staten Island; Ponds (Oakland), N.J.; Pompton Plains, N.J.; Schraalenburgh, N.J.; and Second River (Belleville), N.J. (See Harmelink et. al., *Reformed Church*, p. 9).
26. Godfridus Dellius to the Classis of Amsterdam, 7 October 1694, *Records*, 2:1106-7.
27. Rev. Henricus Selyns to the Classis of Amsterdam, 30 September 1696, *Records*, 2:1171.
28. "Proceedings of the Consistorial Meeting to elect a Second Minister, and Elders, Deacons, and Church-Wardens, for the Dutch Reformed Church of Jesus Christ, at New York, held in the years 1697 and 1698," *Records*, 2:1189-1213.
29. Rev. Rudolphus Varick to the Classis of Amsterdam, 9 April 1693, *Records*, 2:1051-52; and Rev. Godfridus Dellius to the Classis of Amsterdam, 7 October 1694, *Records*, 2: 1106.
30. Ibid.
31. Rev. Rudolphus Varick to the Classis of Amsterdam, 9 April 1693, *Records*, 2:1051.
32. Ibid.; Rudolphus Varick to the Classis of Amsterdam, 27 June 1693, *Records*, 2:1067; and Godfridus Dellius to the Classis of Amsterdam, 7 October 1694, *Records*, 2:1106-7.
33. Tanis, *Dutch Calvinistic Pietism*, p. 44.
34. Rev. Rudophus Varick to the Classis of Amsterdam, 9 April 1693, *Records*, p. 1051. This comment may not imply any direct knowledge of a link between Bartholf and Koelman. Rather, it might simply be a general smear against Bartholf because he, like Koelman, sometimes diverged from strict ecclesiastical policies and procedures.
35. Tanis, *Dutch Calvinistic Pietism*, pp. 44-45.
36. The church of New Castle (South River) to the Classis of Amsterdam, 25 September 1682, *Records*, 2:824.
37. DeJong, *The Dutch Reformed Church*, p. 173, and Leiby, *United Churches*, p. 18.

38. Timothy L. Smith, "Congregation, State, and Denomination: The Forming of the American Religious Structure," *The William and Mary Quarterly*, 3rd series, 25 (April 1968): 159-60, 173.
39. Boel, *Complaint*, p. 32.
40. The earliest evidence of van Dieren in New York is a letter dated 7 March 1721. See "The Lutheran Church in New York 1649-1772: Records in the Lutheran Church Archives at Amsterdam, Holland," trans. Arnold J. H. van Laer, *Bulletin of the New York Public Library* 49 (November 1945): 832. (These records were published in eleven parts in the *Bulletin of the New York Public Library* from January 1944 [vol. 48] to May 1946 [vol. 50]. Hereafter they are cited as *L.C.N.Y.*, and unless otherwise indicated page numbers refer to volume 49.)
41. Rev. Wilhelm C. Berkenmeyer to the Amsterdam Consistory, 1 November 1725, *L.C.N.Y.*, p. 106.
42. Rev. Michael C. Knoll to Johann B. van Dieren, 5 November 1734, *L.C.N.Y.*, p. 835. "Doctor Boehm" is Anton Wilhelm Boehme, who was pastor of the Royal Chapel of St. James in London from 1705-22. For background on both Boehme and the Royal Chapel see Harry J. Krieder, *Lutheranism in Colonial New York* (New York, 1942), pp. 9-10.
43. Muhlenberg, *Journals*, 1:237.
44. See list of "Letters and Writings of the Pastor and Church Council, 1696-1717, received by W. C. Berkenmeyer," *Protocol of the Lutheran Church in New York City*, trans. and ed. Simon Hart and Harry J. Kreider (New York: New York Synod, 1958), pp. 49-50 (hereafter cited as *Protocol*).
45. *Protocol*, p. 50. and *L.C.N.Y.*, p. 107.
46. *L.C.N.Y.*, p. 106.
47. Rev. Andrew Hesselius to Rev. Justus Falkner, 3 July 1721, *L.C.N.Y.*, p. 16.
48. Rev. Wilhelm C. Berkenmeyer to Rev. Michael C. Knoll, 25 April 1735, *L.C.N.Y.N.J.*, pp. 77-78. Van Dieren's ordination was questioned by Berkenmeyer first over the simple fact of whether or not it had occurred. Later, granting that van Dieren had been ordained by Henkel, Berkenmeyer questioned the validity of ordination at the hands of one man. He also went on to question Henkel's own ordination.
49. Rev. Wilhelm C. Berkenmeyer to the Amsterdam Consistory, 1 November 1725, *L.C.N.Y.*, pp. 106, 108.
50. The Consistory and leaders of the Lutheran Church at New York to the Amsterdam Consistory, 27 April 1725, *L.C.N.Y.*, p. 92; and Rev. Wilhelm C. Berkenmeyer to the Amsterdam Consistory, 1 November 1725, *L.C.N.Y.*, pp. 103, 110.
51. "Minutes of the Amsterdam Consistory," 4 July 1725, *L.C.N.Y.*, p. 96; and The Amsterdam Consistory to the Lutheran Church at New York, 10 July 1725, *L.C.N.Y.*, pp. 97-98.
52. Rev. Wilhelm C. Berkenmeyer's account on his arrival in New York and his plans for his first meeting with the Church Council, September 1725, *Protocol*, p. 12.

53. Rev. Wilhelm C. Berkenmeyer to the Amsterdam Consistory, 1 November 1725, *L.C.N.Y.*, pp. 103, 110-11.
54. Account of the visit of Rev. Wilhelm C. Berkenmeyer to the Lutheran Congregation at Hackensack, New Jersey, 5-11 October 1727, *Protocol*, pp. 98-99.
55. Ibid.; and Account of the delegation from Hackensack, New Jersey, including John B. van Dieren, with Rev. Wilhelm C. Berkenmeyer, in New York City, 24 October 1727, *Protocol*, pp. 101-2.
56. Ibid., p. 103.
57. The Amsterdam Consistory to Rev. Wilhelm C. Berkenmeyer, 26 May 1730, *L.C.N.Y.*, p. 660.
58. Rev. Wilhelm C. Berkenmeyer to Rev. Jonas Lidman, 28 September 1730, *Protocol*, p. 178.
59. Ibid.; and Rev. Wilhelm C. Berkenmeyer to Rev. Johann Friedrich Winkler, Senior of the Lutheran Ministerium of Hamburg, 4-6 November 1731, *L.C.N.Y.N.J.*, pp. 21-22.
60. Rev. Michael C. Knoll to Wilhelm C. Berkenmeyer, 25 February 1733, *L.C.N.Y.N.J.*, p. 28; and "Account of what took place in controversy between me [Rev. Wilhelm C. Berkenmeyer], Rev. Michael C. Knoll, and Johann V. van Dieren, [October 1734]-Aug. 1736," in Rev. Wilhelm C. Berkenmeyer to the Amsterdam Consistory, 19 Aug. 1736, *Protocol*, p. 248.
61. Report from Rev. Wilhelm C. Berkenmeyer to Rev. Johann F. Winckler, 17 September 1734, *L.C.N.Y.N.J.*, p. 64.
62. "Account of . . . controversy . . . [October 1734]-Aug. 1736," in Rev. Wilhelm C. Berkenmeyer to the Amsterdam Consistory, 19 Aug. 1736, *Protocol*, p. 248.
63. Johann Michael Schutze to the Amsterdam Consistory, 15 April 1733, *L.C.N.Y.*, pp. 816-17.
64. Report from Berkenmeyer to Winckler, 17 September 1734, p. 54.
65. "Account of . . . controversy . . . [October 1734]-Aug. 1736," p. 248.
66. Rev. Michael C. Knoll to Johann B. van Dieren, 5 November 1734, *L.C.N.Y.*, pp. 830-38.
67. Ibid., p. 838.
68. Rev. Wilhelm C. Berkenmeyer to Rev. Johann C. Wolf of Hamburg, 20 June 1735, *L.C.N.Y.N.J.*, p. 94.
69. Rev. Wilhelm C. Berkenmeyer to Rev. Johann F. Winckler, 19 Aug. 1736, *L.C.N.Y.N.J.*, p. 116.
70. Report of Rev. Wilhelm C. Berkenmeyer to Rev. Johann F. Winckler, 17 September 1734, *L.C.N.Y.N.J.*, p. 56.
71. Rev. Wilhelm C. Berkenmeyer to Rev. Johann F. Winckler, 4-6 November 1731, *L.C.N.Y.N.J.*, p. 21.
72. Theodore G. Tappert, "The Church's Infancy 1650-1790," E. Clifford Nelson, ed., *The Lutherans in North America* (Philadelphia: Fortress Press, 1975), p. 45.
73. Rev. Michael C. Knoll to Johann B. van Dieren, 5 November 1734, *L.C.N.Y.*, p. 832.

74. *Blood Will Out, or an Example of Justice in the Tryal, Condemnation . . . and Execution of Thomas Lutherland, Who Barbarously Murthered the Body of John Clark of Philadelphia, And was Executed at Salem in West-Jersey the 23rd of February, 1691* (Philadelphia: William Bradford, 1692).
75. Kai T. Erickson, *Wayward Puritans: A Study in the Sociology of Deviance* (New York: John Wiley & Sons, Inc., 1966), pp. 195-96.

CHAPTER FOUR

1. H. Richard Niebuhr, *The Social Sources of Denominationalism* (New York: Henry Holt and Company, 1929; reprint ed., New York: Meridian Books, New American Library, 1975).
2. Winthrop S. Hudson, "Denominationalism as a Basis for Ecumenicity: A Seventeenth-Century Conception," in Russel E. Richey, ed., *Denominationalism* (Nashville: Abingdon, 1977), p. 22.
3. Andrew Greeley, *The Denominational Society* (Glenview, Ill.: Scott, Foresman and Company, 1972), p. 1.
4. Robert E. Park and Ernest W. Burgess, *Introduction to the Science of Sociology*, 3rd ed. (Chicago: Univ. of Chicago Press, 1969), pp. 508-9.
5. Coser, *Social Conflict*, p. 8.
6. See W. B. Gaillie, *Philosophy and the Historical Understanding* (London: Chatto and Windus, 1964), chapter 8.
7. Acrelius, *New Sweden*, p. 365.
8. George Keith, *Truth Advanced in the Correction of Many Gross & Hurtful Errors; Wherein is occasionally opened & explained many great and peculiar Mysteries and Doctrines of the Christian Religion* (New York: William Bradford, 1694), p. 137.
9. Jonathan Dickinson, *Remarks Upon a Pamphlet Entitled, A Letter to a Friend in the Country; containing the Substance of a Sermon preached at Philadelphia, in the Congregation of the Rev. Mr. Hemphill. Wherein the Terms of both Christian and Ministerial Communion are so stated, that all Impositions in religious Concerns are exploded, a proper Enclosure proposed for the Security of each religious Society; and the Commission of the Synod justified in their Conduct toward Mr. Hemphill.* (Philadelphia: Andrew Bradford, 1735), pp. 1-2, 26.
10. Edwards, *Baptists in New Jersey*, p. 32.
11. John Dewey, *Experience and Education* (New York: Collier Books, 1963), pp. 38-39.
12. Joseph Morgan, *The Great Concernment of gospel Ordinances, manifested From the great effects of the well Improving or Neglecting of them. Delivered in a Sermon at the Ordination of Reverend Mr. Jonathan Dickinson at Elizabeth-Town, the 29th of September 1709.* (New York: William and Andrew Bradford, 1712), p. 15.
13. Acrelius, *New Sweden*, p. 302.
14. Ibid., p. 401.

15. See Martin E. Marty, *The Public Church: Mainline-Evangelical-Catholic* (New York: Crossroads, 1981).
16. For the best description of demographic patterns in colonial New Jersey see Wacker, *Land and People*.
17. Edwards, *Baptists in New Jersey*, pp. 31-32.
18. See Victor W. Turner, *The Ritual Process* (Chicago: Aldine Publishing Co., 1966; reprint ed., Ithaca, N.Y.: Cornell University Press, 1977), especially pp. 94-130.
19. Keith, *New England's Spirit*, p. 38.
20. Keith, *Truth Advanced*, pp. 1, 137.
21. Richard Webster, *A History of the Presbyterian Church in America* (Philadelphia: Joseph M. Wilson, 1857), pp. 335-38.
22. Ibid., p. 337.
23. See Peter Berger's discussion of the importance of sociological factors in maintaining a given structure of beliefs, *Sacred Canopy*, pp. 49-51.
24. Joseph Morgan, *The Duty and Mark of Zion's Children. A Discourse at Freehold, New Jersey, Upon the Sorrowful Occasion of the Death of the Young and very Hopeful Joseph Morgan, of Yale Coll., B. A. who Departed this Life the 28th of November, 1723* (New London, Conn.: T. Green, 1725), p. 8.
25. Ibid., p. 10.
26. Morgan, *Kingdom of Basaruah*, pp. 1-69.
27. Ibid., pp. 70-71.
28. Ibid., pp. 87, 94.
29. Ibid., pp. 96-98.
30. Ibid., pp. 101-2.
31. Boel, *Complaint*, p. 49.
32. Ibid., p. 78.
33. Ibid., p. 63.
34. Ibid., p. 92.
35. See, for example, Pomfret, *Colonial New Jersey*; Tanis, *Dutch Calvinistic Pietism*; and Wertenbaker, *Middle Colonies*.
36. Quoted in Karl J. Weintraub, *Visions of Culture* (Chicago: University of Chicago Press, 1966), p. 277.
37. John Pierson, *Funeral Sermon Preached at Elizabethtown October 9, 1747 Occasioned by the Death of the Rev. Mr. Jonathan Dickinson* (New York: James Parker, 1748), p. 20.
38. See Jonathan Dickinson, *A Defense of Presbyterian Ordination. In Answer to a Pamphlet, entitled, A Modest Proof of The Order and Government settled by Christ, in the Church* (Boston: Daniel Henchman, 1724).
39. Dickinson, *Remarks Upon a Pamphlet*, p. 3-4.
40. Ibid., p. 3.
41. Ibid., pp. 4-5.
42. Ibid., pp. 5-6.
43. Ibid., pp. 5-6, 14.

44. Baptist Church, *A Confession of Faith Put forth by the Elders and Brethren of Many Congregations of Christians (Baptised upon Profession of their Faith) In London and the Country. Adopted by the Baptist Association met at Phildelphia Sept. 25, 1742. The Sixth Edition. To which are added, Two Articles viz. Of Imposition of Hands, and Singing of Psalms in Publick Worship. Also a Short Treatise of Church Discipline* (Philadelphia: B. Franklin, 1743).
45. For a good discussion of this process see Butler, *Power, Authority, and the Origins of American Denominational Order*, especially chapter 4.
46. *Minutes of the Philadelphia Baptist Association from A.D. 1707, to A.D. 1807*, ed. A. D. Gillette (Philadelphia: American Baptist Society, 1851), p. 31.
47. Ibid., pp. 42-43.
48. Ibid., p. 35.
49. Ibid., p. 68.
50. Abel Morgan, *Anti-Paedo-Rantism; or, Mr. Samuel Finley's Charitable Plea for the Speechless Examined and Refuted; the Baptism of Believers Maintain'd; and the Mode of it by Immersion Vindicated* (Philadelphia: B. Franklin, 1747), p. 158.
51. Ibid.
52. Reprinted in *N.J.A.*, volume 6.
53. Carl Bridenbaugh, *Gentleman's Progress: The Itinerarium of Dr. Alexander Hamilton 1744* (Chapel Hill: University of North Carolina Press, 1948), pp. 34-35.

CHAPTER FIVE

1. See Edward Shils, "Center and Periphery," in *Center and Periphery*.
2. Emile Durkheim, *The Elementary Forms of the Religious Life* (New York: The Free Press, 1965), p. 470.
3. Maurice Powicke, *The Reformation in England* (New York: Oxford University Press, 1961), p. 14.
4. David Little, *Religion, Order, and the Law* (New York: Harper and Row, 1969), p. 135.
5. William Haller, *Foxe's Book of Martyrs and the Elect Nation* (London: Cape, 1963), pp. 224-25.
6. Little, *Religion, Order, and Law*, p. 134.
7. See Eliade, *The Sacred and the Profane*, especially chapter 2.
8. Ibid., p. 138.
9. *N.J.A.*, 1:57.
10. See *Grants*, pp. 121-22.
11. Gov. William Burnet in the Assembly, 7 March 1722, *N.J.A.*, 5:25.
12. Ibid., 5:25-26.
13. Smith, *History*, p. 414.
14. Gov. William Burnet in the Assembly, 7 March 1722, *N.J.A.*, 5:27.

15. See Perez Zagorin, *The Court and The Country: The Beginning of the English Revolution* (New York: Atheneum, 1970).
16. Scott's *Model* is reprinted in full in William Whitehead, *East Jersey Under the Proprietary Governments* (Newark: New Jersey Historical Society, 1875), p. 373.
17. Ibid., pp. 377, 381.
18. Ibid., pp. 378-79.
19. Ibid., pp. 379, 386-87.
20. Ibid., pp. 429-30.
21. See for only one example Ahlstrom, *A Relgious History of the American People*.
22. *Records of the Town of Newark*, pp. 76-77.
23. Ibid., pp. 83-84.
24. John Barclay, Arthur Forbes, and Gawen Lawrie to the Scots proprietors, 26 Jan. 1684, Smith, *History*, p. 186.
25. See the Society of Friends, *A General Epistle*, p. 18, and William Penn, Gawen Lawrie, and Nicholas Lucas, "A Cautionary epistle," 1676, in Smith, *History*, p. 88.
26. The phrase comes from Richard John Neuhaus, *The Naked Public Square: Religion and Democracy in America* (Grand Rapids: Wm. B. Eerdmans, 1984).
27. *Grants*, p. 14.
28. Ibid., p. 394.
29. Ibid., p. 425.
30. Burr, "Religious History of New Jersey," p. 248.
31. *Grants*, pp. 474-75.
32. *N.J.A.*, 2:206.
33. Jeremiah Basse, *History of the Church at Burlington, New Jersey*, in Hills, *Church at Burlington*, p. 138. The entire text of Basse's short history is reprinted on pp. 127-39.
34. Samuell Jennings, Speaker of the Assembly to Governor Cornbury, 8 May 1707, *N.J.A.*, 3:174.
35. Governor Cornbury to the Assembly, 12 May 1707, *N.J.A.*, 3:182.
36. Col. Robert Quary to the Lords of Trade, 16 June 1703, *N.J.A.*, 2:544.
37. See Jeremiah Basse in the Assembly, 15 Jan. 1716, quoted in Richard S. Field, *The Provincial Courts of New Jersey with Sketches of the Bench and Bar* (New York: New Jersey Historical Society, 1849), p. 101; the Assembly to Governor Lewis Morris, 6 March 1746, in Lewis Morris, *The Papers of Lewis Morris, Governor of New Jersey from 1738-1746* (New York: George P. Putnam, 1852), p. 302; and Griffin Jenkins, *A Brief Vindication of the Purchassors Against the Propritors in a Christian Manner* (New York: Peter Zenger, 1745-46; reprint in *N.J.A.*, vol. 6), 6:287.
38. Field, *Provincial Courts*, pp. 101-2.
39. Ibid.
40. Morgan, *Zion's Children*, pp. 6, 18.
41. Joseph Morgan, *The Nature of Riches, Shewed from the Natural Reasons of the Use and Effects thereof: Together with some Improvements made upon the*

consideration of the Nature and Effects of Riches (Philadelphia: B. Franklin, 1732), pp. 3-5.
42. *N.J.A.*, 6:280-81.
43. Ibid., 6:282.
44. Ibid., 6:273, 277.
45. Smith, *History*, p. 424.
46. Edwards, *History of the Baptists*, p. 61.
47. Ibid., p. 66.
48. The Assembly to Governor Lewis Morris, 18 April 1745, Morris, *Papers*, p. 237.
49. The Assembly to Governor Lewis Morris, 6 March 1746, Morris, *Papers*, p. 302.
50. Smith, *History*, p. 434.
51. *Grants*, p. i.

CONCLUSION

1. Kenneth A. Lockridge, *Settlement and Unsettlement in Early America* (New York: Cambridge University Press, 1981), p. 1.
2. See George G. Willison, *Saints and Strangers* (New York: Raynal and Hitchcock, 1945).
3. See Erickson, *Wayward Puritans*; W. Clark Gilpin, *The Millenarian Piety of Roger Williams* (Chicago: University of Chicago Press, 1979); K. B. Stoever, *"A Faire and Easie Way to Heaven"* (Middletown, Conn.: Wesleyan University Press, 1978); and Larzer Ziff, *Puritanism in America* (New York: Viking Press, 1974).
4. See C. C. Goen, *Revivalism and Separatism in New England, 1740-1800* (New Haven: Yale University Press, 1962); William G. McLoughlin, *New England Dissent, 1630-1833*, 2 vols. (Cambridge: Harvard University Press, 1971).
5. In religious affairs, Boston differed most notably from other New England towns in that churches in the city always relied on voluntary financial support rather than a prorated church tax.
6. Donald G. Mathews, *Religion in the Old South* (Chicago: University of Chicago Press, 1977), p. 9.
7. Ibid., p. 5.
8. Ibid., p. 7.
9. See Rhys Isaac, *The Transformation of Virginia 1740-1790* (Chapel Hill, N.C.: University of North Carolina Press, 1982).
10. George L. Smith, *Religion and Trade in New Netherlands* (Ithaca: Cornell University Press, 1973).
11. This is in fact exactly what did occur when the founding of King's College fanned a public discussion about relations among the various religious groups present in the city. See Carl Bridenbaugh, *Mitre and Sceptre* (New York: Oxford University Press, 1962), especially pp. 138-70.

12. Some of these generalizations could be modestly revised in the light of Richard Pointer's *Protestant Pluralism and the New York Experience* (Bloomington, Ind.: Indiana University Press, 1988), but in the main they still hold.
13. See Gilpin, *The Millenarian Piety of Roger Williams*.
14. Nash, *Quakers and Politics*, p. 14.
15. Lemon, *The Best Poor Man's Country*, p. 98.
16. See Daniel J. Boorstin, *The Americans: The Colonial Experience* (New York: Vintage Books, 1958), pp. 33-70.
17. Lemon, *The Best Poor Man's Country*, p. 21.
18. See Richard Bauman, *For the Reputation of Truth: Politics, Religion, and Conflict Among the Pennsylvania Quakers, 1750-1800* (Baltimore: The Johns Hopkins Press, 1971).
19. See John F. Wilson, *Public Religion in American Culture* (Philadelphia: Temple University Press, 1979), pp. 7-8.

Bibliography

PRIMARY SOURCES

Acrelius, Israel. *A History of New Sweden*. Translated by William M. Reynolds. Philadelphia: Historical Society of Pennsylvania, 1874.

Archives of the State of New Jersey. First Series, 48 vols. Newark, 1880-1949.

Baptist Church. *A Confession of Faith Put forth by the Elders and Brethren of Many Congregations of Christians (Baptised upon Profession of their Faith) In London and the Country. Adopted by the Baptist Association met at Philadelphia Sept. 25, 1742. The Sixth Edition. To which are added, Two Articles viz. Of Imposition of Hands, and Singing of Psalms in Publick Worship. Also a Short Treatise of Church Discipline*. Philadelphia: B. Franklin, 1743.

_____. *Minutes of the Philadelphia Baptist Association from A.D. 1707 to A.D. 1807*. Edited by A. D. Gillette. Philadelphia: American Baptist Publication Society, 1851.

Boel, Henricus. *Boel's Complaint Against Frelinghuisen*. Translated and edited by Joseph Anthony Loux Jr. Rensselaer, N.Y.: Reformed Church Historical Society, 1979.

Blood Will Out, or an Example of Justice in the Tryal, Condemnation, Confession, and Execution of Thomas Lutherland, Who Barbarously Murthered the Body of John Clark of Philadelphia, And was Executed at Salem in West-Jersey the 23rd of February, 1691. Philadelphia: William Bradford, 1692.

Dickinson, Jonathan. *A Defense of Presbyterian Ordination. In Answer to a Pamphlet, entitled, A Modest Proof of The Order and Government settled by Christ, in the Church*. Boston: Daniel Henchman, 1724.

_____. *Remarks Upon a Pamphlet, Entitled, A Letter to a Friend in the Country; containing the Substance of a Sermon preached at Philadelphia, in the Congregation of the Rev. Mr. Hemphill. Wherein the Terms of both Christian and Ministerial Communion are so stated, that all Impositions in religious Concerns are exploded, a Proper Enclosure proposed for the Security of each religious Society; and the Commission of the Synod justified in their conduct toward Mr. Hemphill.* Philadelphia: Andrew Bradford, 1735.

_____. A Sermon Preached at the Funeral of Mrs. Ruth Pierson, Wife of the Reverend Mr. John Pierson, Minister of the Gospel at Woodbridge, in New Jersey. New York: William Bradford, 1733.

Ecclesiastical Records of the State of New York. 7 vols. Albany: New York State, 1901-16.

Edwards, Morgan. *Materials Towards a History of the Baptists in New Jersey.* Philadelphia: Thomas Dodson, 1792.

Friends, Society of. *A General Epistle given forth by the People of the Lord, called Quakers, That all may know we own none to be of our Fellowship, or to be reckoned or numbered with us, but such as fear the Lord and keep faithfully to his Heavenly Power.* Philadelphia: William Bradford, 1686.

_____. *A Testimony and Caution to such as do make a Profession of Truth, Who are in scorn called Quakers, and more especially such who profess to be Ministers of The Gospel of Peace, That they should not be concerned in Worldly Government.* Philadelphia: William Bradford, 1693.

Keith, George. *The Heresie and Hatred Which was falsely Charged upon the Innocent Justly returned upon the Guilty.* Philadelphia: William Bradford, 1693.

_____. *New England's Spirit of Persecution Transmitted to Pennsylvania, and the Pretended Quaker found Persecuting the True Christian-Quaker, in the Tryal of Peter Boss, George Keith, Thomas Budd, and William Bradford.* Philadelphia: William Bradford, 1693.

_____. *Truth Advanced in the Correction of Many Gross & Hurtful Errors; Wherein is occasionally opened & explained many great and peculiar Mysteries and Doctrines of the Christian Religion.* New York: William Bradford, 1694.

Leaming, Aaron, and Jacob Spicer, eds. *The Grants, Concessions and Original Constitutions of the Province of New Jersey.* Philadelphia: W. Bradford, 1751; reprint ed., Somerville, N.J.: Honeyman and Company, 1881.

Lutheran Church. *Protocol of the Lutheran Church in New York City.* Translated and edited by Simon Hart and Harry J. Kreider. New York: New York Synod, 1958.

"Lutheran Church in New York, 1649-1772: Records in the Lutheran Church Archives at Amsterdam, Holland." Translated and edited by Arnold J. H. van Laer. *Bulletin of the New York Public Library* 48 (1944): 31-60, 409-

18, 417-84, 761-76, 907-29; 49 (1945): 3-29, 89-113, 559-86, 649-70, 813-51; 50 (1946): 409-27.

Lutheran Church in New York and New Jersey, 1722-1760: Lutheran Records in the Ministerial Archives of the Staatsarchiv, Hamburg, Germany. Translated by Simon Hart and Harry J. Kreider. Ann Arbor, Mich.: United Lutheran Synod of New York and New England, 1962.

Makamie, Francis. *An Answer to George Keith's Libel Against a Catechism Published by Francis Makamie.* Boston, 1694.

Morgan, Abel. *Anti-Paedo-Rantism; or, Mr. Samuel Finley's Charitable Plea for the Speechless Examined and Refuted; The Baptism of Believer's Maintain'd; and the Mode of it by Immersion Vindicated.* Philadelphia: B. Franklin, 1747.

Morgan, Joseph. *The Duty and Mark of Zion's Children. A Discourse at Freehold, New Jersey, Upon the Sorrowful Occasion of the Death of the Young and very Hopeful Joseph Morgan, of Yale Coll., B.A. Who Departed this Life the 28th of November 1723.* New London, Conn.: T. Green, 1725.

_____. *The Great Concernment of gospel Ordinances, manifested From the great effects of the well Improving or Neglecting of them. Delivered in a Sermon at the Ordination of Reverend Mr. Jonathan Dickinson, at Elizabeth-Town, the 29th of September 1709.* New York: William and Andrew Bradford, 1712.

_____. *The History of the Kingdom of Basaruah.* Edited by Richard Schlatter. Cambridge: Harvard University Press, 1946.

_____. *The Nature of Riches, Shewed from the Natural Reasons of the Use and Effects thereof: Together with some Improvements made upon the consideration of the Nature and Effects of Riches.* Philadelphia: B. Franklin, 1732.

Morris, Lewis. *The Papers of Lewis Morris, Governor of New Jersey from 1738-1746.* New York: George P. Putnam, 1852.

Muhlenburg, Henry Melchior. *The Journals of Henry Melchior Muhlenburg.* 3 vols. Translated by Theodore G. Tappert and John W. Doberstein. Philadelphia: Evangelical Lutheran Ministerium of Pennsylvania and Adjacent States, 1942.

Pierson, John. *Funeral Sermon Preached at Elizabethtown October 9, 1747 Occasioned by the Death of the Rev. Mr. Jonathan Dickinson.* New York: James Parker, 1748.

Records of the Town of Newark, 1666-1836. Newark: New Jersey Historical Society, 1864.

Smith, Samuel. *The History of the Colony of the Nova-Caesarea, or New Jersey.* Burlington, N.J.: James Parker, 1765; reprint ed., New York: Arno Press, 1972.

Willsford, John. *A Brief Exhortation to all who profess the Truth.* Philadelphia: William Bradford, 1691.

SECONDARY WORKS

Ahlstrom, Sydney E. *A Religious History of the American People.* New Haven: Yale University Press, 1972.

Albanese, Catherine L. *America: Religions and Religion.* Belmont, Calif.: Wadsworth Publishing Co., 1981.

Andrews, Charles M. *The Colonial Period of American History.* 4 vols. New Haven: Yale University Press, 1934-38.

Balmer, Randall. *A Perfect Babel of Confusion: Dutch Religion and English Culture in the Middle Colonies.* New York: Oxford University Press, 1989.

Bauman, Richard. *For the Reputation of Truth: Politics, Religion, and Conflict Among the Pennsylvania Quakers, 1750-1800.* Baltimore: Johns Hopkins Press, 1971.

Boorstin, Daniel J. *The Americans: The Colonial Experience.* New York: Vintage Books, 1958.

Bridenbaugh, Carl. *Mitre and Sceptre.* New York: Oxford University Press, 1962.

Burr, Nelson R. *The Anglican Church in New Jersey.* Philadelphia: Church Historical Society, 1954.

_____. "The Religious History of New Jersey Before 1702." *Proceedings of the New Jersey Historical Society* 56 (July and October 1938): 169-90, 243-66.

Butler, Jon. "Gospel Order Improved: The Keithian Schism and the Exercise of Quaker Ministerial Authority in Pennsylvania." *William and Mary Quarterly*, 3rd ser., 31 (July 1974): 431-52.

_____. *Power, Authority, and the Origins of American Denominational Order: The English Churches in the Delaware Valley 1680-1730.* Philadelphia: American Philosophical Society, 1978.

Clark, Samuel A. *The History of St. John's Church, Elizabethtown, New Jersey.* New York: Thomas N. Stanford, 1857.

Cody, Edward James. "Church and State in the Middle Colonies." Ph.D. dissertation, Lehigh University, 1970.

DeJong, Gerald F. *The Dutch Reformed Church in the American Colonies*. Grand Rapids, Mich.: William B. Eerdmans Publishing Company, 1978.

Ellison, Harry C. *Church of the Founding Fathers of New Jersey*. Cornish, Maine: Carbrook Press, 1964.

Field, Richard S. *The Provincial Courts of New Jersey with Sketches of the Bench and Bar*. New York: New Jersey Historical Society, 1849.

Frost, J. William. *The Quaker Family in Colonial America: A Portrait of the Society of Friends*. New York: St. Martin's Press, 1973.

Gerlach, Larry. *Prologue to Independence: New Jersey in the Coming of the American Revolution*. New Brunswick: Rutgers University Press, 1976.

Gilpin, W. Clark. *The Millenarian Piety of Roger Williams*. Chicago: University of Chicago Press, 1979.

Goen, C. C. *Revivalism and Separatism in New England, 1740-1800*. New Haven: Yale University Press, 1962; reprint ed., Hamden, Conn.: Archon Books, 1969.

Haller, William. *Foxe's Book of Martyrs and the Elect Nation*. London: Cape, 1963.

Harmelink, Herman III. "Another Look at Frelinghuisen and His 'Awakening.'" *Church History* 37 (December 1968): 423-38.

Harmelink, Herman III, William W. Coventry, and Sharon Thomas Scholten. *The Reformed Church in New Jersey*. N.p.: The Synod of New Jersey, 1969.

Hills, George Morgan. *History of the Church in Burlington, New Jersey*. Trenton, N.J.: W. S. Sharp, 1876.

Hofstadter, Richard. *America at 1750*. New York: Alfred A. Knopf, Inc., 1971.

Isaac, Rhys. *The Transformation of Virginia 1740-1790*. Chapel Hill, N.C.: University of North Carolina Press, 1982.

Jamison, Wallace N. *Religion in New Jersey: A Brief History*. Princeton: D. Van Nostrand Company, Inc., 1964.

Jones, W. Northey. *The History of St. Peter's Church in Perth Amboy, New Jersey*. N.p.: W. Northey Jones, 1924.

Kammen, Michael. *People of Paradox*. New York: Oxford University Press, 1972.

Kirby, Ethyn Williams. *George Keith 1638-1716*. New York: D. Appleton-Century Company, 1942.

Kreider, Harry J. *Lutheranism in Colonial New York*. New York, 1942.

Leiby, Adrian C. *The United Churches of Hackensack and Schraalenburgh, New Jersey, 1686-1822*. River Edge, N.J.: Bergen County Historical Society, 1976.

Lemon, James T. *The Best Poor Man's Country: A Geographical Study of Early Southeastern Pennsylvania*. Baltimore: Johns Hopkins Press, 1972; reprint ed., New York: W. W. Norton & Company, 1976.

Little, David. *Religion, Order, and the Law*. New York: Harper and Row, 1969.

Lockridge, Kenneth. *Settlement and Unsettlement in Early America*. New York: Cambridge University Press, 1981.

Lodge, Martin. "The Great Awakening in the Middle Colonies." Ph.D. dissertation, University of California, Berkeley, 1964.

McLoughlin, William G. *New England Dissent 1630-1833*. 2 vols. Cambridge: Harvard University Press, 1971.

MacWhorter, Alexander. *A Century Sermon*. Newark: W. Tuttle and Company, 1807.

Maring, Norman H. *The Baptists in New Jersey: A Study in Transition*. Valley Forge, Pa.: Judson Press, 1964.

Matthews, Donald G. *Religion in the Old South*. Chicago: University of Chicago Press, 1977.

Miller, John C. *This New Man, the American*. St. Louis: McGraw-Hill Book Company, 1974.

Nash, Gary B. *Quakers and Politics: Pennsylvania, 1681-1726*. Princeton: Princeton University Press, 1968.

Pointer, Richard W. *Protestant Pluralism and the New York Experience: A Study of Eighteenth-Century Religious Diversity*. Bloomington, Ind.: Indiana University Press, 1988.

Pomfret, John E. *Colonial New Jersey*. New York: Charles Scribner's Sons, 1973.

_____. *The Province of East New Jersey, 1609-1702*. Princeton: Princeton University Press, 1962.

Powicke, Maurice. *The Reformation in England*. New York: Oxford University Press, 1961.

Smith, George L. *Religion and Trade in New Netherland*. Ithaca: Cornell University Press, 1973.

Stoeffler, F. Ernest, ed. *Continental Pietism and Early American Christianity*. Grand Rapids, Mich.: William B. Eerdmans Publishing Company, 1976.

Stoever, K. B. *"A Faire and Easie Way to Heaven."* Middletown, Conn.: Weslyan University Press, 1978.

Tanis, James. *Dutch Calvinistic Pietism in the Middle Colonies*. The Hague: Martinus Nijhoff, 1967.

Tanner, Edwin P. *The Province of New Jersey 1664-1738*. New York: Columbia University Press, 1908.

Tappert, Theodore G. "The Church's Infancy 1650-1790." In *The Lutherans in North America*, edited by E. Clifford Nelson. Philadelphia: Fortress Press, 1975.

Taylor, Benjamin, C., ed. *Annals of the Classics of Bergen*. New York: Board of the Dutch Reformed Church, 1857.

Trinterud, Leonard J. *The Forming of an American Tradition: A Reexamination of Colonial Presbyterianism*. Philadelphia: The Westminster Press, 1949; reprint ed., New York: Arno Press, 1970.

Wacker, Peter O. *Land and People: A Cultural Geography of Preindustrial New Jersey*. New Brunswick: Rutgers University Press, 1975.

Webster, Richard. *A History of the Presbyterian Church in America*. Philadelphia: M. Wilson, 1857.

Wertenbaker, Thomas Jefferson. *The Founding of American Civilization: The Middle Colonies*. New York: Charles Scribner's Sons, 1938; reprint ed., New York: Cooper Square Publishers, 1963.

Whitehead, William A. *East Jersey Under the Proprietory Governments*. Newark: New Jersey Historical Society, 1875.

Willison, George C. *Saints and Strangers*. New York: Raynal and Hitchcock, 1945.

Wilson, John F. *Public Religion in American Culture*. Philadelphia: Temple University Press, 1979.

Wolf, Stephanie Grauman. *Urban Village: Population, Community and Family Structure in Germantown, Pennsylvania, 1683-1800*. Princeton: Princeton University Press, 1976.

Zagorin, Perez. *The Court and The Country: The Beginning of the English Revolution*. New York: Atheneum, 1970.

Ziff, Larzer. *Puritanism in America*. New York: Viking Press, 1974.

Zuckerman, Michael, ed. *Friends and Neighbors: Group Life in America's First Plural Society*. Philadelphia: Temple University Press, 1982.

Zwierlein, Frederick J. *Religion in New Netherlands*. Rochester, N.Y.: John P. Smith Printing Company, 1910.

OTHER WORKS CITED

Arendt, Hannah. *On Revolution*. New York: Viking Press, 1963.
Bellah, Robert N., and Phillip Hammond. *Varieties of Civil Religion*. San Francisco: Harper and Row, 1980.
Berenson, Bernard. *Aesthetics and History*. New York: Pantheon, 1948; Garden City, N.Y.: Doubleday and Company, 1954.
Berger, Peter L. *Invitation to Sociology*. New York: Anchor Books, 1963.
_____. *The Sacred Canopy: Elements of a Sociological Theory of Religion*. New York: Doubleday and Company, 1967; Anchor Books, 1969.
Chadwick, Owen. *The Secularization of the European Mind in the Nineteenth Century*. New York: Cambridge University Press, 1975.
Coser, Lewis A. *The Functions of Social Conflict*. New York: The Free Press, 1956.
Douglas, Mary. *Purity and Danger*. New York: Frederick A. Praeger, 1966.
Durkheim, Emile. *The Elementary Forms of the Religious Life*. Translated by Joseph Ward Swain. New York: George Allen and Unwin, 1915; reprint ed., New York: Free Press, 1965.
Eliade, Mircea. *The Sacred and the Profane*. Translated by Willard R. Trask. New York: Harcourt, Brace and World, 1959.
Erikson, Kai T. *Wayward Puritans: A Study in the Sociology of Deviance*. New York: John Wiley and Sons, Inc., 1966.
Festinger, Leon. *A Theory of Cognitive Dissonance*. Stanford: Stanford University Press, 1957.
Fischer, Claude S. *To Dwell Among Friends: Personal Networks in Town and City*. Chicago: University of Chicago Press, 1982.
Fox, Edward Whiting. *History in Geographic Perspective*. New York: W. W. Norton and Company, 1971.
Geertz, Clifford. *The Interpretation of Cultures*. New York: Basic Books, 1973.
Greeley, Andrew. *The Denominational Society*. Glenview, Ill.: Scott, Foresman and Company, 1972.
Hoffer, Eric. *The True Believer*. New York: Harper and Brothers, 1951; reprint ed., New York: Mentor Books, 1958.
Hooker, Richard. *The Works of Mr. Richard Hooker*. 3 vols. Edited by John Keble. Oxford: Clarendon Press, 1874.
Hudson, Winthrop S. "Denominationalism as a Basis for Ecumenicity: A Seventeenth-Century Conception." In *Denominationalism*, edited by Russell E. Richey. Nashville: Abingdon, 1977.

Isaacs, Harold R. *Idols of the Tribe.* New York: Harper and Row, 1975.
Lippmann, Walter. *A Preface to Morals.* New York: Macmillan Company, 1929.
Marty, Martin E. *The Public Church: Mainline-Evangelical-Catholic.* New York: Crossroads, 1981.
Mead, Sidney E. *The Lively Experiment: The Shaping of Christianity in America.* New York: Harper and Row, 1963.
Miller, Perry. *The New England Mind: The Seventeenth Century.* New York: Macmillan Company, 1939; reprint ed., Boston: Beacon Press, 1961.
_____. *The New England Mind: From Colony to Province.* Cambridge: Harvard University Press, 1953; reprint ed., Boston: Beacon Press, 1961.
Montesquieu, Baron de. *The Spirit of the Laws.* 2 vols. Translated by Thomas Nugent. New York: Haftner Publishing Company, 1949.
Neuhaus, Richard John. *The Naked Public Square: Religion and Democracy in America.* Grand Rapids, Mich.: William B. Eerdmans Publishing Co., 1984.
Niebuhr, H. Richard. *The Social Sources of Denominationalism.* New York: Henry Holt, 1929; reprint ed., New York: Meridian, 1975.
Park, Robert E., and Ernest W. Burgess. *Introduction to the Science of Sociology.* Third Edition, revised. Chicago: University of Chicago Press, 1969.
Purchas, Samuel. *Microcosmus or The Historie of Man.* London, 1619; reprint ed., New York: Da Capo Press, 1969.
Redfield, Robert. *The Little Community.* Chicago: University of Chicago Press, 1960.
Roberts, Brian K. *Rural Settlement in Britain.* Hamden, Conn.: Archon Books, 1977.
Sennett, Richard. *Authority.* New York: Alfred A. Knopf, 1980.
Shils, Edward. *Center and Periphery: Essays in Macrosociology.* Chicago: University of Chicago Press, 1975.
Smith, Timothy L. "Congregation, State, and Denomination: The Forming of an American Religious Structure," *William and Mary Quarterly,* 3rd, ser., 25 (April 1968): 155-76.
Troeltsch, Ernst. *The Social Teaching of the Christian Churches,* 2 vols. Translated by Olive Wyon. New York: Macmillan, 1931; reprint ed., New York: Harper and Row, 1960.
Turner, Victor. *The Ritual Process.* Chicago: Aldine, 1966; reprint ed., Ithaca: Cornell University Press, 1977.

Weber, Max. *The Sociology of Religion*. Boston: Beacon Press, [1922] 1964.
White, Hayden. *Metahistory: The Historical Imagination in Nineteenth-Century Europe*. Baltimore: Johns Hopkins Press, 1973.
Wolf, Eric R. *Peasants*. Englewood Cliffs, N.J.: Prentice-Hall, 1977.

Index

Acrelius, Israel, 89, 90, 91, 116, 122-23
Actes and Monuments, 152
Americanization, 4, 5
The Anglican Church in New Jersey, 5
Anglicans
   conflict with Puritans in Elizabethtown, 72-73
   cooperate with Baptists in Middletown, 91
   cooperate with Congregationalists in Elizabethtown, 73-74
   cooperate with Presbyterians in Elizabethtown, 74
   early settlement, 46
   led by Southern gentry, 179-80
   in Monmouth County, 56
   in New England, 178
   religious establishment proposed after royalization, 44-46
   in Southern colonies, 179-81
   threaten Quakers, 64
Antonides, Vincenius, 103
Apostasy
   as threat to religious tribalism, 61
Arminianism, 129
Atheists
   proposed restrictions on, 38-39
Auren, Jonas, 91
Aylmer, John, 152

Bailey, John, 27
Baptists
   American characteristics of, 5
   baptismal doctrine of, 141, 145
   clash with Presbyterians in Haightstown, 171-72
   congregational mergers in Cohansey, 125-26, 132
   cooperate with other religious groups in Middletown, 91
   and denominationalism, 118-19, 139-45
   inconsistent behavior, 14
   in Monmouth County, 56
   in Rhode Island, 183
   in Southern colonies, 180
Barclay, John, 159, 171
Bartholf, Guilium, 92-101, 121
   character of, 97-99
   criticizes Society of Friends, 100
   disagreement with Theodorus Jacobus Frelinghuisen, 99-100
   disregards ecclesiastical procedures, 196n
   as forerunner of Theodorus Jacobus Frelinghuisen, 98
   and generic religion, 99-101
   ministry of, 100
   pietism, 101
Basse, Jeremiah, 164-65, 167-70
Belcher, Jonathan, 64
Berenson, Bernard, 17
Bergen, New Netherlands
   religion in, 24
Bergen, N.J.
   Dutch Reformed Church established in, 33
   religious establishment allowed in, 31-32
Berger, Peter, 8, 54, 65, 79
Berkeley, John, 26-27, 33, 36, 46
Berkenmeyer, Wilhelm Christoph, 102, 103-6, 107, 109, 197n

Bjork, Eric, 91
Boehme, Anton Wilhelm, 101-2, 197n
Boel, Henricus, 75, 78, 133
Boston
  churches rely on voluntary financial support, 203n
  religious pluralism in, 178
Bradford, William, 110
A Brief Vindication of the Purchassors Against the Propritors, in a Christian Manner, 145-46, 170-71
Brooke, John, 62, 72-73
Brooks, Timothy, 125
Burgess, E.W., 115
Burlington
  Quakers threatened in, 64
Burnet, William, 50, 154-55
Burr, Nelson, 3-4, 5, 6, 92
Butler, Jon, 69
Byllynge, Edward, 33, 36, 39-40

Carteret, George, 26-27, 33, 36, 38, 46
Carteret, Philip
  as governor, 26-32
  declares Elizabethtown seat of New Jersey government, 72
  and English public piety, 153-54
  influences development of moral society, 35
Catholics
  challenges to public officials, 63
  civil restrictions on in East New Jersey, 39, 42
  in Rhode Island, 183
  in Southern colonies, 180
Charles II, 23-24
Charles XII, King of Sweden, 91
Christianity
  and natural law theory, 20
Civil Religion, 12, 16, 149-51, 176
Clark, John, 110
Clergy
  as educators in denominationalism, 120-22
  blamed for religious divisions, 87
  discourse defines public piety, 169-72
  displaced in Enlightenment natural religion, 175
  Guilium Bartholf, 92-101
  role in generic religion, 86-87
  role in religious tribalism, 54, 65-66, 86
  salaries of, 97
  town-sponsored ministers, 25
Cognitive Dissonance
  and churchly tribalism, 72
Cohansey
  congregational mergers in, 132
  development of denominationalism, 125-26, 140-43
  relations among denominations in, 118-19
  tax revolt in, 63
College of New Jersey (Princeton University)
  public funding for, 64
Colonies, American
  competition for English settlers, 157-59
  construct public framework of neighborliness, 175-76
  development of, 2
  hierarchical structures affect religion in South, 179-81
  legal structures, 22-23
  religion as search for community, 99
  religious structures, 177-85
  royalization of, 43
  struggle to define public piety, 150-51
  tensions between English court and country in, 156
  world view, 20-21
Commins, Dr., 89
The Concession and Agreement of the Lords Proprietors of the Province of New Caesarea, or New Jersey, 27-28, 30, 31, 32, 36, 157, 161, 163
A Confession of Faith . . . Adopted by the Baptist Association Met at Philadelphia September 25, 1742, 140-41
Congregational Church
  challenges Catholic officials, 63
  establishment in Newark, 30-31
  shares meetinghouse with Anglicans in Elizabethtown, 73-74
Conversion
  and denominationalists, 118
  religious tribalism as threat to, 61-62
Cornbury, Edward Lord, 42, 44, 45-46, 47-48, 165-66, 173
Corwin, Edwin T., 98
Coser, Lewis, 58, 62, 63, 74-75, 82, 115

INDEX

Cotton, John, 29

Danielle, Pierre, 55
Davenport, John, 29
Delavall, John, 59
Dellius, Godfridus, 93, 95-96, 97-98
Denominationalism, 13-14
   adherence to tradition in, 122-24
   as adaptation to religious diversity, 113
   authority within, 120-22
   becomes dominant viewpoint, 147
   behavioral etiquette of, 144-47
   characteristics of, 115-24
   in Cohansey, 125-26
   defined, 15-16
   development of, 124-44, 133-35
   diversity as foundation of, 138
   education in, 120-22
   and future optimism, 116-17, 121-22
   generational differences, 135-36
   and George Keith, 126-28
   and Joseph Morgan, 128-32
   as opposite of sectarianism, 114
   organizational concerns, 118
   and proselytizing, 118
   as public and diverse Christian church, 123-24
   reasons for development, 113-15
   and relationships among rivals, 118-19
   and religious competition, 115-19
   rules as response to diversity, 122-23
   rules of conduct, 139-44
   second-generation, 135-36
   and sermons, 121-22
   sheds traditional orthodoxy, 113
   as solution to diversity, 124
   supports religious freedom, 117-18
   theology of, 136-39
DesMarest, David, 55, 85, 88
Dewey, John, 121
Dickinson, John, 73-74
Dickinson, Jonathan, 117-18, 121, 136-39, 140
Dilthey, Wilhelm, 150
Dissonance, Cognitive
   and churchly tribalism, 72
Diversity, Cultural, 8
Diversity, Religious, 34
   after royalization, 42-49
   allowed to develop in New Netherlands, 24, 25
   as basis for pluralism in New Jersey, 184-85
   as catalyst for religious competition, 115
   colonists adapt to, 1, 2, 7, 10, 12, 14-15, 16
   colonists construct public framework of neighborliness, 166-67, 169-73, 175-76
   defined, 10-11
   denominationalism as solution to, 124-44
   denominationalists adjust to, 119
   denominational rules as response to, 122-23
   denominations as adaption to, 113
   effect on churchly tribalism, 72
   as foundation of denominationalism, 138
   and freedom of religion, 1
   generic religion as adjustment to, 87, 88
   George Keith on, 128
   as incentive for settlement, 21-22
   integrated, 12
   Jonathan Dickinson on, 137-39
   Joseph Morgan on, 131-32
   leaders mandate public peaceableness, 161
   legal framework for, 19-51
   legal protection for, 27-28
   in New England, 177-79
   in New York, 181-82
   as paradigm for American diversity, 10
   in Pennsylvania, 183-84
   as public concern, 35
   and public framework of neighborliness, 149
   in Rhode Island, 182-83
   segregated, 12
   in Southern colonies, 179-81
   tribalism as reaction to, 53-54, 57, 74-75, 86
   upheld in New Jersey, 49-50
   See also Pluralism, religious
Douglas, Mary, 60
DuBois, Abraham, 146
DuBois, Gualtherus, 75, 76
Dumont, Pieter, 82, 133
Durkheim, Emil, 150-51
Dutch Reformed Church
   Americanization of, 5

217

clerical response to Leisler's Rebellion, 93-94
and Guilium Bartholf, 92
and Theodorus Jacobus Frelinghuisen, 75-83, 133-35
Huguenots split from, 55
legally established during Dutch rule, 33
in Monmouth County, 56
New Jersey churches break from New York clergy, 93-95
New York clergy oppose Guilium Bartholf's ordination, 97-98
religious practices protected in New Netherlands, 24
response to diversity in New York, 181-82
theological disputes within, 76-77

East New Jersey
imposes Catholic civil restrictions, 39, 42
proposed religious restrictions in, 38-39
proposes public office religious test, 39
proprietors' role in royalization, 43
Quaker proprietors reorganize colony, 38
rejection of proposed constitution, 38-39
restricts irreligious behavior, 36-37
sabbatarianism in, 36-37
sale of proprietary rights to, 38
Eaton, Theophilus, 29
Edwards, Morgan, 91, 118-19, 125, 171-72
Eldridge, 172
Eliade, Mircea, 153
Elizabethtown
Anglicans and Congregationalists share meeting house, 73-74
breakdown of religious tribalism in, 72-74
founding of, 26
Quakers attacked in, 59-60
religious cooperation in, 136
religious homogeneity ended, 27, 31
England
colonization of America, 157-59
Enlightenment changes public piety, 174-76
governmental policy toward religion, 28
Lords of Trade support New Jersey Society of Friends, 49
public piety influences American colonies, 150-62, 165-66, 168, 173-76

religious policy of, 47
role in governance of New Jersey, 23
royalization of American colonies, 43
tensions between court and country, 156
Enlightenment
changes public piety, 174-76
Erikson, Kai, 110
Essex County
intermarriage in, 57
Execution
of Thomas Lutherland, 110-11

Falkner, Justus, 102, 103, 104
Fenwick, John, 33, 36
Festinger, Leon, 72
Finley, Samuel, 145
Fisser, Hendrik, 78
Fletcher, Benjamin, 94
Fletcher, Seth, 59-60
Forbes, Arthur, 159
The Forming of an American Tradition: A Re-Examination of Colonial Presbyterianism, 5
Foxe, John, 152
Franklin, Benjamin, 6, 184
Freeman, Bernard, 75, 82, 133
Frelinghuisen, Theodorus Jacobus
disagreement with Guilium Bartholf, 98-100
opposed by denominationalists, 133-35
and religious tribalism, 75-83
French Reformed Church
formation of, 55-56
Freud, Sigmund, 64-65

Gaillie, W.B., 116
Geertz, Clifford, 9
George I, 154-55
George II, 173
Gerlach, Larry, 55
Glorious Revolution, 93, 154
Great Awakening, 118
effect on religious diversity, 12
in New England, 178
Greeley, Andrew, 114-15
Hackensack
Dutch Reformed Church in, 94-95

Huguenots in, 55-56
Haightstown
    religious conflict in, 171-72
Hamilton, Alexander, 146
Harriman, John, 72-73
Hayman, Nicholas, 81
Henkel, Anthony Jacob, 102, 197n
Henry VIII, 152
History of the Kingdom of Basaruah, 130-32
Hofstadter, Richard, 45
Hooker, Richard, 20
Hudson, Winthrop S., 114-15
Huguenots
    form French Reformed Church, 55-56
Hunter, Robert, 42, 63

Immigrants
    colonial recruitment of, 157-59
    settlement patterns of, 56-57, 182
    restrictions on in West New Jersey, 163
Indians. *See* Native Americans
Ingoldsby, Governor Richard, 48
Innes, Alexander, 91-92

James, Duke of York, 23-24, 25, 27, 28, 39, 46
James, Thomas, 26
Jamison, Wallace N., 5-7, 8-9
Jenkins, Griffin, 145-46, 170-71
Jenkins, Nathaniel, 50
Jennings, Samuel, 39
Jews, 146-47, 183
Jurisdictions, Religious, 133-35

Kammen, Michael, 21
Keith, George, 58, 59, 117
    causes Quaker Keithian schism, 69-71
    and denominationalism, 126-28
Kelsay, 125
Killingsworth, Thomas, 125
King's College (Columbia University), 203n
Kingwood
    Baptists in, 143-44
Knoll, Michael Christian, 101-9
Koelman, Jacobus, 98

Labadie, Jean de, 98
Land and People, 7-8
Law
    after royalization, 42-49
    and colonial development, 22-23
    development of legal code, 23
    development of religious codes, 29
    effect of royalization on, 22, 46
    enforcement of religious codes, 31-32
    framework for religious diversity, 19-51, 49
    and informal establishment of religion, 35
    nationalism, 20
    natural theory of, 19-20
    and opposing religious groups, 63
    and privatization of religious pluralism, 16
    prosecutes sins against God, 163
    protects rival religious groups, 58
    and religion, 14, 21-22
    rights of Quakers, 47-49
    Western understanding of, 19-20
Lawrie, Gawen, 33
Leaming, Aaron, 50, 176
Leisler, Jacob, 93-94, 97
Leisler, Jacob, Jr., 93
Levi-Strauss, Claude, 57
Liberty
    foundations for religious, 22-34
Lidman, Jonas, 105
Locke, John, 175
Lockridge, Kenneth, 177
Lovelace, John Lord, 42, 48
Lucas, Nicholas, 33
Lucretius, 19
Lupardus, 96
Lutherans
    dispute over Johann Bernhard van Dieren, 104-6
    Old World characteristics of, 5
    oppose ordination of Johann Bernhard van Dieren, 102
    in Pennsylvania, 184
    pluralism in rural New York, 182
    pragmatic traditionalism of Swedish colonists, 122
    Swedish clergy in New Jersey, 58
    Swedish practice generic religion, 89-91
    Swedish settlement patterns, 56-57
Lutherland, Thomas, 110-11

Makamie, Francis, 58, 61
Marty, Martin, 124
Mather, Increase, 59
Mathews, Donald G., 179-80
Melyen, Joanna, 136
Melyen, Samuel, 73
The Middle Colonies, 4-5
Middletown
   Baptists cooperate with other religious groups, 91
   Baptists seek clarification on denominationalism, 142-43
Mill, John Stuart, 20
Miller, Perry, 2
The Model of the Government of the Province of East New Jersey in America, 157-59
Molenaar, Ary, 77-83
Monmouth County
   development of denominationalism, 128
   early settlement of, 26
   generic religion in, 91
   religious diversity in, 31, 56
Montesquieu, Charles, Baron de, 19, 20, 21, 50
Monteux, Pierre, 66
Montgomerie, John, 49
Morgan, Abel, 145
Morgan, Joseph, 76, 121, 128-32, 169-72
Morris, Lewis, 172-74
Moses, His Judaicalls, 29
Muhlenberg, Henry Melchior, 83-84
Muller, Peter, 123

Nationalism
   and understanding of law, 20
Native Americans
   Anglican Church policy toward, 180
   hostilities affect colonial legal codes, 22-23
   New Jersey Quaker proprietors and, 34
Neighborliness
   as public ethic, 16
   as public solution to pluralism, 149, 166-174, 175-76
   outside tensions threaten, 173
Newark
   early settlement of, 29-30
   religious restrictions in, 30-31

   Society of Friends in, 58-60
New England
   migrants flock to Rhode Island, 182
   religious pluralism in, 177-79
New England's Spirit of Persecution Transmitted to Pennsylvania, 70
New Haven Colony
   colonists in migrate to Newark, 29-30
   expansion of, 29
New Netherlands
   religious diversity allowed in, 24-25
Newton, Isaac, 175
New York
   commerce influences religious structure, 181-83
   Leisler's Rebellion, 93-94
   local religious establishments in, 182
   religious diversity in, 181-82
   settlement patterns, 182
Nicolls, Richard, 49
   as governor, 23-27
   land grants in Monmouth County confirmed, 31
Niebuhr, H. Richard, 114-15
North Carolina
   religious dissenters in, 180
Nucella, 96
Nutt, 172

Ortega y Gasset, Jose, 135

Park, Robert, 115
Peck, Jeremiah, 26
Penn, William, 68, 185
   cautions zealous New Jersey Society of Friends, 159-60
   encourages diversity in Pennsylvania, 183-84
   role in division of East and West New Jersey, 33
Pennsneck
   Swedish Lutherans in, 89-90
Pennsylvania
   development of hostile factions in, 184
   religious diversity in, 183-84
   settlement patterns in, 183-84
Philadelphia Baptist Association

counsels local congregations on doctrinal disputes, 140-44
Pierson, Abraham, 30
Pierson, John, 66, 136
Piety, Public, 14, 16
  as gauge of Baptist fellowship, 144
  and Christian imagery, 176
  clergy elucidate, 169-72
  defined, 149-51
  development of, 151, 160-66
  and Edward Lord Cornbury, 166
  English influence on, 150-62, 165-66, 168, 173-76
  Enlightenment influence on, 175-76
  in generic religion, 87
  and Guilium Bartholf, 98-99
  Koelmanism, 98-99
  "ordinariness" of New Jersey, 157-60, 175-76
  and peaceableness, 161-64
  and political critique, 172-74
  restructuring of, 149-51
  tenets of, 167-69
Pluralism, Religious
  in Boston, 178
  colonists adapt to, 16
  defined, 10-11
  effect of laws on, 14
  in rural New York, 182
  types of, 1, 11-12, 177-85
  See also Diversity, religious
Pointer, Richard, 204n
Porter, Abraham, 89
Powicke, Maurice, 152
Presbyterians
  Americanization of, 5
  clash with Baptists in Haightstown, 171-72
  cooperate with Anglicans in Elizabethtown, 74
  cooperate with Baptists in Middletown, 91
  and denominationalism, 118-19, 144-45
  favored by Governor Jonathan Belcher, 64-65
  in Monmouth County, 56
  in Pennsylvania, 184
  in Southern colonies, 180
Protestantism

informal establishment of, 34-42
religious freedom secured after royalization, 43-44
Purchas, Samuel, 35
Puritans
  as English revolutionaries, 153, 156
  aspirations for New Haven Colony, 29
  declension of New Jersey settlers, 159
  migrate to New Jersey, 24-25
  propose religious restrictions, 50
  religious establishments of, 25-26
  in Rhode Island, 182
  settle Elizabethtown, 72
  in Southern colonies, 180
  strict religious laws of, 177-79
  tighten religious codes in East New Jersey, 36

Quakers. *See* Society of Friends
Quary, Robert, 166
Queen Anne, 44-45, 48
Quintipartite Deed, 33

Raccoon
  Swedish Lutherans erect church in, 90-91
Redfield, Robert, 57
Reformation, 152
Reid, John, 159
Religion
  Americanization of, 4, 5
  as search for community, 99
  attempts to establish homogeneity of, 53
  civil, 12, 16, 149-51, 176
  co-joined with political structures, 160-61
  colonial New Jersey as harbinger of future developments, 185
  colonists' influence on world view, 16
  competition viewed as beneficial, 115-16
  creation of informal establishment, 22
  defined, 6-7, 8-10
  disregard for English restrictions on, 47
  early provisions for freedom of, 46-47
  English governmental policy toward, 28
  foundations of liberty, 22-34
  freedom of, 1, 117-18
  hardening of opposition to establishment, 46

221

informal establishment of, 34-36
and law, 14, 29, 35-40
legislature's role in, 35-40
liminal experiences in, 126
linked with virtue after New Jersey royalization, 42
and pluralism, 1, 10-11
popular, 15
privatization of, 34, 176
proprietors' role in, 31-32
provisions for establishment of, 28-29
restrictions on, 30-31, 39, 41-42
Roger Williams on, 183
state-supported practice, 42
traditional orthodoxy in colonies, 113
See also Diversity, religious; Religions, generic; Tribalism, religious

Religion, Generic
appeal of, 110-11
as adjustment to religious diversity, 88
characteristics, 85-87
clergy's role in, 86-87
compared with denominational religion, 113
defined, 15, 87
demographic patterns of development, 88-92
development of, 85-86, 124-44
and diversity, 86
and Guilium Bartholf, 92-101
in harsh environment, 100
New Jersey poverty as catalyst for, 86
and sermons, 121-22
serves needs of subsistence farmers, 108-9
similarities to peasant religion, 87-88

Religion, Peasant
similarities to generic religion, 87-88

Religion in New Jersey: A Brief History, 5-7
"The Religious History of New Jersey before 1702," 3-4

Rhode Island
religious pluralism, 182-83
Royalization, 22, 42, 43, 44-46

Sabbatarianism, 110-11, 141
institution of, 35, 36-37
of Jonas Auren, 91
in West New Jersey, 41

Sacramentalism
in generic religion, 87
Guilium Bartholf and, 101
Schermerhoorn, Lucas, 79-81
Schutze, Johann Michael, 103, 105
Schuurman, Jacobus, 76, 80
Scott, George, 157-59
Sectarianism
as opposite of denominationalism, 114
denounced by Jonathan Dickinson, 117
and Keithian schism, 71
in Pennsylvania, 184
in Rhode Island, 183
and tribalism, 15, 67-68
Selyns, Henricus, 93, 95-96, 98
Sennett, Richard, 66
Settlement and Unsettlement in Early America, 177
Shaefer, Peter, 89-90
Shils, Edward, 88
Simmel, Georg, 62, 82
Skinner, William, 74-75, 76
Slaughter, Henry, 94
Slavery, 180
Smith, George L., 181
Smith, Samuel, 1, 50, 155, 171
Smith, Timothy L., 99
The Social Science of Denominationalism, 114
Society for the Propagation of the Gospel, 46, 58, 62, 64
Society of Friends
and apostasy, 61
as leaders of West New Jersey, 68-69
attacks against, 58-60, 64
condemnation of George Keith, 126-27
dismissed by Guilium Bartholf, 100
A General Epistle, 61
influence diminishes after royalization, 46
institute informal religious establishment in West New Jersey, 41-42
Keithian schism, 69-71
legal rights of, 47-49
meetings disturbed by ranters, 163
in Monmouth County, 56
in Newark, 58-60
in New England, 178
office holding by members of, 47-49
in Pennsylvania, 183-84

religious tribalism and, 68, 71
in Rhode Island, 183
role in establishment of West New Jersey, 33-34
in Southern colonies, 180
and Swedish colonists, 56
and tribalism, 15
William Penn cautions zealous members, 159-60
Spicer, Jacob, 50, 176
The Spirit of the Laws, 19, 20
Stockdale, William, 69-70
Stuyvesant, Peter, 24-25, 29-30
Suffrage
religious restrictions in Newark, 30-31
Sweden
colonists from, 56-57, 58
Sybrand, Johannes Hannes, 103, 104

Talbot, John, 58-59, 61, 64, 66
Tanis, James, 76, 98
Tennent, John, 83
Tennent, William, Jr., 83
Tennent, William, Sr., 83
Tollstadius, Lars, 90-91, 195n
Townley, Colonel, 73
Treat, Robert, 29-30
Tribalism, Religious
as reaction to religious diversity, 53-54
as social mediator, 54
and authoritarianism, 66, 78, 80, 82, 123
cessation in Elizabethtown, 72-74
churchly, 72-75
clergy's role in, 54
compared with denominational religion, 113
and conflict, 115
defined, 15, 54
development of, 56, 57, 58, 60-61, 68, 85-86, 124-44
dichotomy of clergy and laity, 65
diversity hinders, 56, 83
and Dutch Reformed Church, 77-83
emphasizes purity, 60-61
facets of, 53
and group rivalries, 58, 63, 66
immigrants attempt to import, 75

impact of Keithian schism on Society of Friends, 69-71
instability of, 67
and intermarriage, 57
maintenance of, 74
negated by Enlightenment natural religion, 175
sectarian, 67-68
and Society of Friends, 58-60
and subculturalism, 55
subdued zealotry of, 160
and Theodorus Jacobus Frelinghuisen, 75-83
threats to, 61-62
traditional absolutes in, 123
widespread effect of, 83-84
Trinterud, Leonard J., 5
Troeltsch, Ernst, 67-68
Truth Advanced in the Correction of Many Gross and Hurtful Errors, 127
Turner, Victor, 126

van Dieren, Johann Bernhard, 101-9
arrival in New York, 197n
ordination questioned by Wilhelm Christoph Berkenmeyer, 104-6, 197n
reasons for success, 108-9
relinquishes Hackensack church to Michael Christian Knoll, 105-7
seeks Reformed ministry at Tappan, 103
Varick, Rudolphus, 93, 94, 95, 97
Vaughan, Edward, 61-62, 64-65, 73-74, 118, 136
Virginia
Anglicans dominate, 180
Voetius, Gisbertus, 98
Vroom, Hendrik, 78, 82, 133

Wacker, Peter O., 7-8, 56
Webb, Joseph, 66
Weber, Max, 65-66
Wertenbaker, Thomas Jefferson, 4-5, 6, 27
West New Jersey
constitution of, 33-34
establishes public morality, 163-64
freedom of religion in, 163
immigration limits imposed, 163

    proprietors' religious role, 34
    Quakers govern in, 68-69
    Quakers institute informal religious establishment in, 41-42
    religious test for officeholders in, 42
    sabbatarianism in, 41
    tightens religious restrictions, 41-42
Whippen, Edward, 89
Whitefield, George, 83
Wightman, Valentine, 118-19, 125
Williams, Roger, 178, 182-83, 183
Willsford, John, 60
Wilson, Peter, 172
Witchcraft
    as capital offense, 35
Woertman, Jan, 81
Woertman, Pieter, 81
Wolf, Eric R., 87-88
Wolf, Johann August, 66-67
Wyckoff, Simon, 82, 133

TITLES IN THE SERIES

Chicago Studies in the History of American Religion

Editors

JERALD C. BRAUER & MARTIN E. MARTY

1. Ariel, Yaakov. *On Behalf of Israel: American Fundamentalist Attitudes toward Jews, Judaism, and Zionism, 1865-1945*
2. Bundy, James F. *Fall from Grace: Religion and the Communal Ideal in Two Suburban Villages, 1870-1917*
3. Butler, Jonathan M. *Softly and Tenderly Jesus is Calling: Heaven and Hell in American Revivalism, 1870-1920*
4. Dvorak, Katharine L. *An African-American Exodus: The Segregation of the Southern Churches*
5. Hardesty, Nancy A. *Your Daughters Shall Prophesy: Revivalism and Feminism in the Age of Finney*
6. Harding, Vincent. *A Certain Magnificence: Lyman Beecher and the Transformation of American Protestantism, 1775-1863*
7. Hewitt, Glenn A. *Regeneration and Morality: A Study of Charles Finney, Charles Hodge, John W. Nevin and Horace Bushnell*
8. Hillis, Bryan V. *Can Two Walk Together Unless They Be Agreed?: American Religious Schisms in the 1970s*
9. Jacobsen, Douglas G. *An Unprov'd Experiment: Religious Pluralism in Colonial New Jersey*
10. Kloos, John M., Jr. *A Sense of Deity: The Republican Spirituality of Dr. Benjamin Rush*

(continued, over)

TITLES IN THE SERIES

11. Kountz, Peter. *Thomas Merton as Writer and Monk: A Cultural Study, 1915-1951*
12. Lagerquist, L. DeAne. *In America the Men Milk the Cows: Factors of Gender, Ethnicity, and Religion in the Americanization of Norwegian-American Women*
13. Markwell, Bernard Kent. *The Anglican Left: Radical Social Reformers in the Church of England and the Protestant Episcopal Church, 1846-1954*
14. Morris, William Sparkes. *The Young Jonathan Edwards: A Reconstruction*
15. Pellauer, Mary D. *Toward a Tradition of Feminist Theology: The Religious Social Thought of Elizabeth Cady Stanton, Susan B. Anthony, and Anna Howard Shaw*
16. Potash, P. Jeffrey. *Vermont's Burned-Over District: Patterns of Community Development and Religious Activity, 1761-1850*
17. Queen, Edward L., II. *In the South the Baptists are the Center of Gravity: Southern Baptists and Social Change, 1930-1980*
18. Schmidt, Jean Miller. *Souls or the Social Order: The Two-Party System in American Protestantism*
19. Shaw, Stephen J. *The Catholic Parish as a Way-Station of Ethnicity and Americanization: Chicago's Germans and Italians, 1903-1939*
20. Shepard, Robert S. *God's People in the Ivory Tower: Religion in the Early American University*
21. Snyder, Stephen H. *Lyman Beecher and his Children: The Transformation of a Religious Tradition*